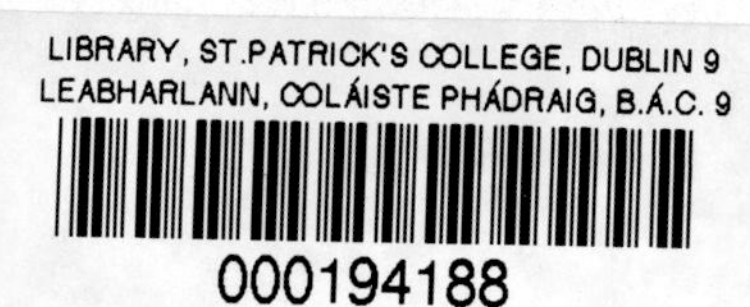

Scarecrow Film Score Guides

Series Editor: Kate Daubney

1. *Gabriel Yared's* The English Patient: *A Film Score Guide*, by Heather Laing. 2004.
2. *Danny Elfman's* Batman: *A Film Score Guide*, by Janet K. Halfyard. 2004.
3. *Ennio Morricone's* The Good, the Bad and the Ugly: *A Film Score Guide*, by Charles Leinberger. 2004.
4. *Louis and Bebe Barron's* Forbidden Planet: *A Film Score Guide*, by James Wierzbicki. 2005.
5. *Bernard Herrmann's* The Ghost and Mrs. Muir: *A Film Score Guide*, by David Cooper. 2005.
6. *Erich Wolfgang Korngold's* The Adventures of Robin Hood: *A Film Score Guide*, by Ben Winters. 2007.
7. *Mychael Danna's* The Ice Storm*: A Film Score Guide*, by Miguel Mera. 2007.
8. *Alex North's* A Streetcar Named Desire*: A Film Score Guide*, by Annette Davison. 2009.
9. *Nino Rota's* The Godfather Trilogy*: A Film Score Guide*, by Franco Sciannameo. 2010.
10. *Miklós Rózsa's* Ben-Hur*: A Film Score Guide*, by Roger Hickman. 2011.
11. *Zbigniew Preisner's* Three Colors *Trilogy: Blue, White, Red: A Film Score Guide*, by Nicholas W. Reyland. 2012.
12. *Franz Waxman's* Rebecca*: A Film Score Guide*, by David Neumeyer and Nathan Platte. 2012.
13. *Jerome Moross's* The Big Country*: A Film Score Guide*, by Mariana Whitmer. 2012.
14. *Leonard Bernstein's* On the Waterfront*: A Film Score Guide*, by Anthony Bushard. 201

Leonard Bernstein's *On the Waterfront*

A Film Score Guide

Anthony Bushard

Scarecrow Film Score Guides, No. 14

The Scarecrow Press, Inc.
Lanham, Maryland • Toronto • Plymouth, UK
2013

SCARECROW PRESS, INC.

Published in the United States of America
by Scarecrow Press, Inc.
A wholly owned subsidiary of
The Rowman & Littlefield Publishing Group, Inc.
4501 Forbes Boulevard, Suite 200, Lanham, Maryland 20706
www.scarecrowpress.com

10 Thornbury Road
Plymouth PL6 7PP
United Kingdom

British Library Cataloguing in Publication Information Available

Library of Congress Cataloging-in-Publication Data

Bushard, Anthony, 1974– author.
Leonard Bernstein's On the waterfront : a film score guide / Anthony Bushard.
pages cm. — (Scarecrow film score guides ; no. 14)
Includes bibliographical references and index.
ISBN 978-0-8108-8137-2 (pbk. : alk. paper) — ISBN 978-0-8108-8399-4 (ebook) 1. Bernstein, Leonard, 1918–1990. On the waterfront. 2. On the waterfront (Motion picture) I. Title.
ML410.B566B93 2013
781.5'42—dc23

2012037142

™ The paper used in this publication meets the minimum requirements of American National Standard for Information Sciences—Permanence of Paper for Printed Library Materials, ANSI/NISO Z39.48-1992.
Manufactured in the United States of America.

For Erica, Zachary, Nicholas, and Daniel

CONTENTS

ILLUSTRATIONS AND TABLES

Examples

EDITOR'S FOREWORD

As the Series of Scarecrow Film Score Guides grows more diverse in its scope, it is interesting to consider the constants that have emerged from the outstanding scholarship the series has inspired. Although the series was established to promote a level of analysis of individual scores that had previously not been attempted, the contextualization of the scoring processes has itself become a major feature of the volumes. The original format of the series included a biographical portrait of the composer, an analytical narrative of the composer's scoring technique, an assessment of the historical and critical context of the film's production and reception, a consideration of the film's musical 'soundscape,' and finally the detailed deconstruction of the written score with the aim of revealing the source of its power and effect. One of the pleasures of being the Series Editor has been to invite authors to write about scores and films whose existence, conception, production, and place in the composer's oeuvre in some way explode the rigidity of this format, thus revealing collaborations, coincidences, and analytical challenges of great insight. The series has thus contrasted the 'classical' and the most modern of compositional techniques, both in musical and logistical terms; it has exposed the mythologies of the 'golden era' and the many external influences the contemporary composer must manage; it has considered the responsibility of an audience in appreciating musical significance across the films of a trilogy; and it has almost exclusively to date focused wide bodies of scholarship and analysis onto a single work in a film composer's oeuvre.

By contrast, this volume on Leonard Bernstein's only film score considers a single contribution to one genre by a figure of extraordinary talent and industry across many genres. It is impossible to speculate what form a larger body of film scores by Bernstein would have taken, for we have too little evidence to be sure. But where studies of Korngold and Steiner have explored the way in which a background outside Hollywood influenced the creation and intentions of film scores at the formative period in film scoring practice, Bernstein's experience was of a very different Hollywood, within a vastly different compositional career. The Hollywood of this era was knowing, self-aware, politically complicated, and explicitly engaged with the outside world in a way that the dream factories of the 1930s only explored in a more implicit and reflective, rather than representative, fashion. Nor did Bernstein compose in complicity with anything like the same escapist illusion that Steiner and Korngold so ably conspired to perpetuate. The challenge in writing about Bernstein is, naturally, that so much has already been written about him, but Dr Bushard has overlaid the different contexts which intersected in the conception, production, and reception of this highly charged film in this deeply symbolic period in both Hollywood and American history. That carefully constructed context then provides a fascinating kaleidoscope through which to appreciate an analysis of the musical language which is at once both incredibly familiar and so powerfully evocative of its complex origins. Bernstein's 'sound' is so recognizable and so distinctive that it would seem to subvert the notion that a film score should not be heard. Yet it is this paradox which makes Bernstein's assimilation and expression of contemporary America in his music so utterly appropriate for this film that so starkly portrayed the real lives of real Americans. And, as ever, whatever the level of musical knowledge of the reader, there is much in this volume to illuminate why Bernstein's music spoke so effectively to this most acclaimed of films.

Dr Kate Daubney
Series Editor

ACKNOWLEDGMENTS

I would like to thank the following organizations for their generosity and willingness to permit me to reprint musical examples from a variety of sources in order to enhance the musical analyses below. All excerpts from *On the Waterfront* that appear in the film are used by permission of Alfred Publishing Company.

Several excerpts (found in Chapter 5) composed by Bernstein and recorded by Columbia ultimately did not make it into the final score. For those examples, and for any unused sketches from the Leonard Bernstein Collection at the Library of Congress, I wish to thank the Leonard Bernstein Estate and Boosey & Hawkes for allowing me to reprint those passages.

Moreover I would like to thank Boosey & Hawkes for granting permission to reprint excerpts (found in Chapter 2) from Leonard Bernstein's *West Side Story*, Benjamin Britten's Four Sea Interludes (Op. 33a) and Aaron Copland's *The Red Pony* Suite and *Billy the Kid* Suite.

The Red Pony: Film Suite by Aaron Copland © Copyright 1951 by the Aaron Copland Fund for Music, Inc. Copyright Renewed. Boosey & Hawkes, Inc., Sole Licensee. Reprinted by Permission.

Billy the Kid: Ballet Suite by Aaron Copland © Copyright 1941 by the Aaron Copland Fund for Music, Inc. Copyright Renewed. Boosey & Hawkes, Inc., Sole Licensee. Reprinted by Permission.

Four Sea Interludes, Op. 33A by Benjamin Britten © Copyright 1944 by Boosey & Hawkes Music Publishers Ltd. Reprinted by Permission.

In addition I am appreciative of G. Schirmer for approval to reproduce the opening (Chapter 2) of Dmitri Shostakovich's Symphony No. 5.

Symphony No. 5 in D Minor, Op. 47 By Dmitri Shostakovich. Copyright © 1939 by G. Schirmer, Inc. (ASCAP). International Copyright Secured. All Rights Reserved. Reprinted by Permission.

Finally, I am grateful to MGB Hal Leonard for permission to reprint brief passages (Chapter 2) from Arthur Honegger's Symphony No. 5 "Di tre re."

Symphony No. 5 "Di tre re" by Arthur Honegger. Copyright © 1951 Éditions Salabert – Paris. Tous droits réservés pour tous pays. Reproduced by kind permission of MGB Hal Leonard s.r.l.

I am also indebted to the AMS 75 PAYS Endowment of the American Musicological Society, funded in part by the National Endowment for the Humanities and the Andrew W. Mellon Foundation, for their generous subvention to cover copyright permission fees. Individually I am most grateful to Troy Schreck at Alfred Music for his extremely prompt and helpful service, Marie Carter, Eleonor Sandresky, and Brent Reno at the Leonard Bernstein Office, John White at Boosey & Hawkes, Kevin McGee at G. Schirmer, and Joseph Howard at Hal Leonard for their extraordinary collective efforts in securing copyright permission for this book.

My connection with Bernstein and his score for *On the Waterfront* goes back more than ten years when I first researched Bernstein's music for the film in a seminar at the University of Kansas taught by Paul Laird. I am grateful for his support of my work over these last ten years and I appreciate immensely his continued mentorship and ongoing friendship. In addition, I am indebted to Scott Murphy for his keen analytical eyes and ears as I turned that seminar paper into something much more substantial. Since that seminar in 2002 I have encountered much help along the way. Mark Horowitz was extremely helpful both as I conducted dissertation research at the Library of Congress in 2005 and more recently as I sought clarification on materials related to *On the Waterfront* in the Leonard Bernstein Collection. During my visit to the Sony Pictures Music Library in 2011, Raul Perez and Rod Davis were extraordinarily kind and unfailingly helpful in making sure I was able to look at as much material as possible. In addition they created a research environment that has been unsurpassed in my experience. While the staff was not—and has not—been able to locate the full orchestral film score, they remain dedicated to finding it and I hope that future researchers will benefit from their determination. I would also like to thank the Hixson-Lied Foundation at the University of Nebraska, Lincoln for their support of my research at Sony Pictures through a Hixson-Lied Faculty Research/Creativity Grant. In addition to the Hixson-Lied Foundation, I am truly thankful for the support of my colleagues at the University of Nebraska, Lincoln School of Music. Your achievements inspire me on a regular basis and your support of my work—from students and faculty to administration and staff—has been overwhelming. My hope is that the following pages live up to your high standards.

As I began the process of disseminating this research, I am grateful to Bill Rosar for first publishing my work on Bernstein in the *Journal of Film Music*, as well as for his encyclopedic knowledge of the film music industry and its people, and for his advice, counsel, and priceless anecdotal information throughout this process that I still benefit from today. In addition I thank Bill, as well as Sarah Cunningham at Intellect Books for their blessing to draw upon articles published in the *Journal of Film Music* and *Studies in Musical Theatre*, respectively, for use in this book. Most importantly I thank Renée Camus for her initial support of this book and Kate Daubney for her ongoing encouragement, insightful editing comments, and persistence in seeing this work through. I cannot imagine a more patient editor and supportive voice and I am profoundly appreciative of her leadership of the Film Score Guide Series. Those sentiments carry over to the entire Scarecrow staff, namely Stephen Ryan, Sally Craley, and Christen Karniski, who each have demonstrated unparalleled understanding of an academic's demanding schedule, especially when that schedule intersects with the myriad activities of one's family life.

In addition to those named here, and the countless dozens I will neglect to mention, none of what follows would have been possible or worthwhile without the undying support of my wife and family. My parents, Steve and Doris, have provided countless means of support that I can never repay as has my brother, Matt, who has never wavered in his encouragement. To my wife, Erica, you are my chief source of inspiration and as paradoxical as it sounds, the hours spent away from you working on this book were spent with you foremost in my thoughts. I am thankful beyond words for your kindness and compassion and for your time sacrificed so that I could "play" in archives in Los Angeles and Washington, D.C. Zachary, Nicholas, and Daniel, your frequent visits to my office to ask me "are you done with your book yet" also kept me on task and the smiles on your faces when I told you I was done is something I'll never forget. As this book demonstrates, *On the Waterfront* was a collaborative effort and none of what follows would have been possible without my family, friends, colleagues, and associates who have supported me along the way.

INTRODUCTION

"You don't understand. I could've had class. I could've been a contender. I could've been somebody instead of a bum, which is what I am, let's face it." Terry Malloy's famous line from *On the Waterfront* summarizes the angst he feels as he struggles to become an individual in a highly conformist environment. As more and more Americans turned away from radio and tuned into the increasingly popular television, they witnessed a time of great contrasts. Victorious soldiers returned home after World War II to resume their civilian lives, and their efforts led to a period of unparalleled economic expansion. However, as the 1950s progressed, there was also much social and political upheaval. Much of this tension resulted from various conflicting ideologies. For instance, government officials assured citizens that atomic weapons and testing would eventually save lives and establish peace throughout the world. However, reports of fallout and widespread destruction did little to ease an anxious and fearful public. U.S. foreign policy fought for democracy and the traditional, American way of life throughout the world in the hopes of halting the spread of Communism. Conversely, in battling domestic Communism, the spirit of freedom was tarnished in the way certain government officials persecuted those who criticized them under the protection of free speech. When these social and political dualities converged, the results reflected what are often cited as side effects of U.S. foreign and domestic policy during the 1950s: fear, paranoia, and alienation.

Films fulfill an important role in popular culture and deal with crucial issues concerning our humanity and the world in which we live. Although the 1950s witnessed a decline in movie audiences, films were still an important avenue by which to provide social commentary as well as political influence. In fact, several movies ran contrary to predominant social, political, and cultural beliefs. Moreover, for reasons addressed below, the movie industry, along with its film scoring component, experienced a transition in their histories as well. Thus, films of the 1950s reflect an intriguing time in the art's history because of the rich variety of emerging and established genres coupled with the competition following the dissolution of the large studios.

For a variety of reasons, *On the Waterfront* offers a particularly interesting case study of both film and music in the 1950s. The film received twelve Academy Award nominations and won eight awards. Among the four nominations that did not win was Leonard Bernstein for Best Original Score. Amidst the adulation for the overall impact and quality of the film, Bernstein's first and only film score has been met with much negative criticism. For instance Roy Prendergast stated:

> In 1954, Kazan called upon the considerable talents of Leonard Bernstein to create the music for his then latest Marlon Brando vehicle, *On the Waterfront*. The collaboration was less than successful, for while *On the Waterfront* is highly regarded among film historians and theoreticians, the music which accompanies it has serious flaws. Indeed, the music for this film is discussed here only because of its popularity in film classes and the mistaken idea that, because the multitalented Leonard Bernstein composed it, the score is a brilliant example of film composing at its best. Unfortunately the contrary is true. Bernstein's lack of experience in the area of film composition tends to destroy the effect, in terms of the picture, of what is some very beautiful music. However, the same material as *film music*, becomes, in many places, intrusive and inept-sounding from a dramatic standpoint.[1]

Edward Murray thought:

> Leonard Bernstein's score for the film, however, is certainly open to criticism. A melodramatic drumbeat announces the approaching death of Joey Doyle. In the tender love scenes, a symphony orchestra threatens to blow Terry and Edie off the roof too. At times we cannot hear the dialogue, thanks to Bernstein's obtrusive, almost operatic, playing. When the cabdriver takes Charlie to his death the music comes up like thunder. Much too often, the pompous score clashes with the visuals. Even with Kazan's and Kaufmann's [*sic*; cinematographer] *poetic* realism, music which would be appropriate for *Tristan and Isolde* seems out of place on the docks of Hoboken.[2]

Even Elia Kazan had this to say about the same scene:

> I think the music hurt that picture, Bernstein's a brilliant guy, but—you remember, the film opens with a kind of drumbeat which puts it right away on a level of melodrama, rather than just showing the murder, the body falling, just showing it—it's strong enough by itself.[3]

In this book I hope to demonstrate—contrary to these negative critical appraisals—that Bernstein's score enhances the drama throughout the score. Through his integration of themes, Bernstein highlights the pain, anxiety, and isolation the protagonist feels when attempting to become an individual in a highly conformist environment.

The first question that should arise before any discussion of a film score is how does music enhance a given film? Aaron Copland, in his discussion of the aesthetics of film music, states that the composer "makes potent through music the film's dramatic and emotional value."[4] Also in this discussion, Copland guides the reader through a discussion of how music intensifies the cinematic experience. The second of these points proved to be especially pertinent to this study: "Underlining psychological refinements—the unspoken thoughts of a character or the unseen implications of a situation."[5] Therefore, given film music's capacity to comment upon, augment, and/or clarify the intentions of the filmmakers, or the intricacies of the narrative, the next question (and perhaps the most important), becomes: How can/does Bernstein's music for *On the Waterfront* interact with the film in the way Copland describes?

Because Bernstein's contribution to *On the Waterfront* is his first and only film score, I have found this question to be particularly challenging. Thus, the following pages are organized in such a way as to answer this question, but in a manner that is somewhat different than what readers of this Film Score Guide Series have come to expect. For instance, Bernstein's considerable renown and the amount of ink spilled recounting his considerable achievements, renders an opening section on his "life and musical background" somewhat superfluous. Rather, Chapter 1 provides a discussion of Bernstein's life and career up to 1954, concentrating on the composer's penchant for the dramatic witnessed in both works for musical theater as well as his programmatic symphonies. Chapter 1 also examines reasons why Bernstein composed only one film score, e.g., his demanding conducting schedule, and posits the idea—suggested elsewhere of course—that everything Bernstein experienced in life entered his musical and artistic vocabulary.

The typical "film scoring technique" chapter promises to look different considering there is no previous or subsequent body of work in Bernstein's career on which to base such a discussion. Instead, Chapter 2 examines Bernstein's overall musical language, focusing on the sphere of influences—e.g., musical theater, jazz, symphonic works, and conducting—that informed Bernstein's "musical memory" akin to "method acting" as espoused by the Group Theater via Elia Kazan and upon which he drew to complete this film score. In other words when Bernstein famously remarked that "he heard music" when he saw an early version of the film, the strains he perceived derived from a diverse web of classical and vernacular influences both past and present. Then, by building on the work of Jack Gottlieb and others, I deal with precedents in Bernstein's music (and the work of others) for the detailed thematic and motivic integration central to the success of his score for *On the Waterfront*. The chapter concludes with a discussion of how *On the Waterfront* impacted Bernstein's music going forward through its influence on the composer's most famous work, *West Side Story*.

While the lone film score of an American musical icon might be enough to warrant a book-length discussion of Bernstein's score for *On the Waterfront*, the composer also plays an important part in the film's social and political context. Kazan's film depicts the struggles of longshoremen to find a voice in the corrupt world of organized crime on the New Jersey docks. Furthermore, the film also functions as a justification for Kazan's confession before HUAC in which he summarized the past activities of his Communist colleagues in the Group Theater. Bernstein was also implicated as a former Communist and walked in some of the same circles with some of the same colleagues as Kazan. In fact the intense connection Bernstein made with Marlon Brando's performance—and an important factor in Bernstein's decision to write music for the film—derived in part from being able to relate to the same pressures exerted on Kazan and hundreds of others in the artistic community throughout the United States. Thus, because this film arguably depends more on its contemporaneous context than any other book in the Film Score Guide series, I devote two chapters to contextual issues in order to provide the general reader with a more thorough grounding in the 1950s sociopolitical landscape. Chapter 3 examines important conflicting ideologies—protecting freedom by silencing subversives (anti-Communism), waging peace to prevent war (nuclear proliferation), and seeking escape through conformity (suburban exodus)—and their impact on the mindset of moviegoers in the 1950s. Chapter 4 applies these issues to a more specific context by discussing the politics of the corrupt waterfront world to which screenwriter Budd Schulberg and Elia Kazan called attention. Further I examine the many similarities between Elia Kazan and Leonard Bernstein, most notably their roles as "informers" in the anti-Communist crusade and how that phenomenon as mirrored by the film's main protagonist underpinned the creation of *On the Waterfront*. Chapter 4 also provides a film synopsis as well as a treatment of the cast and the genesis of the film.

Chapter 5 combines a treatment of the various *On the Waterfront* "scores"—namely the conductor parts and other materials at Sony Pictures (Culver City, CA), as well as the short score and other sketches at the Library of Congress—along with a thorough reading of the film's narrative as it pertains to the aforementioned sociopolitical undercurrents and how Bernstein's music comments effectively throughout the film to produce a most worthy example of modern film scoring. In revisiting Terry's famous lament that opened this introduction, it is my hope that the reader of this book will come to the same conclusion that I have made in almost ten years of close contact with Bernstein's first and only film score: He could've been a contender!

1

LEONARD BERNSTEIN'S MUSICAL AND DRAMATIC BACKGROUND TO 1954

As a fourteen-year-old in Boston, Leonard Bernstein met a fellow aspiring pianist named Mildred Spiegel and their shared love of music made them fast friends. Later in life, Spiegel reminisced "Lenny had a natural inclination for the spotlight. . . . He had a fascination with unique people and artistic projects, and needed to have many projects going on at once."[1] Spiegel's keen remembrance calls attention to two facets of Bernstein's life that could be viewed both as character strengths and weaknesses. Bernstein was a gifted speaker, equally comfortable explaining sonata form to children and their parents in his *Young People's Concerts* as he was lecturing a room of musical intellectuals on the intersection of music and language at the Harvard Norton Lecture Series. However, Bernstein's need to be loved by those closest to him as well as the general public resulted in broken relationships and hurt feelings for many who knew him. Bernstein was also an immensely talented artist who excelled at various times as a composer, conductor, concert pianist, writer, educator, and entrepreneur. Yet, critics and mentors alike pointed out that he could never become a success in any of those disciplines while he tried to master them simultaneously. Regardless, examining Bernstein's life and music remains a fascinating exercise in part because of these character dualities, as well as the degree to which Bernstein struggled to achieve an identity despite these dualities. Fittingly, the story of one individual—Terry Malloy—and his fight to re-forge a purpose in life inspired Bernstein to score *On the Waterfront* yet, because Bernstein was involved in so many projects before, during, and after those spring months in 1954, he never composed another film score.

This complex set of dualities and these multiple roles make Leonard Bernstein one of the most interesting figures in the twentieth century musical world and studies of his life and music have only increased since his death in 1990. There have been numerous biographies, dissertations, articles, interviews, and photographs documenting Bernstein's contributions to and impact upon music, art, society, and politics in the twentieth century in both the United States and abroad. In addition, the more than 400,000 items that comprise the Library of Congress's Leonard Bernstein Collection should alleviate any worries that Bernstein scholarship will wane anytime soon. So the present challenge is to present Bernstein's life in such a way as to tell a story that hasn't been told already. With that task in mind, this chapter aims to provide a look at Bernstein's life leading up to his collaboration with Elia Kazan to produce the score for *On the Waterfront*. In order to manage the discussion I will focus on those seminal events in his life that will inform his work on *On the Waterfront* and provide clues as to why—despite Bernstein's exemplary work on the score—he only produced one film score.

Early Life in Boston

"Moynik, moynik!" young Bernstein shouted, and it was "moynik" or "music" that he received from the Bernstein family's Victrola to ease the toddler's cries.[2] While one would encounter difficulty suggesting Leonard Bernstein came from a "musical family," he demonstrated a genuine interest in music heard on the family's record player and was equally mesmerized by the static-filled strains of popular music he heard on the radio. In addition to the pop tunes, Jewish songs accompanied by organ also profoundly affected young Bernstein. As Bernstein remembered, "[Isadore Glickstein, synagogue cantor] would begin to sing the ancient tunes . . . and then the organ would start and then the choir would begin with its colors, and I just began to get crazed with the sound of choral music."[3] Despite Bernstein's interest in and love for music, his parents never compelled him to study music formally, nor presented him with anything outside of record players, radio, and religious music. Bernstein's father was much too busy with his burgeoning beauty supply business to be bothered with Leonard's musical instruction and when his sister Clara gave the family a piano, it stayed in a hallway in favor of the sofa.[4] Yet for young Bernstein, what his father considered a useless piece of furniture opened a new and exciting world for him. No longer was he confined to tapping out tunes on an imaginary keyboard on the family's windowsill. Instead he provided full voice to his record and radio favorites. Through his teachers and in his own explorations he was able to feed his musical imagination through masterpieces in the Western classical tradition, quickly assimilating the inner workings of melody and harmony. Eventually Bernstein's musical talent outpaced that of his teacher, Frieda Karp, and he began instruction with a more expensive teacher at the New England Conservatory. The prospect of having to triple his payments for piano lessons enraged Bernstein's father, thus Leonard's budding passion for music quickly became a wedge between father and son. Despite his father's reluctance to pay for lessons, young Leonard funded his own lessons by teaching neighborhood children and performing on weekends with what Bernstein called a "jazz band,"[5] demonstrating the resourcefulness and entrepreneurial spirit that would later be a hallmark of his mature career.

Upon entering the renowned Boston Latin School, Bernstein was already exhibiting the habits of a polymath that would define him as an adult. While Bernstein was an immensely talented individual, his education at Boston Latin should not be underestimated for shaping the figure he became later in life. Boston Latin provided a curriculum of intense rigor. With an attrition rate of sixty-seven percent (for the six years inclusive of seventh through twelfth grades), many students could not handle the demands of daily Latin translation, essays, oral examinations, and participation in academic clubs. Bernstein succeeded admirably, earning a variety of academic prizes in addition to membership in the French, Physics, and Glee clubs, as well as a performer in the school's symphony orchestra. Samuel Bernstein surely prized these academic triumphs of his eldest son and perhaps gave the father hope his son would be cured of his musical fever.[6]

In reality Bernstein's academic training only bolstered his musical progress. In order to seek refuge from the academic grind and tension with his father, Bernstein combined his fertile imagination, desire for companionship, and growing love of the spotlight to fuel his musical pursuits. Through a mutual friend, Eddie Ryack, Bernstein met and found his first student in Sid Ramin, who later orchestrated *West Side Story*. The two became so close that Ramin even became initiated in the imaginary world of Rybernia, populated by Bernstein, his younger siblings Shirley and Burton, and Ryack. As Burton Bernstein explains, "Rybernian" was the official language based on the Yiddish of elder members of the Bernstein family as well as the distinct Boston dialect of their Roxbury neighborhood:

> The influences on this language were legion. They were mainly my father and his friends with their peculiar accents from the old world. A lot of Yiddish was thrown in. Relatives of all kinds, some outrageously funny. . . . All accents were funny and derisive. It was a very derisive kind of humor. And one of the accents that was funny to all three of us, because we had them ourselves, was the Boston accent.

> And it was a constant joke right up to the end for Lenny and Shirley and me.[7]

Eventually Bernstein was able to enliven his piano repertoire in a similar manner. He often brought arrangements of operas from the library and directed his sister Shirley in four-hand versions of Italian opera. Soon thereafter when the Bernstein family vacationed in nearby Sharon, young Bernstein began organizing productions of opera and musical theater with friends and neighbors in Sharon. From *Carmen* to *The Mikado* and *H.M.S. Pinafore*, Bernstein demonstrated a gift for organizing a cast, leading a group of relatively inexperienced performers, and producing shows that found him functioning as director, choreographer, and impresario. This was no small feat as his production of *H.M.S. Pinafore* included a chorus of forty.[8] While Bernstein was at Harvard, he continued directing musical dramas at Camp Onota in northwest Massachusetts, overseeing a production of *The Pirates of Penzance*. Clearly these early experiences in Sharon and Camp Onota provided the foundation for his dramatic collaborations at Harvard and later as he made his mark on Broadway. Combined with his successful piano studies, now with Helen Coates—who would become his personal secretary and one of his closest confidants—Bernstein saw a musical career in his future and distanced himself further from his father's wishes. As Humphrey Burton notes in quoting an essay Bernstein wrote in his last year at Boston Latin:

> There stands ready for my claiming a fairly stable business, over a decade old and offering excellent means for my development and improvement. On the other hand, I care nothing for it, but am exceedingly interested in music. In fact there is never a time when I do not prefer playing my piano to any other sort of work or recreation. It is inexplicably true that because of rather than in spite of home discouragement, I am filled all the more with the desire for a musical life. . . . I would probably attempt a Harvard training because of the superb musical training there. . . . At the same time I would not omit the liberal arts training, as general knowledge is essential to success in any field.[9]

Harvard and a Series of Fortunate Events

In the fall of 1935, Bernstein indeed attended Harvard and was well positioned for success there. Bernstein's time at Harvard was defined by several experiences in which the student demonstrated a knack for being in the right place at the right time. Continuing his habits from

Boston Latin, Bernstein continued to be an academic and social gourmand. In addition to piano studies with Heinrich Gebhard and counterpoint with Arthur Tillman Merritt, Bernstein sought membership in various fraternal, social, and academic organizations, also using these groups for ways to further his musical ambitions.

One of these clubs helped facilitate an encounter with one of Bernstein's most influential mentors. Early in 1937, Bernstein attended a concert of the Boston Symphony Orchestra led by guest conductor Dimitri Mitropolous. Bernstein was totally enamored with Mitropolous's performance and when he was asked by some students from a Harvard Greek organization to perform at a reception for Mitropolous the next day, Bernstein took advantage of this cosmic serendipity. When Mitropolous heard Bernstein's playing, he was equally taken with the young composer and invited him to attend his rehearsals that week with the Boston Symphony Orchestra. The experience impacted Bernstein profoundly and was recorded in an essay during his junior year entitled "The Occult," which survives today in *Findings* (1982). In the fictional account of this week in 1937, Bernstein conveys with flowery prose how Mitropolous—as "Eros Mavro"—saw in Bernstein the potential for greatness and made clear to Bernstein that:

> You must make me very proud of you one day. . . . It is plain to me that you have every talent for a composer. You are sensitive in an ideal way—I know, do not say a word. You must work, work very hard. You must devote all your time to your art. You must keep yourself pure. Do not let friends spoil you with flattery. You have everything to make you great; it is up to you only to fulfill your mission.[10]

This idealized account of a supposed conversation between Bernstein and Mitropolous shows the seriousness with which Bernstein heeded the flamboyant conductor's request. Throughout, "The Occult" speaks to the confusion of the week spent with Mitropolous and how the conductor's words seemed to "clarify" the bewilderment and conflict that Bernstein felt.[11] While Mitropolous saw in Bernstein the potential for a great composer, it is likely that in the company of Mitropolous's presence—and his genuine love of directing productions going back to his pre-adolescence—Bernstein saw in himself the beginnings of a great conductor.

That same year Bernstein also encountered someone who would exert an even more profound influence on his career than Mitropolous. On 14 November 1937, Bernstein attended a dance recital in New York and sat, unknowingly at first, next to Aaron Copland. Bernstein had recently mastered Copland's challenging Piano Variations (1930) and it quickly became one of his favorite pieces, so he was already quite familiar with both Copland's music and his reputation as the foremost new voice in American music. Yet Bernstein was surprised when this "odd-looking man in his thirties, a pair of glasses resting on his great hooked nose" challenged the lionized image of "a cross between Walt Whitman and an Old Testament prophet, bearded and patriarchal" that he had carried with him thus far.[12] The concert also coincided with Copland's birthday so he invited Bernstein and everyone else in their row to a party at his apartment. True to his continual desire for the spotlight, Bernstein made the most of the opportunity by accepting Copland's challenge to play the Variations at the party, thus introducing himself to several of New York's most culturally-connected individuals. As he did at the reception with Mitropolous, Bernstein made a lasting impact on all in attendance, especially Copland, who like his mentor Nadia Boulanger, began to nurture Bernstein's personal and professional aspirations:

> I would show Aaron the bits and pieces, and he would say, "All that has to go . . . . This is just pure Scriabin. You've got to get that out of your head and start fresh. . . . This is good; these two bars are good. Take these two bars and start from there." And in these sessions he taught me a tremendous amount about taste, style, and consistency in music. . . . Through his critical analyses of whatever I happened to be working on at the moment, Aaron became the closest thing to a composition teacher I ever had.[13]

Bernstein was also privileged enough to observe some of Copland's works, including his film scores for *Of Mice and Men* (1939) and *Our Town* (1940), long before anyone heard those scores in theaters. Copland offered the sort of support for Bernstein's musical development that was missing from his biological father. Copland's impact on Bernstein's career lasted well into the future and his influence on Bernstein's musical language will be explored in greater detail in Chapter 2.

In meeting and developing relationships with Mitropolous and Copland on either end of 1937, Bernstein educated himself in a way that transcended his courses and activities at Harvard. Through his talent and their connections, Bernstein entered a world of possibilities of which few aspiring artists could dream. That said, the young composer/conductor still depended on his beloved Harvard for opportunities to showcase his talent. Despite studying with the most prominent members of Harvard's musical faculty, such as Merritt, Walter Piston, and Edward Burlingame Hill, it was aesthetics professor David Prall whom Bernstein most admired. It was Prall who purchased the score of Copland's Piano Variations for Bernstein and it was Prall who opened Bernstein's eyes to a new way of thinking about art that embraced both objective and subjective points of view. Moreover, Prall's assertion that art is best understood from a multifaceted, interdisciplinary perspective embraced Bernstein's equally diverse artistic interests and underpinned what some have noted as Bernstein's eclectic musical style.[14] Not surprisingly Bernstein actively sought opportunities in which he could employ this interdisciplinary spirit.

In April of 1939, Bernstein conducted (in what amounted to his true debut) and provided incidental music for a production of Aristophanes's *The Birds*, produced by Harvard's Classical Club. The fifth century BCE work was presented in the original Greek, but was connected to the present through set designs depicting Harvard and its immediate environs, as well as through Bernstein's music. The play came at a busy time for Bernstein because he was also writing his senior thesis, entitled "The Absorption of Race Elements into American Music," in which he made the case for an assimilation of jazz and blues idioms into concert music (according to Bernstein, exemplified in the works of George Gershwin and Copland) to create a more genuine sense of American music. Thus, *The Birds* offered a working laboratory in which Bernstein could employ the theories he was positing in his thesis. Some characters declaimed their lines in a blues style, while Bernstein also wrote jazzy material for the chorus such that one preview noted that, "the musical idioms of our day have been employed to serve the humor of Aristophanes and to provide a point of interest in their own right."[15] Yet, Bernstein was not content to confine his stylistic palette to jazz and made references to a recent performance of Indian classical music, as well as Verdi's *Rigoletto*, all to make more relevant the virtually unintelligible Greek language.[16] From composition to conducting, from setting text to coaching soloists and chorus, Bernstein demonstrated to those in attendance at the premiere (Copland among them) the potential for success in collaborative dramatic projects.

As if completing his thesis and staging *The Birds* was not enough, Bernstein also brought Marc Blitzstein's *The Cradle Will Rock* (1937) to Harvard. Bernstein had seen the play in New York the previous year and was certainly aware of the work's famous premiere. In June 1937, Orson Welles, Blitzstein, and John Houseman along with the cast and audience arrived at the Maxine Elliot Theater for the premiere but, because federal funding of the play was pulled due to political pressure, the ensemble found the theater locked and surrounded by federal guards. Bravely, the cast walked twenty blocks away to the Venice Theater and performed the play without staging. Moreover, the musician's union refused to allow the musicians to participate so Blitzstein played a piano reduction on stage and the actors united with him from within the house. Because of Blitzstein's ability to convey effectively

American vernacular speech patterns set to music, it is likely Bernstein viewed him as an ideal role model in his efforts to stage *The Birds*. Perhaps to curry favor with his newfound inspiration, and with the help of the Harvard Student Union,[17] Bernstein was able to obtain enough institutional support to present the *The Cradle Will Rock* at Harvard. With only two weeks to prepare the play Bernstein worked feverishly with the student cast, but the results were a success and Bernstein was even able to convince Blitzstein to attend the Harvard debut. In fact, one of the unexpected hits of the Harvard production was the role of Moll, played by Bernstein's sister Shirley, only fifteen at the time.

The confluence of events that comprised Bernstein's Harvard years is nothing short of amazing. As one author put it, "[I]n four years Bernstein had become a cosmopolitan modernist, an intimate of two celebrated musicians, and a propagandist for the new American music. Had he a presentiment in that spring of 1939 that he would take the title of creative artist upon his own shoulders?"[18] Bernstein enjoyed the enviable problem of demonstrating vast potential across the artistic spectrum so much that the most difficult question for him upon graduating from Harvard was what to do now?

Bernstein on the Podium

After struggling as a freelancer in New York City—most notably at the Village Vanguard in Greenwich Village with The Revuers, comprised of future collaborators Adolph Green and Betty Comden—Bernstein decided that perhaps conducting was the answer. Through Copland's intercession, Bernstein obtained an interview with Fritz Reiner at the Curtis Institute in Philadelphia in the fall of 1939. Here Bernstein collided with an institution which, from Mary Curtis Bok (the institute's founder) down to the Curtis faculty, stressed working in "a background of quiet culture" and producing works that emphasized the "quality of the work rather than quick, showy results."[19] Despite the clash of cultures, Bernstein endured and in the spring of 1940, upon Copland's urging, Bernstein applied for conducting classes with Serge Koussevitzky at the newly formed Berkshire Music Center. Armed with recommendations from Reiner, Roy Harris, William Schuman, and Copland, Koussevitzky warmly accepted and allowed Bernstein invaluable practical experience conducting one of the finest student orchestras in the United States for six weeks.[20]

In Koussevitzky, Bernstein found a kindred spirit and grew to view the Boston Symphony Orchestra conductor as another paternal musical figure. While much of Bernstein's conducting theatrics can be derived from Mitropolous, Koussevitzky stressed zealously the conductor's role as a vital conduit between the composer's intentions and the orchestra's realization of those intentions; to Koussevitzky a sacred connection. Bernstein also learned from Koussevitzky a heightened sense of showmanship, "When Koussevitzky stepped out on the stage . . . no matter what the music was going to be, it was going to matter because he was performing it. Nobody in his audience could fail to perceive that and you listened . . . to each strand and caress and inflection and breath of the music."[21] Following Bernstein's graduation from Curtis in 1941; he again went to Tanglewood and by 1942 became Koussevitzky's assistant.

Bernstein moved back to New York City and after a series of minor conducting opportunities, Artur Rodzinski, then musical director of the New York Philharmonic, contacted Bernstein in the spring of 1943 about an assistant conductor opportunity with the Philharmonic. By late summer the proposal became a reality and on 14 November, Bernstein again found the stars aligning in his favor. The day before the Sunday afternoon concert, Bernstein learned that the scheduled conductor, the renowned Bruno Walter, had fallen ill and might not be able to conduct. Moreover, snow kept Rodzinski from making the journey to New York from his home in Stockbridge, leaving Bernstein to conduct the matinee. Bernstein briefly reviewed the scores with Walter and without a rehearsal conducted the orchestra in front of a packed hall that included his family and thousands more over nationally broadcast radio. The concert was a major success and made headline news in the *New York Times* the next day. Yes, Bernstein delivered brilliantly under immense pressure, but more importantly, an American-born, American-trained conductor—in a field whose chief exemplars were entirely born and trained in Europe—led the most prominent orchestra in the United States and did so convincingly and with much flair.

In between composing pieces for both Broadway and the concert sphere, Bernstein made a few more appearances with the New York Philharmonic from 1943-1945. In addition to the steady diet of orchestral favorites, Bernstein also conducted more contemporary works by Bernard Herrmann, Maurice Ravel, and Dmitri Shostakovich[22] and by the end of 1944 had made appearances in Pittsburgh, Boston, Montreal, Chicago, Cincinnati, Los Angeles, and Detroit.[23] Based on his conducting successes in New York and elsewhere, and combined with the heightened celebrity status he enjoyed following the dual 1944 triumphs of both *Fancy Free* and *On the Town*, Bernstein was an ideal choice to direct the New York City Symphony upon Leopold Stokowski's departure. The job promised to be daunting given the limited budget, but the opportunity to plan an entire season without interference was one Bernstein could not pass up. In his three years as the New York City Symphony leader, Bernstein demonstrated diverse programming and a penchant for conducting the most contemporary pieces, presenting no fewer than fifty twentieth-century works between 1945-1947.[24] When he wasn't conducting the New York City Symphony, Bernstein went on to endear audiences abroad in England, France, Belgium, the Netherlands, and Israel. This latter tour stop had a profound impact on Bernstein and established a long professional and personal relationship with the country.

As important as Bernstein's 1943 debut with the New York Philharmonic had been for young, American-born conductors, his well-received tour of Europe in the later 1940s was arguably more significant because it shattered the notion that an American conductor could not achieve success outside of his homeland. Yet, Bernstein's renown and dedicated following was not enough to convince the Boston Symphony Orchestra's administration to hire him following Koussevitzky's retirement announcement in 1948, going with Charles Munch instead. Bitterly disappointed yet undeterred, Bernstein accepted an advisory post in his beloved Israel with the Israel Philharmonic. Koussevitzy was also distraught that his protégé would not be able to succeed him at the Boston Symphony Orchestra post so it was fitting that when Koussevitzky died shortly before the opening of Tanglewood's 1951 season, Bernstein assumed control of conducting studies in his mentor's absence. In his work throughout the world, and especially at the New York City Symphony and Tanglewood, Bernstein's musical interpretations breathed new life into the world of conducting that drew upon a sense of dynamism characteristic of the postwar worldview. More importantly, contemporary composers found in Bernstein a willing champion of their works and a composer who was already beginning to realize his fullest potential.

Bernstein the Dramatist

As Bernstein leaped his way through orchestra halls in Europe, audiences and critics began to realize that this was a different sort of conductor than they had ever seen before. Yet from his days at Harvard throughout the 1940s, Bernstein had shown so much compositional promise that Virgil Thomson opined, perhaps presciently following Bernstein's triumphs at the podium that "It would be a pity if our brightest young leader [compositionally] should turn out to be just a star conductor."[25] A detailed account of Bernstein's compositions following his time at Harvard is beyond this brief account of his life up to the point he commenced work on *On the Waterfront*. Rather, I will treat only those acclaimed works prior to 1954 that also most closely informed the *On the Waterfront* score musically and dramatically.

Symphonies 1 and 2

Despite the several months of frustration that followed Bernstein after his Harvard graduation, he was able to begin work on what would become his first symphony. As Bernstein indicates in the notes accompanying the published score, 1939 found him outlining a piece for soprano (later mezzo soprano) and orchestra based on an excerpt from the Lamentations of Jeremiah. When Bernstein returned to New York in 1942 following his graduation from the Curtis Institute, he also renewed his connection to the work, prompted by a composition contest sponsored by the New England Conservatory. Bernstein composed two new movements ("Prophecy" and "Profanation") and used the song composed in 1939 as the central portion of the third movement. Bernstein worked feverishly to finish by the contest's 31 December deadline and the result is impressive given Bernstein's relative inexperience with large-form orchestral works. Eventually Bernstein was able to get the work published and impressed his Curtis mentor Fritz Reiner enough for the seasoned veteran to allow Bernstein to conduct the premiere of his symphony with the Pittsburgh Symphony Orchestra in January 1944.

Opinions about the high level of theatricality in Bernstein's musical output are pervasive and well-documented. Yet, his own comments regarding the "programmatic" nature of the Jeremiah Symphony reveals much about the way he approached the score for *On the Waterfront*:

> As for the programmatic meanings, the intention is not one of literalness, but of emotional quality. Thus the first movement (Prophecy) aims only to parallel in feeling the intensity of the prophet's pleas with his people; and the scherzo (Profanation) to give a general sense of the destruction and chaos brought on by the pagan corruption within the priesthood and the people. The third movement (Lamentation), being a setting of poetic text, is naturally a more literary conception. It is the cry of Jeremiah, as he mourns his beloved Jerusalem, ruined, pillaged and dishonored after his desperate efforts to save it.[26]

Bernstein's description makes the symphony seem like incidental music for the text from Jeremiah. In the same way a film score at its best enhances the film for which it is written, Bernstein's music enlivens the essence of the biblical text.

In order to connect the movements into a cohesive whole, Bernstein derived much of the symphony's primary thematic material from Hebrew songs and liturgical chants. For instance, the first movement's opening theme derives from the High Holy Day liturgy and undergoes a dark, often dissonant treatment. The second movement displays a jazzier sentiment and is the movement most closely indebted to his studies with Copland. Replete with vigorous, irregular rhythms this material suggests the Bernstein of Broadway. The final movement includes a moving setting of Jeremiah's lamentations and suggests through its restatement of themes from the first movement, that the initial prophecy has been realized.

A lament of a different sort served as the source for Bernstein's Second Symphony. Symphony No. 2, "The Age of Anxiety" drew upon W.H. Auden's extensive eponymous poem that chronicled the sort of isolation, itinerancy, and alienation prevalent in post–World War II society. Bernstein identified strongly with the spirit of Auden's poem as he too floated between conducting engagements, composition commissions, relationships both personal and professional, each an ongoing effort to establish his identity. The poem chronicles the travails of four individuals—three men and one woman—who meet at a bar in New York City. The group talks, drinks, listens to news of the war, and through their discussion (and a subsequent dream sequence) attempts to discover meaning in life. Later, the quartet continues the party at the female character's (Rosetta) apartment. Two of the men leave, after which Rosetta and the remaining male—Emble—attempt and fail to consummate their casual relationship. The two wake up the next morning and continue their lives as if nothing happened.

Bernstein began the work in 1948, commissioned by the Koussevitzky Music Foundation, and true to the wandering spirit of the poem's protagonists, Bernstein composed the work at various times and places throughout the United States and Israel. He finally finished the piece on 20 March 1949, a few weeks before the premiere with Koussevitzky—the work's dedicatee—and the Boston Symphony Orchestra featuring Bernstein as the soloist.[27]

Bernstein identified strongly with Auden's work, so much so that he placed himself into the symphony, personified by the piano. In fact, when he revised the work in 1965, he extended the role of the piano beyond its place in the 1949 original version, especially with respect to its function in the "Finale." Throughout—and especially in the revised edition—the musical texture suggests a piano concerto rather than a symphony, and demonstrates Bernstein's redefinition of the symphonic genre begun with the "Jeremiah" Symphony and continued with his Symphony No. 3, "Kaddish." Just as he had done with his first symphony, Bernstein attempted to capture the essence of the work's literary source, here the restless spirit of a world in chaos. In addition, the degree to which Bernstein strived to capture the spirit and images of Auden's work was even more evident than it was in his first symphony:

> If the charge of "theatricality" in a symphonic work is a valid one, I am willing to plead guilty. I have a suspicion that every work I write, for whatever medium, is really theater music in some way, and nothing has convinced me more than these new discoveries of the unconscious hand that has been at work all along in The Age of Anxiety.[28]

Bernstein organized the symphony largely along Auden's formal parameters. The first part, comprised of "The Prologue," "The Seven Ages," and "The Seven Stages" follows the action through the end of the dream sequence. Part II begins with the taxi ride to Rosetta's apartment with "The Dirge," which then leads to "The Masque" and the symphony closes with "The Epilogue." "The Prologue" opens with a plaintive duet between clarinets followed by an extensive descending scale. This latter passage links to a chorale-like presentation in the piano, and thus the first of six variations that comprise "The Seven Ages." "The Seven Stages" opens with a slow, plodding theme reminiscent of the *Dies irae*, that comes back in various guises throughout the second series of variations amidst frenzied activity in the piano. Some have suggested[29] that the first part of the symphony best demonstrates the reading of the work as a concerto (given the prominence of the piano part throughout the variations), whereas the second part manifests itself more symphonically. To that end, the "Dirge" (slow)-"Masque" (fast)-"Epilogue" (slow) form reflects recent precedents in Stravinsky's *Symphony in Three Movements* and adopts a form (slow-fast-slow) favored by Copland.[30] The brooding "Dirge," with its dark string writing sets up the frenetic "Masque," which demonstrates one of Bernstein's most virtuosic displays of melding concert and jazz influences. The "Epilogue" attempts to come to terms with the evening's events by recalling material from the "Prologue" and—in a departure from the resigned tone of Auden's poem—offers optimism for the new day.

Fancy Free and *On the Town*

In the years between his first and second symphonies, Bernstein debuted and made a big splash in the dance and musical theater realms with the ballet *Fancy Free* (1944) and the musical spin-off, *On the Town* (1944). In Bernstein's first major work, the "Jeremiah" Symphony, the composer drew extensively from musical materials that helped to define who Bernstein was: namely Jewish liturgical music, but also jazz. From his early adolescent bands to his paid job as a transcriber of jazz solos, Bernstein was one of only a few composers who both admired and played jazz. The score for *Fancy Free* depended upon the contemporary jazz idiom—as well as other vernacular references—and in choreographer Jerome Robbins Bernstein found a collaborator who wanted to convey the same sense of the contemporary vernacular in dance. More importantly as it pertains to Bernstein's work for *On the Waterfront, Fancy Free* demonstrates his potential to underscore images—here Robbins's choregraphy—in an effective manner, and throughout enhances effectively the work's narrative.

Robbins approached Bernstein about the project in late 1943 and the two artists—born roughly two months apart—were excited to realize that their collective artistic visions of representing their beloved New York City through music and dance were closely aligned. Bernstein thrived in the collaborative environment that Robbins and his Ballet Theatre colleagues provided, working closely with Robbins and the dancers and changing the score, sometimes spontaneously, based on rehearsal discussions. The ballet premiered on 18 April 1944 at the Metropolitan Opera House and was an immediate success, so much so that the season was lengthened and Bernstein toured with the company for two more weeks in 1944.

The ballet's story concerns three sailors granted a leave of absence from their obligations and their attempt to realize this break to the fullest. While at a bar, an attractive woman passes by and they each attempt to win her over. Unimpressed she leaves, but two of the sailors pursue her further, leaving the third behind. This third sailor meets another woman and after regaling her about his military life, they dance a *pas de deux*. The first two sailors, having convinced the first woman to rejoin them at the bar, return and make it an incompatible party of five. In order to even the odds, the three men dance their way to the women's hearts, and impressed by each, the women join the men in a group dance. Before the scene gets too violent the women leave the men to decide the competition on their own. The men decide to bemoan their situation by ordering more drinks, but before finishing them notice yet another woman passing by and the chase begins again, rounding out the drama.

While the ballet incorporates plentiful jazz references, they are but one stylistic component of a piece that also makes reference to Stravinsky, Copland, Shostakovich, Hindemith, and Gershwin, and ranks among Bernstein's most eclectic. In addition to these elements, the piano interjects frequently into the proceedings, as if commenting from a piano at the bar on the action between the dancers, and foreshadows the autobiographical role of the piano in Bernstein's Second Symphony. As Paul Laird notes regarding *Fancy Free*:

> The ballet, after all, was written by a pianist who often played jazz, blues, and boogie-woogie, a natural show-off who spent many parties entertaining at the piano. Here the piano has a similar function, sometimes dominating the proceedings with unmistakably American party music, rudely interrupting more "classical" sections. One is tempted to see Bernstein himself sitting at the piano bench in the orchestra, urging the sailors along as they seek pleasure on their short leave.[31]

The ballet opens to the strains of "Big Stuff," a slow blues song written by Bernstein with Billie Holiday in mind, accompanied by a bass line replete with dotted rhythms and evocative of contemporaneous bass lines from similar blues ballads. The opening song is then interrupted by four rim shots in the percussion and a syncopated melody in brass, scored to suggest a big band. The stride texture in the piano along with the frequent interjections of the percussion complete the jazzy reference. As "Scene at the Bar" opens, the previous material thins and one is left with a series of open harmonies in the clarinets that call to mind Copland's most pastoral moments, only to be interrupted again by the faint strains of the piano. A dissonant chord high in the winds gives way to a strutting figure in the piano that capitalizes on the bluesy juxtaposition of major and minor third scale degrees, known well to Bernstein as a defining feature of Copland's Piano Variations. Through the rest of the section, both syncopated and "straight" rhythmic patterns play against each other, broken by strident horn fanfares. The "Pas de Deux" recalls the opening tune of the ballet passed between instruments in the winds and brass. After a section distinguished by shifting meters, Bernstein builds the entire orchestra into a grand presentation of the "Big Stuff" theme into what one commentator called, "a commercially inspired figure . . . that sounds like an introduction fanfare for a cheesy cabaret act."[32]

Because the Russian influence on American dance in the first half of the twentieth century was so pervasive, it is no wonder that Bernstein chose to combine his vernacular influences with frequent allusions to Igor Stravinsky. In the subsequent competition scene, Bernstein employs material that recalls Stravinsky's penchant for stacking ostinatos, something that Bernstein employs throughout *On the Waterfront* as well. As the sailors each take their turn in front of the two ladies, the "Galop" finds Bernstein calling upon Stravinsky's neoclassical tendencies through frequent bitonal dissonant clashes. Bernstein demonstrates the softer, more romantic side of the second sailor in the "Waltz," but departs greatly from the Viennese favorite, once again through shifting meters and dotted rhythms more closely aligned with jazz. Similar to the rim shots in "Opening Dance" Bernstein uses the *tresillo* rhythm[33] of the *rumba* in the low strings to call attention to the final sailor's passionate display in the "Danzón." A theme then enters in the winds and foreshadows a similar texture in the "Cha Cha" of *West Side Story* (1957). Besides the *rumba*, Bernstein employs other dances that the audience would have recognized immediately as ballroom favorites going back to the first decades of the twentieth century. The "Finale" recycles the syncopated, brass-laden material from the "Competition Scene" and the open harmonies from the "Scene at the Bar," until a lonely, stride piano is overtaken by a rousing, yet brief climax (again from the "Competition Scene") signaling the beginning of yet another journey for the sailors—all the way to Broadway.

Shortly after *Fancy Free* premiered at the Met, plans were already under way to make a Broadway musical based on the ballet. *Fancy Free* set designer Oliver Smith thought the ballet would make a great musical and offered to produce it. Robbins and Bernstein were both excited about the possibility and began work immediately. For his part, Bernstein ensured that his former Village Vanguard Revuers—Green and Comden—were part of the collaborative team as lyricists and writers of the book. Because the artistic team had never produced a Broadway musical, they sought the demonstrated expertise of George Abbott to direct the show. Based on his success with Rodgers and Hart musicals, such as *Pal Joey* (1940), Abbott molded the original work—which came together rather quickly given the show's connection with *Fancy Free*—into a Broadway-worthy musical that eventually premiered in December 1944.[34]

For *On the Town*, Bernstein fused jazz and other vernacular styles with the Broadway song and dramatic tradition, to create a thoroughly integrated show in which music, acting, and dance all contributed to the plot's realization, and ultimately the show's success. Moreover Bernstein's appropriation of contemporary jazz idioms contributed much to the drama's authenticity, an aspect echoed in the realistic plot and character motivations. As described by Comden and Green at the time:

> The main thing was that having decided on three sailors we wanted them to come off as people. No matter how extravagantly treated, we wanted them to possess the qualities and attitudes of the servicemen we had seen coming into the city for the first time and at least touch on the frantic search for gaiety and love, and the terrific pressure of time that war brings. Our intention was not to bludgeon these points

> home, but to provide whatever fun and merriment we had to give with some basis of contemporary truth.[35]

Thus, jazz, blues, and Latin American music became important methods through which Bernstein was able to emphasize the youthful exuberance, highly charged sexual innuendos, and the soul of New York City central to *On the Town*'s success. It is this same sense of the vernacular that informs Bernstein's "urban" scoring throughout *On the Waterfront* and without examining the entire musical, a few notable examples bear this out quite effectively.

While Bernstein did not recycle any music from *Fancy Free* in *On the Town,* the musical opens in very much the same way as the ballet. After a slow blues song, a series of dissonant "alarms" signal 6:00 AM followed by material that recalls Copland's Concerto for Piano and Orchestra (1926; particularly the second movement), the sailors jump from their ship and utter the now-famous rocket-like call to action, "New York, New York!" The syncopated melody above a repetitive bass figure evokes contemporaneous swing bands and the imitative handling of the theme—an uncommon device for Broadway at the time and one Bernstein employs for the "Main Title" music in *On the Waterfront*—creates much musical intensity to open the show. As the lyrics of the song's "A" section speed past, one notices that, similar to the layering of riffs in arrangements personified by Count Basie's bands of the 1930s, it is the rhythmic intensity of the riffs (and thus the eager anticipation of the sailors) that is more important than the text. This action is then intensified in the opening dance number, which finds Bernstein employing the same thematic material from the song, the riffs—as they did for Basie—facilitate an exciting opening scene.

After Gabey chases after the elusive "Miss Turnstiles," Chip more than meets his match with an "experienced" cab driver named Hildegard Esterhazy, who convinces Chip in "Come Up to My Place" that the only place worth seeing in New York is the inside of her apartment. While several of the tunes in *On the Town* ("Lonely Town," "Lucky to be Me," and "Some Other Time") conform to the conventional, thirty-two measure, AABA Broadway ballad form, "Come Up to My Place" plays with that paradigm and uses jazz to emphasize Hildy's wanton morality. Chip opens each "A" section by asking Hildy to see prominent landmarks throughout New York, accompanied by a motoric rhythm suggestive of stride pianists like James P. Johnson, Willie "the Lion" Smith, and Earl Hines (particularly Hines's 1939 recording of "Piano Man"). After each request, Hildy begins the second "A" section with a question clarifying where Chip wants to visit and as Chip answers, Hildy abruptly stops the cab, stopping Chip (and the "A" section) in mid-sentence. The rude gesture signals the beginning of the "B" section and a change in musical style to a slow, seductive blues texture where Hildy falsely informs Chip that each place on his list no longer exists. The "A" section returns each time and Hildy makes her pleas (now spoken) more obvious. This clever setting of music and text continues until Hildy's insistence to "go to my place" increases in direct proportion to Chip's desire to go anywhere else. Bernstein follows the increasingly rapid exchange between Chip and Hildy with an equally quick alternation between riffs that brings the number to an exciting close.

Later we find Chip and Hildy back at her apartment in "I Can Cook Too," a number indebted to Gershwin classics like "Fascinatin' Rhythm" from *Lady Be Good* (1924). The song, at a fast tempo and with much syncopation in the melodic line, contains several blues references both musically and textually. Hildy's melody incorporates alternating major and minor thirds that are mirrored harmonically in the accompaniment. Most noticeable are the humorous *doubles entendres* that compare food and kitchen conveniences to Hildy's most sexually appealing body parts—for instance, "Yes I can roast too, my chickens just ooze, my gravy will lose you your mind"—reminiscent of more overt sexuality in versions of "Shave 'em Dry" by blues singers Ma Rainey and Lucille Bogan from 1924 and 1935 respectively. Again Bernstein plays with conventional Broadway forms by juxtaposing Hildy's boasts (in ABA form) with what functions as a bridge (C section repeated) wherein Hildy proves her case. She starts the bridge by telling the audience what "some girls" do and "one-ups" those labels—accepting a challenge mirrored aurally when Bernstein modulates up one whole step—by saying she can do all those things . . . and cook too! Here and throughout *On the Town*, Bernstein incorporates vernacular elements—especially jazz and blues—in an effort to more authentically convey urban New York life in the 1940s. This concern for the vernacular also informs his score for *On the Waterfront*, though much more subtly than the 1940s successes of *Fancy Free* and *On the Town*.

Trouble in Tahiti and *Wonderful Town*

Bernstein met Felicia Montealegre Cohn at a party early in 1946 and by the end of the year the two were engaged. Despite the white hot intensity that led to such an early commitment, Bernstein's demanding conducting and composing schedule (not to mention his omnivorous sexual appetites) cooled the relationship and eventually led to a dissolution (albeit temporarily) of their engagement. An aspiring actress, Montealegre found solace in her career and was further comforted through an affair with stage and screen actor Richard Hart. Yet, when Hart died unexpectedly in January of 1951, it was Bernstein to whom Montealegre turned to help pick up the pieces.[36] Based in large part on Felicia's persistence, the couple renewed their engagement in the summer of 1951 and by September were married. Following a whirlwind honeymoon in Mexico, the newlyweds announced in early 1952 that Felicia was pregnant with their first child, Jamie.

Throughout much of 1951, amidst the rapid progression from engagement to marriage to pregnancy—all in the span of seven months—Bernstein had been composing a dramatic work that was at odds with the domestic bliss witnessed by the public. Bernstein's first opera, *Trouble in Tahiti* (1952), insinuated that behind the saccharine exterior of the suburban existence, many "normal" families experienced a sense of discontent and lack of fulfillment in their daily lives. While Bernstein began the work before he entered into marriage with Felicia, and experienced a creative surge on the work during their honeymoon, progress slowed early in 1952. Fortunately, Bernstein became visiting professor at Brandeis University and was charged with leading the Festival of Creative Arts at which *Trouble in Tahiti* was scheduled to appear, giving Bernstein a more tangible reason to complete the work on time. Bernstein premiered the work during the festival in June, but was disappointed with the results. After reworking the opera's final scenes, Bernstein conducted the opera in performances at Tanglewood and in a televised performance in November 1952.

While the piece did have some success (especially following Bernstein's edits) most critics found the work shallow and did not grasp the significance of *Trouble in Tahiti* as a polemic against the paradise envisioned in the suburban experience. In fact Bernstein's work is an important early salvo against corporate conformity and suburban complacency that predates more contemporaneous accounts in Sloan Wilson's *The Man in the Gray Flannel Suit* (1955) and Richard Yates's *Revolutionary Road* (1961)[37] and has been revisited most recently in television's *Mad Men*.[38] More importantly, Bernstein re-engages these issues, albeit in an urban setting, in his score for *On the Waterfront*.

The opera opens with a trio of singers describing a picturesque day in suburbia, in which the sun kisses all that it touches. Bernstein even interrupts the trio's strains with the fanfare, "Suburbia!" to the tune of "New York, New York!" Life couldn't be better and the scene recalls a similar depiction of domestic utopia in Greenbelt, Maryland, featured in the documentary *The City* (1939).[39] Musically Bernstein relies on his mastery of popular styles, infusing the trio's material with swing rhythms and close harmonies in parallel movement reminiscent of popular trios like the Boswell Sisters. Bernstein even indicates in the "Notes on Production" found in the work's 1953 vocal score that the trio is "refined and sophisticated in a high-priced dance-band tradition."[40] The trio functions both as a Greek chorus and a Siren song recurring throughout the work and in each appearance soothing the listener with pleasing melodies and exalting the wonders of suburban living and the accompanying modern conveniences.

Bernstein juxtaposes the trio's sweet, innocent-sounding interjections against more angular, declamatory textures reminiscent of dramatic works by Blitzstein and Bertolt Brecht,[41] found in the opera's more dystopic domestic scenes of one particular family and their dissolving marriage within the little white house. Sam, Dinah, and their son Junior[42] appear to be an average suburban family, but Dinah's bad batch of coffee sparks a heated confrontation between Sam and Dinah thus initiating the audience into their troubled marriage. Dinah accuses Sam of having an affair and Sam shrugs it off as nonsense. Dinah encourages Sam to attend Junior's school play, but he can't be involved with such trivial matters because of his conflicting handball championship later that day. When Dinah reminds Sam how much it would mean to Junior, Sam insists that the boy will be fine and will understand. Sam and Dinah are clearly unsatisfied and desire to talk things over, but ultimately fall short because they don't know how to communicate. Instead, they retreat to their seemingly predetermined societal roles—Dinah the homemaker visits her therapist and later escapes through a B movie called *Trouble in Tahiti* while Sam climbs the corporate ladder and releases tension on the handball court. Sam and Dinah even run into each other between appointments only to invent reasons why they can't have lunch together. The final scene finds Sam and Dinah back at home, following dinner and with Junior supposedly in bed, when Sam decides to try and resolve the issues raised during breakfast while the trio interjects between each line of dialogue. Yet, rather than discuss their problems, Sam suggests escaping to a new movie called *Trouble in Tahiti* and Dinah joins him without protest.

As several scholars have noted, the autobiographical implications in *Trouble in Tahiti* are difficult to ignore. Bernstein's father's name was Sam and Sam's mother was named Dinah.[43] Sam Bernstein was a successful businessman and provided much for his family, but his upward mobility happened sometimes at the expense of his family. For instance, Sam's disinterest in Leonard's early musical endeavors and his chiding of music as a distraction finds its way into the opera when the character Sam chooses his handball tournament over seeing Junior in a school play. In addition, both Shirley and Burton Bernstein have each commented that their parents formed a less than perfect union. Their anecdotes—one about Sam's tirade when Jennie asked for money and the other a supposed extramarital affair that Sam was having[44]—were both represented in the breakfast dialogue between Sam and Dinah in the opera. That Bernstein projected his life into his first opera should also come as no surprise given his previous "dramatic roles" as a pianist in both *Fancy Free*, and Symphony No. 2 "The Age of Anxiety." Further, and expounded upon below in Chapter 4, Bernstein's experience with the House Committee on Un-American Activities and his potential blacklisting certainly informed his contribution to *On the Waterfront*. Although not as directly autobiographical, his next major work turned once again to his beloved New York City for its subject material, during a time in the composer's life when the world lay open before him.

As opposed to the difficulty Bernstein had in finally finishing *Trouble in Tahiti* for its premiere at Brandeis, he completed *Wonderful Town*—along with the help of Comden and Green—in a matter of weeks late in 1952. The close friends derived the musical from a 1940 play by Joseph Fields and Jerome Chodorov that itself was based on a book by Ruth McKenney called *My Sister Eileen* (1938) in which McKenney recounted stories of her youth in Ohio and eventual move to Greenwich Village. Through tryouts in New Haven, Connecticut, the team was able to fine-tune the rapidly conceived show and brought in Jerome Robbins to help with choreography and Sid Ramin to orchestrate the musical. The work premiered on 26 February 1953 and became a major success through 559 performances.

The opportunity to work on a show that took place at the very time Bernstein, Comden, and Green appeared as The Revuers at the Village Vanguard (The Village Vortex in *Wonderful Town*) was one the team could not pass up. In addition their intricate knowledge of the music, lexicon, and popular culture of New York City in the 1930s represented a valuable asset in completing a landmark work in Broadway history and in such a short time. Yet in their depiction of 1930s New York, Bernstein, Comden, and Green used many of the same musical materials from their depiction of 1940s New York in *On the Town*, namely jazz and Latin American music. For instance, "Christopher Street," employed a riff common to 1930s bandleader Eddie Duchin. "Swing" was mostly faithful to swing exemplars like Benny Goodman and even included a scat-based call and response section redolent of Cab Calloway or Ella Fitzgerald, whereas "Conga!" waxes nostalgically for the dance's heyday in the late 1930s.[45]

Yet, the conga is not the only 1930s phenomenon to which Bernstein yearned to return in *Wonderful Town*. Both *Trouble in Tahiti* and

Wonderful Town entered the musical landscape at a difficult political time for musicians, artists, and other intellectuals. Although I will explore this issue in much greater detail in Chapter 3, it is worth mentioning here that HUAC propagated a culture of fear within the artistic community that intensified following World War II. During 1952-1953, many of Bernstein's closest associates—for instance, Jerome Robbins, Aaron Copland, and David Diamond—as well as Bernstein himself had been or would be asked to divulge information about their ties to leftist and/or Communist organizations during the 1930s. In addition, those most responsible for creating *On the Waterfront*, namely Elia Kazan and Budd Schulberg, had also testified before HUAC. So while there is much in common stylistically between Bernstein's major compositions from the 1940s and 1950s, the two New York-based Broadway productions, *On the Town* and *Wonderful Town*, offer a window into Bernstein's mindset as he began work on *On the Waterfront* in early 1954. Whereas *On the Town* attempted to establish a national identity that resonated on an international level during the height of World War II, *Wonderful Town* (and *Trouble in Tahiti* for that matter) deal with matters of identity on a domestic scale. As Katherine Baber clarifies:

> Ultimately, *Wonderful Town* more directly explores what is at stake in the struggle for American identity on a *domestic* stage than on an international one. . . . Furthermore, the ostensibly All-American values of equality, progress, and other ideals of the New Deal era, which had been defended so vigorously abroad [during World War II], were called into question in domestic politics during the Cold War.[46]

As a newly domesticated Bernstein looked ahead to *On the Waterfront*, *Candide* (1956), and *West Side Story* (1957), what becomes clear is the struggle for American identity in his music is a manifestation of Bernstein's—and by extension the individual's—struggle to remain autonomous in an increasingly homogenous society. When Bernstein first became interested in music, he did not limit himself solely to the Western canon, but sought opportunities to play jazz and blues as well. He excelled musically at both Boston Latin School and Harvard University, yet his love of the liberal arts and his voracious intellectual curiosity compelled him to seek out opportunities—like his classes with David Prall—to add depth to his musical knowledge. In his senior thesis he questioned the nature of American music, exemplified for years by fellow New Englanders Horatio Parker, John Knowles Paine, and Edward MacDowell, and instead pointed to Aaron Copland and George Gershwin, among others, as composers who were more thoroughly "American" because of their appropriation of vernacular styles. Further, Bernstein enjoyed composing in both "serious" and "popular" arenas and when he was advised to focus on one, he bristled at the suggestion and found a way to infuse his "popular" works with more serious elements and *vice versa.* As a budding conductor he gravitated towards maestros like Mitropolous and Koussevitzky who both commanded the attention of the orchestra and audience through their highly extroverted conducting styles. Bernstein excelled at both conducting and composing and although his chief mentors—Copland and Koussevitzky—believed that he needed to focus on one to be truly successful, he persevered to contribute profoundly in both arenas. Bernstein was pulled in numerous directions both personally and professionally and though he struggled mightily at times—and at the expense of those closest to him—establishing and maintaining his identity was a paramount concern.

Paradoxically, Bernstein was able to establish a unique compositional voice because of his keen ability to assimilate the tendencies of everyone and everything. Like a method actor, Bernstein was able to summon past musical experiences in order to solve each new compositional problem. Pieces he conducted, people he knew, composers with whom he studied, books he had read, all were potential sources for new compositions. Chapter 2 examines those elements that best represent Bernstein's musical style and that are employed most prominently in his score for *On the Waterfront.*

2

LEONARD BERNSTEIN'S COMPOSITIONAL METHOD IN *ON THE WATERFRONT*

In October 1946, Bernstein commented insightfully on the degree to which he was already being pulled between artistic impulses, and offered an early credo emphasizing his need to focus on one project at a time:

> It is impossible for me to make an exclusive choice among the various activities of conducting, symphonic composition, writing for the theater, and playing the piano. What seems right for me at any given moment is what I must do, at the expense of pigeonholing or otherwise limiting my services to music. I will not compose a note while my heart is engaged in a conducting season; nor will I give up writing so much as a popular song, while it is there to be expressed, in order to conduct Beethoven's *Ninth.* There is a particular order involved in this, which is admittedly difficult to plan; but the order must be adhered to most strictly. For the ends are music itself, not the conventions of the music business; and the means are my private problem.[1]

Further, Bernstein often demonstrated a laser-like focus when completing works like *Wonderful Town* and *On the Waterfront* in a matter of a couple months. While Bernstein's professed dedication to the task immediately at hand is admirable, there is considerable evidence that suggests he experienced difficulty adhering to the above manifesto. For instance, while concertizing on the piano was never a long-term emphasis of his career, the instrument factors prominently in works like *Fancy Free* and Symphony No. 2, "The Age of Anxiety." In addition, his first two symphonies demonstrate indebtedness to vernacular styles, while his musical theater works frequently employ contrapuntal textures uncommon in Broadway in the 1940s and 1950s. During his final days at Harvard, he was able to complete simultaneously incidental music for *The Birds* as well as his senior thesis. Furthermore, these multivalent and competing interests represent an important reason why Bernstein never composed another film score and caused Bernstein to lament later in life that, "I feel I've written very little. Considering my other activities, it is explicable. I mean one understands right away. But the fact remains that the list is short."[2]

What Bernstein alluded to in 1946 and at various points throughout his career was his interest in a wide range of musical and artistic pursuits that led scholars, and Bernstein himself, to call his music "eclectic." As Bernstein divulged in an oft-cited interview with Paul Laird in 1982:

> LAIRD: You've said yourself that your music is eclectic.
> BERNSTEIN: With a certain amount of pride, I think.
> LAIRD: Would you consider Copland your greatest influence?
> BERNSTEIN: I think Copland is very eclectic, very. Because he was strongly influenced, for example by Stravinsky, who was the most eclectic composer that ever lived himself. . . . If you go into anybody, including Bach, Beethoven, you can make out a case for eclecticism. The greater the composer, the better case you can make out for his eclecticism.
> LAIRD: So to you, every composer is to some extent eclectic.
> BERNSTEIN: Every painter, every poet, everybody.
> LAIRD: You've got to be basing your work on what's coming before it.
> BERNSTEIN: Otherwise you don't exist. Who are you if you're not the sum of everything that's happened before? Everything you've experienced at least, not everything that's happened, but everything that has been significant in your experience, unconsciously mainly.[3]

What might seem like a fair retrospective assessment—Bernstein's last point regarding a "sum of experiences"—was actually something the composer suggested in his senior thesis to explain jazz's assimilation into contemporary American concert music:

> If we are true to our conviction that the music a man produces is the sum total of all his experience—conscious and subconscious, prenatal, amatory, social, visual, to say nothing of musical—then we are necessarily led to acknowledge that a composer who hears a certain kind of music around him all the time will show the effect of this force in his own music, regardless of his attitude toward it.[4]

Numerous authors have discussed Bernstein's musical language as communicated through his musical theater writing and in more symphonically conceived pieces.[5] Bernstein's melodies possessed a great deal of lyricism, yet also included wide leaps and irregular phrasing that made them challenging to execute. Bernstein enlivened those melodies by incorporating shifting accents and meters typical of Latin American music and jazz. His harmonic vocabulary tended towards the conventional, but he colored it with added tones and modal shadings, and later in his career experimented with twelve-tone music. Bernstein was an exquisite orchestrator, evidenced across his output by the increased role he gave to the percussion as well as the prominence of the voice in some of his orchestral pieces. By extension, the voice's presence in his first and third symphonies provides evidence of a reconsideration of that primarily instrumental genre. Many of these same characteristics also find their way into his score for *On the Waterfront*. Clearly Bernstein breathed much life into both his concert music (through incorporation of vernacular elements) and his musical theater pieces (via techniques more closely associated with "serious" music), but his overall musical language shares much in common with other prominent twentieth century composers including (among others) Aaron Copland, Béla Bartók, Igor Stravinsky, Samuel Barber, Arthur Honegger, and Benjamin Britten. What then makes his music so distinctively "Bernstein-ian?"

Recalling the quotation that opened this chapter two important points stand out as they pertain to the score for *On the Waterfront*: eclecticism through a "sum of experiences" and a "strict order." In other words, Bernstein drew upon time spent with Copland or Blitzstein, pieces he conducted, works he played on the piano, and songs he heard on records or at nightclubs all as research or source material from which he created new works. In addition, Bernstein organizes many of his larger musical projects by introducing small musical building blocks and expanding them methodically to create a cohesive, wholly integrated structure. For the remainder of this chapter I hope to demonstrate that Bernstein's score for *On the Waterfront* represents a particularly intriguing case study 1) for his ability to draw from a diverse range of experiences akin to a method actor's ability to channel affective memory into given role and 2) for thematic integration of both music and drama that was uncommon in Hollywood film scoring at the time and foreshadowed the same thematic and dramatic integration that was integral to the success of *West Side Story* three years later.

Bernstein's Method

In the above interview when Bernstein was asked whether Copland was his greatest influence, he immediately deflected the question and instead answered with a defense of not only Copland's eclecticism, but also the diverse influences felt by the most renowned composers in the Western canon. Clearly Copland exerted a considerable influence upon Bernstein's musical development beginning with their first meetings together in the late 1930s. In addition to informal studies with Copland, Bernstein also connected with New York's artistic and intellectual elites, including influential critic Virgil Thomson and author/composer Paul Bowles.[6] Copland also initiated Bernstein into the Group Theater, where he met Copland's close friend and co-founding member Harold Clurman, Clifford Odets, and Elia Kazan.[7]

While Clurman helped start The Group, it was Lee Strasberg who trained the company's actors in "The Method." Strasberg and Clurman both lamented the state of American theater in the early 1920s in which acting and the play's true message was subordinate to one's stage presence. Strasberg sought a new way of realizing drama based largely on his interest in Constantin Stanislavsky's theories espoused in *My Life in Art* (1924). As David Thomson put it:

> Stanislavsky was at war with the tradition of stylish, or stylized, impersonation based upon sound stagecraft more than inner inquiry. He was interested in a deeper exploration of motivation, need, desire, and fear in a character—the subtext—and in the kind of ensemble process in which all the players were asking the same kind of questions, bound by similar rules.[8]

Two years before Strasberg met Clurman, he witnessed this phenomenon in action when he saw Stanislavsky's Moscow Art Theatre and noticed that:

> [A]ll the actors, whether they were playing leads or small parts, worked with the same commitment and intensity. No actors idled about posing or preening (or thinking about where they might dine after the performance). More important, each actor seemed to project some sort of unspoken, yet palpable, inner life for his or her character. This was acting of a sort one rarely saw on the American stage.[9]

This experience inspired Strasberg to study at the American Laboratory Theater led by two of Stanislavsky's students, Richard Boleslawsky and Maria Ouspenskaya. Strasberg learned at the Laboratory that in the same way actors prepared their bodies through dance and other movement exercises, they could also better inhabit their roles through mental training. One of the more powerful and influential of these mental tools was what became known as "affective memory" devices. To Stanislavsky's quest for "inner inquiry" Strasberg implemented a:

> [P]sychoanalytic probing in which the personality of the actor himself might be mined for a character's inscape. Thus casting was all the more reliable if a company director knew his players well enough to have unearthed their own personal problems. If he could then harness those traumas to certain roles, not only was a play enriched, but the director began to assume the role of personal teacher or analyst to the actors.[10]

Eventually, stage actors came to study with Strasberg and along with Clurman they formed the Group Theater in 1931. Following the huge success of plays like *Men in White* (1933) and *Waiting for Lefty* (1935) the Group became the most prominent theater company in the United States. When an increasing number of Group members left for Hollywood and unstable finances left the Group in a precarious position, it eventually disbanded in 1941. Not deterred Strasberg picked up the pieces and along with Elia Kazan, Robert Lewis, and Cheryl Crawford formed the Actor's Studio in 1947.

Thus, the Group Theater, Actor's Studio, and method acting, were each important facets of the artistic world that Bernstein inhabited beginning in the late 1930s. While Copland was Bernstein's first connection to the Group Theater, their philosophies, and left-leaning politics, he experienced their chief principles through other means as well. Marc Blitzstein was a Group member in the latter part of the 1930s and as mentioned in Chapter 1, Bernstein depended heavily on Blitzstein as an early mentor and experienced the sort of agitprop theater the Group produced when he helped stage Blitzstein's *The Cradle Will Rock* at Harvard. When Robert Lewis helped establish the Actor's Studio, among the first class admitted was longtime Bernstein collaborator Jerome Robbins.[11] Later, when Robbins attempted to create a truer sense of animosity between Jets and Sharks in *West Side Story* by segregating the actors offstage as well,[12] he adopted a technique previously employed by both Strasberg and Kazan.[13] Beyond these personal connections, the directorial work of Strasberg, Kazan, and Lewis dominated the theater industry in the 1940s and early 1950s such that their success would have been impossible for Bernstein to ignore as someone who was equally important to musical theater's development at the same time.

Another way in which Bernstein connected with the Group Theater/Actor's Studio phenomenon occurred through a shared sense of realism through improvisation. Bernstein's interest in jazz dates back to his youth and elements of jazz enter his work compositionally in his incidental music for *The Birds*. More broadly, Louis Armstrong's Hot Five and Hot Seven recordings between 1925 and 1928 opened eyes in more "serious" artistic circles regarding the implication of improvisation on other artistic disciplines. Armstrong interrogated the "text"— in the form of blues or Tin Pan Alley songs—and improvised a new melody while still remaining faithful to the original text. Later, bop artists like Dizzy Gillespie and Charlie Parker in an effort to reinvigorate jazz improvisation in the early 1940s, appropriated many of the same "texts" as Armstrong, but replaced the original melodies through new improvisation and obscured the harmonic progressions with more complicated chord changes resulting in a more personalized and relevant text. In order to realize these new texts convincingly bop improvisers were able to draw upon an encyclopedic knowledge of thousands of tunes/songs gained through daily exposure to the material in swing bands. Then in after hours workshops—or more appropriately jam sessions—players fashioned new interpretations of classic texts that could be presented on smaller stages throughout New York City. Strasberg asked his students to think similarly about the text, often stating, "Words are decorations on the hem of the skirt of action"[14] in order to encourage actors to alter textual delivery appropriate to their emotions and inner reading of the text.

Intimate understanding of the text—or a variety of texts—in order to create a new version is a chief Group Theater maxim and an important part of Stanislavsky's foremost principle. In his second of eight lectures in 1957 that eventually comprised *Method—Or Madness?*, Robert Lewis displayed for the audience a chart of forty tenets created by Stanislavsky in 1934 arranged (according to Lewis) like a large pipe organ. The axiom that underpinned the entire process was "Work on One's Self."[15] Lewis went on to convey to the gathered audience what Stanislavsky supposedly meant:

> I think what [Stanislavsky] probably means is that when you are expressing yourself in a part, somehow all your reactions to life, all the ideas and feelings that you have stored up, come out in one way or another. Therefore you should work to enlarge your knowledge of the world, the people in it, and their characters and relationships. Also, you should sharpen your observance of situations in life, develop your imagination and sensitivity, because those are the things which you store up to feed you in whatever you do in your work. The process goes on all the time with all artists, but one should make a continuing effort in that direction. It is so basic that it is put down as the foundation of [Stanislavsky's] whole edifice.[16]

Reflecting on Bernstein's career through Lewis's words it would seem he adopted Stanislavsky's chief command and sought every day to realize it as a call to embrace the eclectic spirit. In his educational endeavors, Bernstein's interest in a vast array of intellectual pursuits is the personification of Prall's emphasis on interdisciplinary inquiry. As a composer both vernacular and serious idioms were capable of producing memorable works of art. As a conductor Bernstein gave life to new works and reinterpreted long-held classics. As the quotation that opens this chapter suggests, Bernstein's "self" was the project at hand, an end to which he was utterly devoted. The "work"—or "private problem"—came when Bernstein absorbed and retained everything around him and channeled the most pertinent streams from that memory reservoir into the project at hand.

When Bernstein accepted work scoring *On the Waterfront* in 1954, he embarked upon his most personal collaboration with the Group Theater/Actor's Studio world. Directed by Kazan and including a principal cast—Marlon Brando, Lee J. Cobb, Karl Malden, Leif Erickson, Eva Marie Saint, and Rod Steiger among others—derived from the Actor's Studio, *On the Waterfront* was a cinematic triumph and a vivid demonstration of the "Method" in action. To the degree that Bernstein's accompanying score depends upon a vast collected memory and textual knowledge of pieces conducted and composers consulted, his first and only foray into film scoring presents a unique case study of what I have termed "method scoring." From the portion of Lewis's lecture on affective memory, "When coming up against a situation in a play requiring a certain emotion, [the actor] can evoke the memory of some similar emotion in his life without thinking consciously about it at all."[17] True, Bernstein agreed to collaborate on the project after much of the principal production had been completed so he would not have seen the nuts and bolts of the "Method" at work. In addition, no evidence exists to suggest Kazan and Bernstein discussed the "Method" or "affective memory" in relation to the score. Yet as will be made clearer in Chapter 4, the two had much in common with each other politically and in their personal connection to the film's chief protagonist, Terry Malloy. The reclamation of one's dignity and the ultimate refusal to conform, thus epitomizing "work on one's self," was central to Terry's character development and of paramount concern for Kazan as a director and Bernstein as a composer/conductor. When Bernstein entered into other compositional genres—for instance incidental music for *The Birds*, his first ballet *Fancy Free*, first musical *On the Town*, first opera *Trouble in Tahiti*, and Symphony No. 1 "Jeremiah"—Bernstein employed the musical texts he knew best. He used jazz to make Aristophanes's Greek in *The Birds* more relevant to a modern audience; jazz and Latin American music in both *Fancy Free* and *On the Town* with Russian orchestral/ballet music in the former; continued with jazz in *Trouble in Tahiti* and also depended upon agitprop dramas by Blitzstein (especially his more authentic American speech settings), Brecht, and operas he had conducted, e.g. Britten's *Peter Grimes*;[18] employed Jewish sacred music experienced during his youth especially during the first and third movements of his Symphony No. 1 "Jeremiah." *On the Waterfront* employs texts from Bernstein's musical memory as well, but perhaps more convincingly than these examples, relies on sources that relate directly towards the film's chief narrative: the triumph of the individual. For the remainder of this chapter I will detail specific case studies in which Bernstein depended upon his compositional and musical memory to create his score. I will also consider an additional scenario, which articulates how Bernstein used *On the Waterfront* as source material for *West Side Story*, both here and in a concluding discussion regarding the legacy of the music in *On the Waterfront*. In the Chapter 5 cue-by-cue analysis of the score, I will also refer to other sources where appropriate in order to demonstrate that Bernstein didn't just compose a score to accompany a film. Rather, he channeled some of his strongest musical memories and created a "character" that spoke through music.

Bernstein and Copland

Given the important role Copland played in Bernstein's life and music it should come as no surprise that Copland factored prominently in the musical memory that helped produce the *On the Waterfront* score. Copland wrote several film scores[19] that comprised a part of his output that Bernstein greatly admired.[20] Yet Copland's film scores influence *On the Waterfront* only minimally. For instance, in Part I of *The City*, which depicts life in a pre-industrialized New England community, one notices a father and son on a wagon arriving at a blacksmith's workshop with a wheel to be fixed. As the wagon pulls up, one hears a leisurely melody in the saxophone, an instrument that seems out of place in this bucolic New England hamlet. Yet as Elizabeth Crist explains:

> Here, [the saxophone] serves as a sonic marker of modernism. A musical hybrid (a wind instrument made of brass) closely associated with jazz, the saxophone connotes modernity itself. Its striking timbre gives the rural theme an urban edge, and thus the agrarian scene is shown to contain the seeds of modernity.[21]

Bernstein uses the saxophone as well in *On the Waterfront* as the instrument that introduces the most prominent motive in the film. Yet as the saxophone seems misplaced and even anachronistic in *The City*, the instrument works quite well connoting the contemporary urban setting and destroying the more pastoral strains of the film's opening title music.

In addition to Copland's triumvirate of ballets (*Billy the Kid*, *Rodeo*, and *Appalachian Spring*) his music for *The Red Pony* was also an important source for future film scorers charged with evoking scenes of the open West.[22] Copland's music for "The Gift" shares much in common with the opening of a cue from *On the Waterfront* entitled "Roof Morning" (see Ex. 5.9 and 5.10). Outwardly Tom Tiflin would appear to have decent parents, but young Tom experiences very little warmth and encouragement from them (paralleled in the way that everyone except Tom ignores Grandpa's long-winded tales about the late nineteenth century west). Tom appears to find a more appealing father figure in Billy Buck (Robert Mitchum), going so far as to mimic Billy's every gesture. In an effort to build a closer relationship with Tom, Fred Tiflin purchases a red pony for his son who is overwhelmed by the gesture. Because Tom disdains his reality, he tends to escape to a fantasy world wherein he leads knights on horseback to battle or conducts an orderly procession of horses in the circus. Thus from Tom's point of view this new pony before him could be just another dream. As Fred exits the stable, leaving Tom to ask Billy how to take care of the horse and help Tom name the pony "Galiban," the audience sees two versions of the same person: Tom and Tom's vision of what he wants to be when he grows up in the form of Billy. Copland accompanies this tender scene with an arpeggiation of perfect fourths in the harp, answered by a minor seventh chord in the harp and strings, followed by more widely-spaced sonorities in the upper winds and strings (Ex. 2.1). The opening pentatonic melody followed by harmonic ambiguity in the upper reaches of the winds, strings, harp, and vibes, promotes a sense of anticipation and expectancy as we share in Tom's surprise at his new gift and wonder if this is just another daydream.

Ex. 2.1. *Red Pony* Suite. "The Gift, " mm. 1-4 (without strings).[23]

On the morning following Joey Doyle's assassination in *On the Waterfront*, the audience sees a boy (also named Tommy) seek out Terry Malloy in a scene that finds Kazan juxtaposing Tommy's innocence and potential against Terry's nightmarish reality. Interestingly, as opposed to Copland's more hopeful strains, Bernstein evokes this sense of loss and instability in Terry's life with similar musical materials as used in "The Gift" (harp, vibes, flutes, and solo oboe) and within an ambiguous yet dissonant harmonic context. (See Ex. 5.9 and the accompanying discussion for more detail.)

Despite these references to Copland's film scores, it is one of his ballets that one hears most prominently in *On the Waterfront*, namely *Billy the Kid* (1938). One commentator even asserted that "[t]here is a touch of the cowboy confrontation on main street here, as Terry Malloy goes down to confront Johnny Friendly. Leonard Bernstein's score underlines the parallel musically by quoting Aaron Copland's *Billy the Kid*."[24] While Bernstein did not actually copy *Billy the Kid*, there is ample musical evidence—especially in the final scene—to cause an uninitiated listener to make such a claim. Moreover, through Crist's reading of the ballet in the context of late 1930s politics, the connection between *Billy the Kid* and *On the Waterfront* goes beyond the music.

As Crist explains, when the western frontier had essentially closed by the early 1880s, the idea of the unsettled West continued to be used as an image of what was possible during times of crisis:

> [T]he myth of the West was born of the frontier's death. Even after the frontier had passed into history, the imagined West could still be used to justify a continuing reliance on individual rather than collective solutions to the problems of modernity. The West, the prairie, the pioneer, and the cowboy—all were cemented as icons of American progress, and together they came to represent a spirit of endless expansion, whether national borders, liberal democracy, or industrial capitalism.[25]

As the Great Depression and the Dust Bowl consumed the 1930s, thousands of Americans were again encouraged to go west in search of economic prosperity. However, New Deal politicians like Franklin Roosevelt and Henry A. Wallace, and intellectuals such as Stuart Chase, realized that the unchecked individualism inherent in the frontier mythology contributed greatly to the onset of the Depression. So they shifted the rhetorical focus from the West as a site of plentiful resources ready to feed ravenous capitalistic appetites towards a place where cooperation and collective action was required to govern more effectively.[26]

Consequently, Billy occupies an ambiguous position in the ballet and in the course of American history. We are drawn to his reckless individualism, but it is that very spirit that must be eliminated if we are to live in peace and protect civilization in the conquered frontier. As Lincoln Kirstein, the Ballet Caravan impresario who commissioned *Billy the Kid* noted, "Billy represented the basic anarchy inherent in individualism in its most rampant form."[27] A microcosm of the group's eventual supplanting of the individual occurs at the opening and closing of the ballet. Amidst a shadowy landscape found in the ballet's set design Copland offers bare fifths in the clarinets and oboes that enhance nicely the land's vastness (Ex. 2.2).

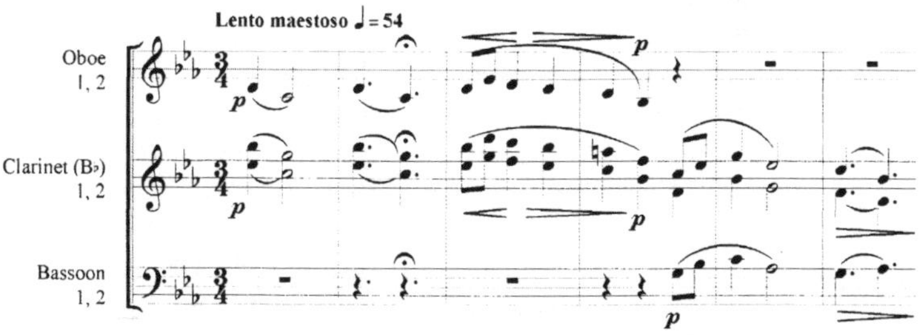

Ex. 2.2. *Billy the Kid*. "Introduction: The Open Prairie," mm. 1-6.[28]

This material gives way to further quintal harmonization in the horns and a syncopated perfect fourth ostinato in the timpani and piano underneath a pentatonic fanfare in the flute that accompanies the first settlers' inexorable movement across the stage (Ex. 2.3). As Crist points out:

> The syncopations accompany the halting, erratic migration of the dancers; the repetitive fragments, uneven rhythms, and static minor-mode harmonies mitigate a sense of progress. . . . The musical deformation of the march casts a pall on the procession, and at times it is not entirely clear whether the dancers (as pioneers) are moving determinedly or reluctantly across the stage from right to left, East to West.[29]

Ex. 2.3. *Billy the Kid.* "Introduction: The Open Prairie," mm. 14-19 (without strings).[30]

Copland increases the musical texture as the appearance of pioneers multiplies rapidly and their movement across the stage overwhelms the surroundings. Among the mass of humanity one notices a woman with a child close by: young Billy is just one among thousands in the westward progression. After the thrilling account of Billy's life and exploits ends with his murder at Pat Garrett's hand, the ballet concludes with a musical reprisal of the great, opening progression that moves ever onwards. From the point of view of Copland's triumphant, relentless, yet ultimately unresolved music (Ex. 2.4), Billy's death was necessary to advance the greater good and echoes Kirstein's sentiments that, "[W]ith a new start across the continent, . . . [Billy's death is] one more step achieved in the necessary ordering of the whole generation's procession. It's a flag-raising, more than a funeral. Billy's lonely wild-fire energy is replaced by the group force of many marchers."[31]

Ex. 2.4. *Billy the Kid*. One measure after R 53 (without strings).[32]

On 8 November 1953 the *Omnibus* television series broadcast a version of *Billy the Kid* with choreographer Eugene Loring as narrator for a nationally televised audience.[33] As farmers and migrant workers were told to seek the West for a better life when the ballet premiered in 1938, the television audience for this *Omnibus* broadcast was again being sold on a new frontier: suburbia. The collective action that was integral to the Popular Front's identity in the 1930s culminated in a nation's coming together to emerge victorious in World War II. The promotion of the group dynamic in *Billy the Kid* and the promise of a better life away from the teeming urban masses depicted in *The City* was being realized in the 1950s in homogenous suburban developments across the country. Bernstein had already commented on suburban discontent and the downside of mass commercialization in his semiautobiographical *Trouble in Tahiti*. Issues of conformity, alienation, anxiety, and the side effects of progress were surely on the minds of many

Americans tuning in to watch the 1953 broadcast of *Billy the Kid*. As "fitting in" and "other-direction" became social paradigms by the early 1950s, it is likely that many admired Billy's bravado and unwillingness to bend to society's norms. Given that frame of reference the parallels between Billy and Terry Malloy are striking. Terry lived in a world bound by a code of silence, thus ensuring the waterfront machine—politically and commercially—ran smoothly. While *Billy the Kid* surveyed the death of the West and promoted collective action as a better means for social and economic well-being, *On the Waterfront* suggested that in a climate where organized corruption enforced conformity upon an oppressed mass, only mobilization behind a strong individual could lead to a better life for all.

Beyond these connections between dramatic narratives and political implications, striking musical similarities exist that suggest *Billy the Kid* was foremost among many other pieces on Bernstein's mind as he began work on the score less than six months after the *Omnibus* broadcast. While the strongest connection occurs at the end of the film there are other similarities as well. The "opening titles" music is comprised of a horn solo that moves pentatonically until the tritone disruption in measure 5 (Ex. 5.1) and is constructed largely in thirds, similar to the pensive pentatonic woodwind fanfare that opens *Billy the Kid*. In order to summon a sense of heroic dignity Bernstein employs the horn and through the modal coloring injects the same sort of timelessness suggested by Copland's languorous melody and bare harmonies that open *Billy the Kid*. Bernstein's lonely yet inquisitive and hopeful melody suggests potential that is ultimately realized in the film's final frames.

After Terry resolves to confront Johnny Friendly, and after he is badly beaten by Friendly and his "posse," Father Barry—with the encouragement of the other workers—convinces Terry to lead the men to work in spite of Friendly's threats to blacklist everyone. As Terry struggles to his feet and stumbles to the cavernous warehouse entry one notices open harmonies in the strings and vibraphones against a lumbering, quartal ostinato in the bass (Ex. 5.52), similar to the accompanimental material found in Ex. 2.3. Loring's paradoxical choreography that closes *Billy the Kid* in which dancers/pioneers are moving west yet looking back to the east, suggests that progress is both inevitable and uncertain. Such ambiguity is mirrored in Boris Kaufman's neorealist cinematography in which the careening subjective point of view allows the audience to feel Terry's struggle to lead the men inside, never quite sure that he will make it. As the shipping boss calls the men to work, Bernstein underscores Terry's vindication—recalling Kirstein's "flag waving of many marchers"—with a brass-dominated recapitulation of themes (Ex. 5.53 and 5.54) that culminate in the same manner as Copland's march of the settlers in *Billy the Kid* (Ex. 2.4). While Copland's music in the opening and closing sections of *Billy the Kid* perhaps best exemplifies the sort of musical source material behind *On the Waterfront*, it is certainly not the only connection; a point that will be emphasized in Chapter 5. Bernstein was also a prominent conductor and he channeled many of the works he interpreted for orchestras around the world into his *On the Waterfront* score.

Bernstein and Conducting

As observed in Chapter 1, by the time Bernstein began work on *On the Waterfront* in 1954 he was already one of the most promising young conductors in the United States and possibly the world. He had already led many of the most renowned orchestras in the world and his leadership of the New York City Symphony allowed him to program a variety of new works, many of which were composed by Americans. Because Bernstein studied with Copland as well as performed and conducted several pieces by his mentor, Copland's music leaves the largest imprint on Bernstein's musical language as it pertains to *On the Waterfront*.

Yet one can also detect a host of other works with which Bernstein was likely quite familiar throughout the score as well. For instance, in addition to *Billy the Kid*'s connection with the "Main Title" music, the wavelike opening figure (mm. 1-4) in the woodwinds that opens Barber's *Knoxville: Summer of 1915* (1947, rev. 1949) as well as subsequent iterations of that material at Rehearsal 22 (mm. 202-214) and, more grandly, at Rehearsal 24 (mm. 218-227) also share much in common with the melodic contour of the Dignity theme (Ex. 5.1 below).[34] Besides American composers like Copland, Barber, or Gershwin, the sharp ear can also detect the influence of Arthur Honegger's music. There is a strong similarity between the accented semitonal "Scotch snap," shifting accents, crisp brass writing, and string ostinato (Ex. 2.5a and 2.5b) during the opening measures of the third movement of his Symphony No. 5 "Di tre re" (1951; like *Knoxville*, premiered by the Boston Symphony Orchestra) and cues like "Scramble" (Ex. 5.12) and "Riot in Church" (Ex. 5.16) that also contained ostinatos and prominent writing for brass, and underscored scenes of intense violence in *On the Waterfront*.[35]

Ex. 2.5a. Arthur Honegger. Symphony No. 5 "Di tre re," 3rd Movement, mm. 2-3 (Trumpets and Strings only).[36]

Ex. 2.5b. Arthur Honegger. Symphony No. 5 "Di tre re," 3rd Movement, mm. 16-17.[37]

Bernstein championed a variety of composers through works he conducted, notably Dmitri Shostakovich's symphonies. Shostakovich's Fifth Symphony (1937) became one of the cornerstone pieces in Bernstein's long conducting career and, not surprisingly, the work contributed in part to *On the Waterfront*'s diverse musical tapestry. For instance, a more obvious connection lies between the thunderous timpani ostinato that opens the final movement and a similarly intense percussive texture that accompanies the film's first images in "Opening Shot to Scream" (see Ex. 5.5). In addition the dark, imitative string writing that accompanies Terry's search for Johnny Friendly after the latter killed Terry's brother Charley ("Throwing the Gun," Ex. 5.39) shares much in common with the equally ominous, contrapuntal string texture in the opening measures of the first movement of Shostakovich's Fifth (Ex. 2.6).

Ex. 2.6. Dmitri Shostakovich. Symphony No. 5, 1st Movement, mm. 1-3.[38]

Another composer and one with whom Bernstein certainly identified was Benjamin Britten and his opera *Peter Grimes* (1945). Bernstein conducted the American premiere of the work at Tanglewood in 1946 and the Four Interludes (Op. 33a) derived from the opera were, like Shostakovich's Fifth Symphony, one of Bernstein's conducting standards until the end of his conducting career. For instance, one could argue that the tumultuous opening of the "Storm" Interlude (2.7a) contributed to the "Violence" music that coincides with the opening images of *On the Waterfront* perhaps more so than the aforementioned Honegger example.[39] Even more to the point is the way in which Britten's "Dawn" Interlude relates to the "Roof Morning" cue following Joey Doyle's death (see Chapter 5, "Roof Morning"). Britten opens that interlude with the flutes and violins in unison answered by an arpeggiated passage in the clarinets, harp, and violas *divisi.* In addition, Britten employs an accented upper neighbor tone (Ex. 2.7b) in the flute solo similar to the one that distinguishes Bernstein's Pain motive (See Chapter 5).

Ex. 2.7a. Benjamin Britten. Sea Interlude No. 4 "Storm" from *Peter Grimes*. Op. 33a, mm. 1-2 (Strings only).[40]

Ex. 2.7b. Benjamin Britten. Sea Interlude No. 1 "Dawn" from *Peter Grimes*. Op. 33a, mm. 1-3.[41]

Of course for "Roof Morning" (Ex. 5.9 and 5.10) Bernstein reverses the texture by providing the arpeggiated ostinato first and the solo second. Given the narrative connection between *Grimes*'s and *Waterfront*'s seaside settings, several critics have noted musical similarities as well.[42] What may have also caught Bernstein's attention was Britten's comment in a 1948 *Time* magazine article that the opera was special to him because it pertains to "the struggle of the individual against the masses. The more vicious the society, the more vicious the individual."[43] It is also possible that Bernstein connected *Grimes* to this particular scene in the film (when the "apprentice" Tommy meets with the troubled Terry) because of the opera's preoccupation with a societal outcast and younger apprentice boys that continue to disappear. While such an intertextual reference is difficult to prove, what is unmistakable is Bernstein's intimate knowledge of *Grimes* and its musical parallels with thematic material employed in *On the Waterfront*, particularly "Roof Morning."

The pieces listed here represent only a sampling of the wide range of pieces from which Bernstein mined to bolster his musical memory. The manner in which Bernstein weaved this diverse array of resources into a cohesive whole represents yet another way in which he relied on previous compositional memory: motivic and thematic integration.

Bernstein and the "Basic Shape"

In Humphrey Burton's magisterial account of Bernstein's life he offers very few substantive comments about the music for *On the Waterfront*. Yet, one of his closing thoughts is that "Bernstein's finest achievement is the thematic integration of the whole score."[44] Here Burton echoes sentiments expressed by Bernstein in a program note that appeared in the *Berkshire* [MA] *Eagle* on 15 July 1955 just before the premiere of the Symphonic Suite from the film:

> The very nature of film music is fragmentary, almost by definition. There are exceptions, of course, such as music for films which are

> pageant-like, or short on dialogue and long on visual effect; in these cases extended musical sections are possible. *On the Waterfront* is not such a picture. Depending, as it does, on highly realistic dialogue, the opportunities for long developed musical sequences are few. In spite of this, I was so intrigued by the atmosphere and power of the film when I saw it in "rough-cut" that I decided to write the score hoping to compensate for the necessary fragmentary quality of the music by strong thematic integration.[45]

For Robert Lewis the "Method" was a technique, something to "stimulate [the] creative process when you need it."[46] In Bernstein's case this "technique" referred to his process of employing smaller thematic cells to construct larger musical ideas. Moreover this phenomenon of Bernstein's compositional style is ably demonstrated in a 1964 dissertation by one of Bernstein's most trusted associates, Jack Gottlieb. In his study, Gottlieb sets out to justify Bernstein's music against what he considers unfair criticism of Bernstein's avowed eclectic style. Gottlieb begins with an organization of intervals frequently used by Bernstein for compositional means followed by an examination of how Bernstein's themes can be broken down to isolate their basic building blocks. Through his painstaking analysis of numerous pieces and hundreds of intervallic formulas, Gottlieb concluded that there is indeed an *Urmotiv* at the heart of several compositions: A descending minor second followed by a descending minor third. Helen Smith cites Gottlieb's *Urmotiv* in her analysis of Bernstein's dramatic works (first in *On the Town*) and likens it to a similar motive favored by Stravinsky (ascending minor second-descending perfect fourth), noting the shared folk like, modal quality between the two interval collections because of the elimination of the second scale degree.[47] Other authors have noted the similarity between Bernstein's cellular construction and Arnold Schoenberg's concept of *Grundgestalt*.[48]

In a chapter entitled, "The Concept of Musical Evolution" Gottlieb examines the Suite from *On the Waterfront* (among other pieces) as the closest Bernstein had come to realizing the "potential of melodic concatenation."[49] Gottlieb's examination of the suite is considerable, but because he does not tie the music to the images—and because Gottlieb does not adequately account for changes Bernstein made in the film score to fit a one movement concert piece—Gottlieb too falls short of realizing the full potential of his analysis. In order to compose his score for *On the Waterfront*, not only did Bernstein integrate compositional building blocks, he also weaved those elements with the film's narrative structure into a truly cohesive musicodramatic entity. This next section will introduce how Bernstein derived main themes from the film from interrelated motivic cells while Chapter 5 will reiterate and demonstrate more fully the following explication of thematic development in more specific cases. Throughout, Bernstein made his decision in a manner consistent with the drama.

During the opening credits, Bernstein sets the mood for the subsequent drama through the horn solo in Ex. 5.1, known as the Dignity theme. As mentioned above, the first four measures of the solo progress in the pentatonic mode until the tritone in measure 5 disrupts the easy-going melody. Given his penchant for vernacular elements, the flatted fifth scale degree in measure 5 could be viewed merely as a "blue" note meant to further call attention to the melody's homespun connotations. Later in this opening sequence, Bernstein reiterates the second half of the melody containing the "blue" note, thus emphasizing its importance at this early stage in the score. Upon further inspection, however, the "blue" note injects more than color into the theme. In Ex. 5.1, the melody progresses within a pentatonic rendering of F natural minor until the C-flat is sounded, thereby changing the complexion of the entire theme. In addition, the tritone created by the descent from the lowered dominant C-flat to the tonic F-natural in Ex. 5.1, m. 5, establishes a sense of melodic instability—a feeling lessened in the subsequent measures. As this opening theme foretells the journey Terry must take towards his redemption, it also perhaps warns of the perils he must endure in order to save himself, thus Bernstein's placement of the tritone within this opening melody seems to hint at Terry's struggle. The change in the melody becomes even more prescient when one considers how it relates to the next theme introduced in the film.

In the opening scene amidst a thunderous ostinato referred to here as the Violence theme (Ex. 5.5), one notices a lamenting strain in the alto saxophone (Ex. 5.6), as Bernstein called it, "a tugging, almost spastic, motive of pain."[50] The plaintive Pain theme in the saxophone (which, among the other intervals that make up the melody) is distinguished by the opening minor second between scale degrees 4 and 3 (in F-major) and introduces a rather dissonant passage whose melodic volatility is an appropriate counterpart to the driving rhythm of the ostinato. Subsequently, one hears development of the first four notes of the aforementioned theme (Ex. 5.6) in the cellos and basses of Ex. 5.7. What is fascinating about this opening sequence, besides the stark juxtaposition of contrasting musical styles and images that elicits much audience excitement, is the way in which Bernstein's music ties the sequence through interdependent themes.

The dramatic climax of the opening theme is the unexpected passage, B-flat, A-flat, C-flat, F-natural (Ex. 5.1, m. 5). This figure is not only important musically, but also cinematically. At the precise moment in the opening credits in which the audience hears this passage, the title of the film appears. Furthermore, when these notes are isolated from the opening theme (Ex. 2.8), one observes how the motive becomes the basis for the opening motive of the Pain theme (Ex. 2.9). Both of the thematic cells begin on B-flat and comprise identical numerical intervals, but different modifiers: major second—minor third—augmented fourth for the former and minor second—minor third—perfect fourth for the latter. The characteristic tritone of the Dignity theme is replaced with a perfect fourth in the Pain theme, and a minor second opens the motive rather than the major second. However, the same basic shape prevails between the two motives. In addition to its similarity to Gottlieb's *Urmotiv*, the semitone opening of the Pain theme is usually on the strong beat with the second note sustained, thus enhancing the prominence of the interval within the context of the theme.

Ex. 2.8. *On the Waterfront.* "Main Title." Motive isolated from opening theme.

Ex. 2.9. *On the Waterfront.* "Opening Shot to Scream." Opening motive of Pain theme.

Since the Dignity theme comments upon Terry's development as an individual, so Bernstein derived the Pain motive from that specific cell of the Dignity theme in order to comment upon those particular aspects of fear and isolation that eventually lead to Terry's triumph. Bernstein further emphasizes the importance of this relationship in the prominent role that the Pain motive plays in enhancing several other scenes throughout the movie, discussed in more detail in Chapter 5.

Bernstein further coordinates thematic materials during a scene in which there is a fight at the church. As this violence ensues Bernstein presents a vigorous ostinato in the violas and clarinets beneath a dissonant melody in the flutes, oboes, and horns, seen in Example 5.15. Bernstein makes the melodic component more dissonant by adding dyads separated by a major second to the notes of the theme (top notes), tightly grouping the three note chords.

As the scene increases in intensity the orchestration becomes denser. The reconfiguration of musical materials associated with the Pain theme in this passage will be discussed more thoroughly later, but for this analysis, most notable is that both cues conclude in a similar manner—fast, descending three-note patterns marked by stepwise motion followed by a large leap (Ex. 2.10 and 2.11)—and that they give rise to another of the film's prominent themes, namely the lyrical theme associated with the love between Terry and Edie.

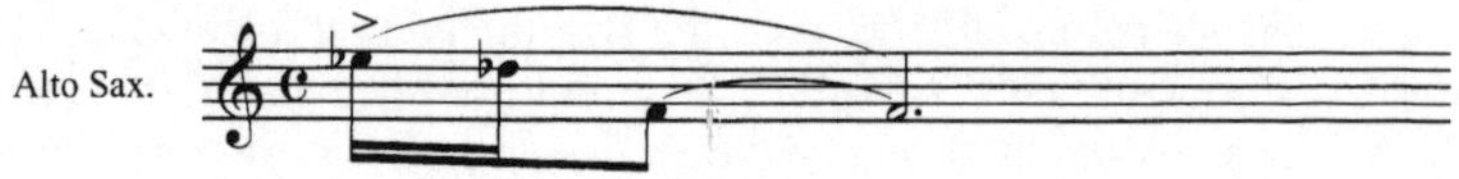

Ex. 2.10. *On the Waterfront.* Closing motive of Pain theme.

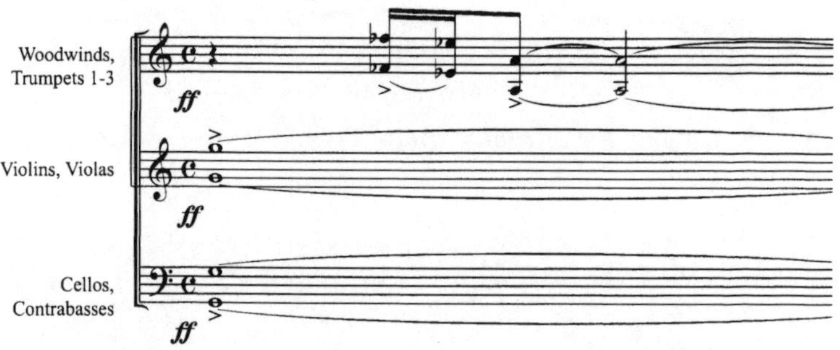

Ex. 2.11. *On the Waterfront,* Conductor Part. "Riot in Church." Closing motive of Riot theme, m. 41.

The Love theme is another important melody and the one that fits most closely with Bernstein's profound lyrical gift. Because it factors into more pertinent scenes later in the film, it is mentioned here to introduce the theme and consider its derivation. The first time the audience encounters the Love theme in its entirety is following the cruel incident at the church. Terry eventually comments upon Edie's awkward appearance as a youth and then he asks her if she remembered him. Edie replies that she recognized him "the first moment I saw you." At this point, one hears an arpeggio in the harp and clarinets and the Love theme in the flutes (Ex. 5.16). Yet their love is bittersweet. Terry, as we learned, lured Joey (Edie's brother) to the roof to be murdered. Edie, however, is ignorant to this fact. Bernstein was conscious of this irony and it is reflected in his score. Recalling Ex. 2.10 and 2.11, one notices the similarity between the closing motive of both the Pain theme and its derivative, the Riot theme. The opening three notes of the Love theme are nearly a retrograde of the final three notes of the Riot theme and, by extension, the Pain theme. In addition, the melodic peak on F-natural (Ex. 5.16; m. 7; flutes) functions as a flatted seventh scale degree and clashes with the expected F-sharp of the G-major scale. In this sense, the note is a blue note similar to the opening Dignity theme (although in that case it was flatted fifth and raised fourth scale degrees).

This relationship works on several levels. Terry just saved Edie from a potentially dangerous situation at the church. In fact, the last three notes of the "Scramble" cue (heard as a co-worker informs Terry that Edie is Joey's sister) foreshadow the first three notes of the Love theme (See "Scramble" in Chapter 5 for more detail). Therefore, in diegetic time, the course of events that brought Terry and Edie together and allowed them to have their first conversation moved sequentially from violent to peaceful. The Dignity, Pain, and Love themes represent the three most prominent musical ideas in Bernstein's score, a fact further emphasized by their collective presence in the triumphant closing sequence. Chapter 5 will detail further how these two facets of Bernstein's musical memory—thematic integration through cellular materials and an impressive recall of an immense number of musical texts—bind the score into a cohesive musicodramatic being. Yet *On the Waterfront* was not the only score in which Bernstein employed his affective memory to create an enduring musical work. Just as Marlon Brando needed Stanley Kowalski to create Terry Malloy,[51] Bernstein relied upon *On the Waterfront* to aid him in composing *West Side Story*.

Bernstein and . . . Bernstein

In the retroactively compiled "Excerpts from a *West Side Story* Log,"[52] which details the early conversations Leonard Bernstein had with Arthur Laurents and Jerome Robbins about a project that would ultimately become *West Side Story*, Bernstein had this (among other things) to say about the genesis of his most famous composition:

> *Beverly Hills, Aug. 25 1955.* Had a fine long session with Arthur today, by the pool. We're fired again by the whole Romeo notion; . . . Suddenly it all springs to life. I hear rhythms and pulses, and—most of all—I can sort of feel the form.[53]

This statement as edited could also be applied to *On the Waterfront*. Numerous scholars and critics have commented on the separate historical and artistic significance of *West Side Story* and *On the Waterfront*, but few have made connections between these Bernstein contributions beyond noting similarities in orchestral timbre, rhythmic intensity, and overlapping of themes. Stephen Lias, in his extensive comparison between Bernstein's film score and the subsequent Symphonic Suite (1955), comments on the "noticeable similarity between Bernstein's musical materials for *On the Waterfront*, and a number of themes from *West Side Story*," which "lead[s] to the inescapable conclusion that Bernstein, whether consciously or not, was drawing on the same core of musical materials for both projects."[54] As evidence of this parallel, Lias points to the Love theme from the film and its recasting three years later in both "Somewhere" and "Something's Coming" (Ex. 2.12a-c).

Love Theme

Ex. 2.12a. *On the Waterfront*. Love theme.

"Somewhere"

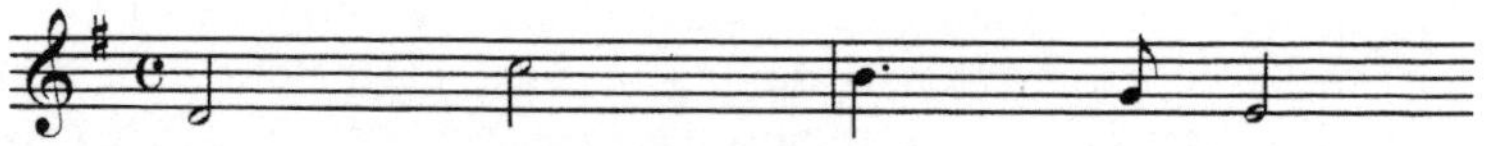

Ex. 2.12b. *West Side Story*. "Somewhere" (Excerpt).

"Something's Coming" (Excerpt)

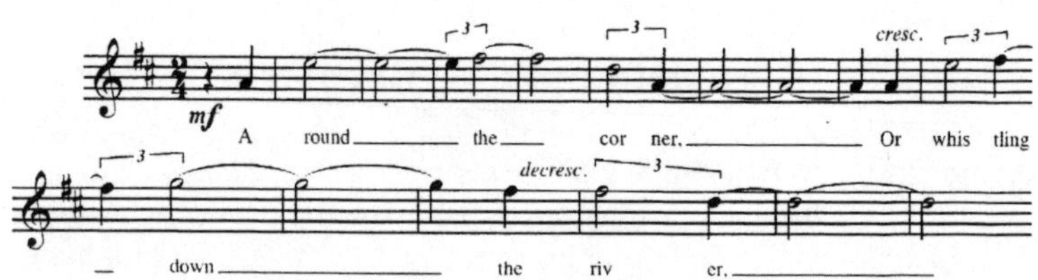

Ex. 2.12c. *West Side Story*. "Something's Coming" (Excerpt).

"Somewhere" has four notes in common with the Love theme and the last three bars of the theme are repeated nearly exactly in "Something's Coming." Elaborating upon Lias's observations, parts of "Somewhere" could be superimposed upon the Love theme. The "Somewhere" motif heard in the trumpets at the end of the musical corresponds with Bernstein's ascending resolution to the opening minor seventh of the Love theme (Ex. 2.13). In addition, were it not for the D natural on bar 4, beat 4 of the Love theme, the opening melody of "Somewhere" could be placed directly over the Love theme.

Ex. 2.13. ***On the Waterfront*****. Love theme with lyrics from** ***West Side Story*****'s "Somewhere" superimposed.**

Using this common ground between the two works as a point of departure, there are other more important ways that *On the Waterfront* serves as a model for *West Side Story* both musically and dramatically. As suggested in the preceding section, one of the reasons *On the Waterfront* maintains a prominent place in the development of film music is the high degree of the thematic integration that Bernstein employs throughout the score. Similarly, an important facet of *West Side Story*'s integral role in the development of musical theater is Bernstein's equally dense network of motivic relationships. As David Bowman points out,

> One of the most impressive features of *West Side Story* is the feeling of almost symphonic integration as the drama unfolds and builds to the inevitable tragic climax. In this it is more akin to Wagner than to the typical musical.[55]

Bowman goes on to cite the important role the perfect fourth, tritône, and minor second play throughout *West Side Story* in this "symphonic integration."[56] To illustrate this, Bowman asks the reader to consider Bernardo's entrance from the "Prologue," in which a solo muted trombone is answered—after five bars of percussion—by the bassoon and horn (Ex. 2.14).

Ex. 2.14. ***West Side Story*****. "Prologue." Bernardo's Entrance.**[57]

Bernstein extended the opening "hunting call" by adding a tritone and answered the figure with an embellished descending major second. In addition, the minor second—just as it does in *On the Waterfront*—appears throughout *West Side Story* as an important structural interval as well. In addition to the passage in Ex. 2.14 above, David Bowman also cites the interval's prominence in the "Cool" ostinato and the second half of the most sacred name in the musical, "Maria," seen below in Ex. 2.15.

Ex. 2.15. *West Side Story*. Minor second in "Cool" ostinato and "Maria" motive.[58]

In each of these figures and their respective songs, the semitone usually ascends. However, the opening phrase of "Somewhere" (Ex. 2.16), like the Pain motive (Ex. 2.9), ends on a descending minor second and with the same rhythm as the Pain motive. Just as Terry's road to redemption is filled with painful moments, the ultimate consummation of Tony's love for Maria is realized through pain and death.

Ex. 2.16. *West Side Story*. "Somewhere." Opening phrase, mm. 123-130.[59]

Thus, just as he does in the "Main Title" music and at subsequent points in *On the Waterfront*, here in the opening "Prologue," Bernstein introduces important motivic material that will pervade the remainder of *West Side Story*. Similarly, Joseph Swain argues that Bernstein's inversion of the opening tritone of "Something's Coming" to become the first interval of "Maria" is "[B]ut the most famous example of a motivic and thematic integration so thorough that by it alone is *West Side Story* set apart from any preceding Broadway musical."[60] Through this thematic integration, Bernstein began to bridge the divide between musical theater and opera and in Geoffrey Block's words, "forged his own dramatic musical hybrid."[61] Thus, by employing a similar model of motivic construction in *On the Waterfront*, Bernstein was able to comment more effectively on the narrative than previous efforts in the medium.

Beyond the shared compositional methods, Bernstein also employed similar musical styles at coinciding points in the respective dramas. For instance, the Love theme is most closely related to Bernstein's melodic language employed in *West Side Story*, particularly "Somewhere" and "Something's Coming." In the case of "Somewhere," similar dramatic contexts exist between the song and the movie theme as well. Tony went to the rumble in order to stop it from ever taking place. At first he is successful, but he ends up holding the knife that murdered Maria's brother Bernardo. When Tony goes to tell Maria the terrible news that Chino has already delivered she strikes Tony repeatedly, enraged not so much at her beloved, but at the current situation.[62] They finally resolve to run away from their troubles to that blissful utopia described in the equally harmonious strains of "Somewhere." So, out of tragedy comes one of the most beautiful moments of the musical. Yet tragedy is what ultimately befalls Tony and Maria and represents a final relationship between the two works. The final strains of *West Side Story*—an ending Bernstein foreshadows in the balcony scene—exhibit a high degree of ambiguity depending upon which version of the musical is being discussed. Out of the frenzied rhythms and activities during "The Dance at the Gym," Tony and Maria each proclaim their love to each other in "Maria" and "Tonight." As the two lovers wish each other (in unison) a pleasant, dream-filled evening, Bernstein foreshadows (Ex. 2.17, mm. 151-154) the heart-wrenching end of the musical. Bernstein then conveys to the audience "[t]his first glimpse of looming tragedy, ironic in that such a disaster could spring from such love [and] is turned into music at the very end of the scene."[63] As Tony's body is carried away Bernstein juxtaposes the tritone formed between the C major chord and octave F-sharps against the ascending whole tone "Somewhere" motive (Ex. 2.18).

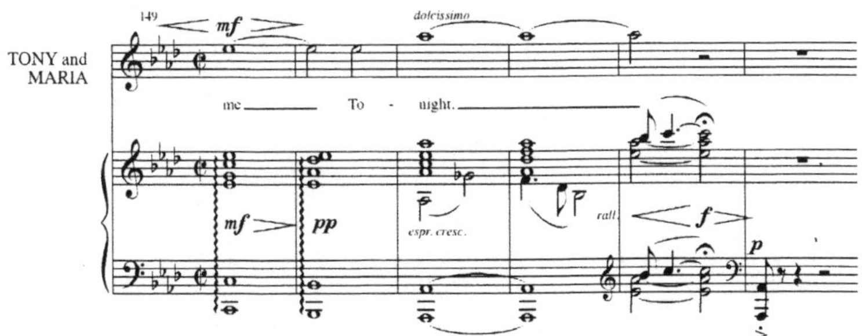

Ex. 2.17. *West Side Story*. "Balcony Scene" (No. 6), mm. 149-154.[64]

Ex. 2.18. *West Side Story*. "Finale" (No. 17), mm. 24-28.[65]

West Side Story became the most enduring part of Bernstein's musical legacy. Moreover, while *On the Waterfront* was certainly an important precursor musically and dramatically, one could argue that Bernstein drew upon both dramatic works and absolute compositions going back to the late 1930s for *West Side Story* in the same way that he mined that material for *On the Waterfront*. Yet given the chronological proximity to *West Side Story*, *On the Waterfront* offered Bernstein an opportunity—perhaps a "dry run"—to weave effectively thematic musical material within a musical vocabulary that borrowed extensively from vernacular musical styles and remained consistent with twentieth-century harmonic and rhythmic tendencies. In addition he was able to fashion these musical aspects such that they commented incisively on a narrative with contemporaneous connections to some of the most important sociopolitical issues of the 1950s. While Chapter 5 will explore in detail how Bernstein welded these materials to create a convincing film score, Chapters 3 and 4 will provide a sufficient contextual basis for understanding *On the Waterfront* and its sociopolitical implications.

3

THE HISTORICAL AND CRITICAL CONTEXT OF *ON THE WATERFRONT*: PART I

In their book, *The Fifties: The Way We Really Were*, Douglas T. Miller and Marion Nowak discuss a 1972 issue of *Newsweek* that longed for hula hoops, 3-D movies, poodle skirts, tail-finned Cadillacs, Howdy Doody, Elvis Presley, and other icons of the 1950s, "a simple decade when hip was hep [and] good was boss."[1] Popular culture in the early 1970s was replete with wistful thinking about the 1950s witnessed in movies like *The Last Picture Show* (1971) and *American Graffiti* (1973), Broadway productions like *Grease* (1971), and television shows such as *Happy Days*, *Laverne and Shirley*, and *M*A*S*H*.

However, like previous and subsequent desires for the halcyon days of old, people tend to remember the good times while denying the existence of the troubles and negative emotions of the past. As Miller and Nowak put it, "Nostalgia is highly selective. No one is staging a House Un-American Activities Revival."[2] Amidst the signs of carefree leisure listed above, there were many ugly realities in the 1950s. Frequent atomic bomb testing, potential Communist subversion, spies, and Sputnik as a symbol of growing Soviet ambition, were each factors that frightened many Americans. This fear also led to the repression both of civil liberties through McCarthyism as well as the less visible pressure to conform on a daily basis.

Following World War II, the United States experienced a period of vast economic expansion and prosperity. One could find employment opportunities in construction of new suburban housing developments, expanded highways for increasing automobile travel, and an explosive production of televisions. Americans also went to more concerts, museums, operas, and purchased more recordings of jazz and classical music. The more leisure time one had to go to the country club or visit the opera house, the higher status level one seemed to occupy. However, this desire for status and prestige often compensated for deeper insecurities. Many found it difficult to match the rapid pace of social and economic change. For instance, the mass exodus from the inner cities to the more attractive suburbs left urban neighborhoods in a state of flux. Furthermore, Americans conformed increasingly to the consumer mindset by finding comfort in abundance. However, as they acquired more and more possessions, they found that a true sense of security was still missing from their lives.

In his book, *The Power of Positive Thinking* (1952), motivational speaker and clergyman, Norman Vincent Peale, detailed what he considered an "epidemic of fear. All doctors are having cases of illness, which are brought on directly by fear and aggravated by worry and a feeling of insecurity."[3] For some people, the fear derived from the ongoing escalation of the Cold War. Others recoiled at the increase in anti-Communism following the rise of the Soviet Union as a dominant world power. As Senator Joseph McCarthy and the House Committee on Un-American Activities looked under every stone for evidence of potential Communist subversives, their efforts engendered a sense of paranoia and even hysteria in much of the American public. Samuel Stouffer conducted a survey for his 1955 study, *Communism, Conformity, and Civil Liberties*, in which he asked a cross section of the population what worried them. Based on a sampling of those interviews, many Americans were concerned about the threat of sabotage by Communists:

> They could *sabotage* our railroads and factories; could ruin our country.
> —Housewife, New York
> They are scattered all over our big factories and are working underground in all of them. Looking for chances of *sabotage*.
> —Farmer, Illinois
> One of their objectives is to infiltrate government, and armed forces, and other vital spots with a view to destruction and *sabotage* when the need for it strikes.
> —Mayor, Massachusetts[4]

While the potential destruction of major bridges, factories, and communication lines occupied the minds of many U.S. citizens, the fear of Communist conversion was almost four times as prevalent.[5] According to many Americans, potential subversion existed because of various societal weaknesses:

> They are getting into schools and teaching the children things and it's the young minds that are easy to influence.
> —Housewife, Nebraska

> They are agitating the Negroes. They always try to work on the man that hasn't had a chance or equal rights with most people.
> —Student, Alabama
> Communists are a danger when they talk to ignorant people. Ignorant people can be used by Communists to get more converts. I think ignorant people are most likely to become Communists, but, still, I always had a feeling that Mr. and Mrs. Roosevelt may have been Communists.
> —Housewife, New Jersey
> They preach against Christ. People who don't believe in Christ are so warped they can do almost anything.
> —Housewife, Texas[6]

Others feared not only Communists and Communist subversion, but also the far-reaching anti-Communism of McCarthy and HUAC. In a different Stouffer survey of the various worries of the average person, several individuals reflected negatively on McCarthy's role in producing a climate of fear:

> I am most worried about what McCarthy is doing to our American way of life.
> —Businessman, Georgia
> McCarthy being allowed to do as he does concerns me greatly.
> —Wife of owner of trucking business, Iowa
> I'm concerned about the fact that McCarthy can pull all the stuff he's pulled. All he develops is the froth on top of the glass and no beer underneath.
> —Newspaper editor, New Jersey[7]

In short, America during the 1950s represented a series of conflicting ideologies: securing freedom abroad while limiting it at home; waging peace to avoid war; promoting an increased sense of community in the suburbs wherein most residents craved anonymity. For this culture, and mindful of the widespread societal cognitive dissonance, *On the Waterfront* was made and its score composed. To understand better how the filmmakers, including Leonard Bernstein, were not only influenced by the film's dramatic intent, but also by the world around them, one must examine more closely the many facets of society in which and for whom the film was produced.

Anti-Communism, HUAC, and Hollywood in the 1950s

Following World War II, the Popular Front struggled to regain the important position it enjoyed before the war as a vehicle of political and economic change in the wake of the Great Depression. The nation emerged from World War II stronger and more unified than ever before and under President Truman's more centrist leadership (as opposed to the New Deal pioneer President Roosevelt) the U.S. further coalesced as a global superpower. Pessimism towards capitalism that existed before the war was put on hold in order to support the war effort and as returning soldiers gradually—if at times awkwardly—found their way back into the workforce, most Americans saw the Depression as a minor setback in capitalism's inevitable comeback.

The Popular Front had always been a large tent under which many individuals from Democrats to Communists were welcome. Yet after the war, this inclusive spirit grew increasingly difficult to sustain as reports of Stalin's atrocities as the leader of the Communist Party became fuel for anti-Communist fervor. Consequently, many liberals discontinued support of their American Communist Party colleagues, who in turn found themselves in the awkward position of supporting a brutal and oppressive regime. Following World War II, a 1945 article (backed by Stalin) by the French Communist Party leader, Jacques Duclos, derided their United States counterparts for diverging from the party-line during its support of the allies during the war. In response, the American party leaders implemented a more militant, anti-capitalist position that grew much more antagonistic towards the United States government. As party chairman William Z. Foster decried in 1947:

> Besides this economic fear [that the Soviet economic model is superior to capitalism], the big American capitalists also have a profound political fear. They view with the gravest alarm the rising democratic tide throughout Europe and the world. In the reactionary spirit of Hitler, therefore, they have embarked upon a crusade to crush democracy and socialism and to set up reactionary political systems that will conform with their plans for establishing world domination by Wall Street.[8]

This postwar political position, combined with a blind eye towards Stalin's corruption, gave anti-Communists, both conservative and liberal, an easy target in the fight against Communist subversion in the United States.

In examining American history, scholars point to a long record of counter-subversive activities preceding anti-Communist rhetoric in the 1950s. Historians believe this arises from an irrational fear that "others," whether Native Americans, Catholics, Freemasons, African Americans, or immigrants, are conspiring to destroy the nation from within. One scholar in particular has suggested a name for this phenomenon: the "paranoid style" of politics. As Richard Hofstadter points out, clinical paranoia is "a mental disorder characterized by systematized delusions of persecution and of one's own greatness."[9] Hofstadter differentiates between this psychiatric definition of paranoia and the paranoid style of politics in that the former believes conspiracies are directed at oneself whereas the latter believes any and all hostilities are aimed at one's country, society, or way of life. Hofstadter then points to various incidents in American history to prove his point. Each of these examples highlights a broad, evil, and effective international scheme designed to perpetrate terrible acts on the general American populace. One of these attacks comes from a sermon given in 1798 preaching against the spread of Freemasonry:

> Secret and systematic means have been adopted and pursued, with zeal and activity, by wicked and artful men, in foreign countries, to undermine the foundations of this Religion, and to overthrow its Altars, and thus to deprive the world of its benign influence on society.[10]

A more contemporary excerpt comes from a speech Joseph McCarthy gave to the Senate on 14 June 1951 in which he blamed then secretary of defense and former Army chief of staff and secretary of state, George Marshall, for involvement in the rise of Communism, specifically in China, but more directly throughout the world:

> How can we account for our present situation unless we believe that men high in this government are concerting to deliver us to disaster? This must be the product of a great conspiracy . . . so immense as to dwarf any previous such venture in the history of man. . . . What can be made of this unbroken series of decisions and acts contributing to the strategy of defeat? They cannot be attributed to incompetence.[11]

Of course, McCarthy did not create the fear nor was he the first to persecute Americans for their political beliefs. The prominence of the anti-Communist movement following World War II and eventually leading to the phenomenon known as McCarthyism had been in existence at least as long as the Soviet state. For instance, J. Edgar Hoover first stepped into the national spotlight after leading the Palmer Raids designed to quell a group of supposed radicals on separate occasions in 1919 and 1920. Moreover, Veterans groups like the American Legion and pro-business associations such as the Chamber of Commerce decried not only Communist targets, but anyone who dared criticize their methods and beliefs, most notably the American Civil Liberties Union, and pitted competing labor organizations against each other. Eventually these civic groups garnered support from conservative members of Congress, who in the 1930s viewed Roosevelt's New Deal as a means of implementing widespread Communism. The success of the New Deal, and conservative abhorrence of such widespread socialism represented an important distinction between Hofstadter's above scenarios and the increasing anti-Communism of the 1930s. While the aforementioned groups viewed Freemasonry and Catholicism as challenges by fringe groups to a predominantly conservative—and thus American—way of life, the New Deal as federal policy threatened to obliterate the American way of life.

After years of lobbying by the aforementioned right-wing groups to examine Communism and halt its spread, Congress approved in 1938 the formation of the House Committee on Un-American Activities. Martin Dies of Texas was the first chairperson and from its inception, the committee was vigorous in its activities. It sought information from American Legion officials, religious groups aghast at Communist atheism, liberals seeking separation from Stalinist propaganda, and former Communist Party officials. These groups formed a rather sophisticated network during the late 1930s and early 1940s. They constantly reminded the American public of the threat of Communism and "educated" them on how to deal with Communists exemplified in a 1948 letter by American Legion national commander James F. O'Neil:

> Never forget the fact that Communists operating in our midst are in effect a secret battalion of spies. . . . Every art of human cunning is therefore necessary on their part to protect themselves and their subversive mission from exposure. So the first step is to disguise, deodorize, and attractively package Moscow's revolutionary products. They are "liberals" at breakfast, "defenders of world peace" in the afternoon, and "the voice of the people" in the evening.[12]

Apparently, the electorate sided with the conservatives as well because in 1946 the Republicans gained both chambers of Congress for the first time since 1928. Crucial to their success was making the anti-Communist issue a main support of their election platform. President Truman, in order to shore up support for his foreign policy agenda and remain strong in the face of domestic and foreign Communism, enacted two important proposals in March 1947. The first requested funds to stop Communist takeovers of Turkey and Greece and became the chief Communist containment policy known as the "Truman Doctrine." Later that month, Truman issued Executive Order 9835,[13] which established government boards that determined the allegiance of current and potential government employees. The effect of these executive branch decisions separated by several days was far-reaching. While the Truman Doctrine proved his commitment to containing Soviet imperialism and sought to comfort Americans regarding the Communist threat, the loyalty review boards actually raised the anxiety and fear of Americans towards Communism. People across the country began to both question the safety of their own jobs and cast suspicion on their co-workers. Furthermore, the boards set a precedent for all other such mechanisms at the local and state levels and in private and public spheres. In addition, because of the order's vague language, no longer were serious crimes like treason the only causes for termination. Membership in the Communist Party or any number of liberal groups, or association with the wrong people represented grounds for loss of employment.

As the Truman Administration fought the spread of Communism abroad, Republican adversaries sought to improve their political standing by claiming that the Truman Administration was filled with Communists. The earlier Dies-led HUAC insinuated similarly with the Roosevelt Administration and with increased national awareness because of the Cold War, the Republicans chose this time to bring anti-Communist politicians like McCarthy and Richard M. Nixon to prominence. In addition, Truman did not seem to be containing the spread of Communism as he had planned. Early defeats came in 1948, following a successful Communist coup in Czechoslovakia. Even worse, in 1949, American confidence was dealt an enormous blow as not only China became a Communist nation, but also the Soviets became the first country other than the United States to detonate an atomic bomb.

The era of liberal dissent that was so prominent in the 1930s and 1940s was all but deceased. Many liberals in wanting to preserve the way of life for which they fought so hard to establish in the New Deal found themselves inundated by a more conservative mindset. As McCarthy and his supporters gained a foothold on the political scene, it became clear that the anti-Communist movement represented dissent in the 1950s. Right-wing opposition differed from the left wing in the 1930s in that the former required strict conformity to their issues. Hofstadter called these practitioners of the paranoid style "pseudo-conservatives." Hofstadter borrowed the term from Theodor Adorno because according to Adorno, while these people may perceive themselves to be conservative, their current disillusionment with American society—and mechanisms for changing that society—has more in common with radicalism than the cooperative spirit indicative of traditional conservatism. In his essay, *The Pseudo-Conservative Revolt—1954*, Hofstadter summarized the prototypical pseudo-conservative. It serves as an important reminder of the mindset behind the actions of McCarthy and his anti-Communist supporters:

> The restlessness, suspicion, and fear shown in various phases of the pseudo-conservative revolt give evidence of the anguish which the pseudo-conservative experiences in his capacity as a citizen. He believes himself to be living in a world in which he is spied upon, plotted against, betrayed, and very likely destined for total ruin. . . . He feels that his liberties have been arbitrarily and outrageously invaded. He sees his own country as being so weak that it is constantly about to fall victim to subversion; and yet he feels that it is so all-powerful that any failure it may experience in getting its way in the world . . . cannot possibly be due to its limitations but must be attributed to its having been betrayed.[14]

As an increasing number of Americans could attest, the inherently conflicted notion of the "pseudo-conservative" and the extent of McCarthy's reach were only gaining power during the first half of the 1950s. By 1952, Truman's inability, in the eyes of the public and conservative detractors, to stop Communism at home and abroad played a big part in Adlai Stevenson's defeat in the 1952 presidential election. For being reelected himself and for doing much to damage Truman's credibility, McCarthy was given control of his own congressional committee, the Investigative Subcommittee of the Committee on Government Operations, which performed the same types of investigations as HUAC. The congressional committee was the primary tool by which anti-Communists were able to expand their attack from a focus on a small political party to a far-reaching reexamination of virtually every facet of American society. So strong was the guilt in being subpoenaed before a committee during the 1950s that most people were fired from their jobs before they appeared in front of a committee. Nowhere was this inquisition felt more strongly or witnessed more visibly than the HUAC investigations of the Hollywood film industry in 1947 and 1951.

Although HUAC was officially investigating Communists in the movie industry who might be infusing their beliefs into films, what they really wanted to curtail was the prominence of liberal and populist subjects and ideas. To HUAC and other anti-Communists, the vast number of artists and intellectuals who played an important part in what ultimately made it to the silver screen had too much control over a medium that was so popular and influential with the general populace.

While in reality, these films often underlined mainstream ideas, HUAC believed that even the slightest hint of left-wing philosophy should be eliminated to reflect "proper American values."[15] Whenever HUAC had attempted to investigate Hollywood Communism up until World War II, the public was not interested and studio bosses did not want to alienate themselves from the actors, writers, and directors that made the Hollywood machine turn. However, in the new Cold War era of the late 1940s, HUAC was able, with the support of influential organizations like the Catholic Church and the American Legion, to be more persistent with their mission. Furthermore, when faced with potential boycotts, studio executives were forced to consider the assets of the studio over the rights of its employees.

After much preliminary fact-finding by congressional investigators and the FBI, HUAC handed out subpoenas in September 1947 stating that the witnesses—of which nineteen were labeled "unfriendly" based largely on current or past Communist Party membership—were to appear in Washington, D.C. The "unfriendly" witnesses took the stand later in October 1947, armed with the assumption that the First Amendment and later the Supreme Court would ultimately side with them. Their testimony followed earlier sessions by producers and "friendly" witnesses. These latter witnesses claimed that Hollywood was doing all it could to contain and remove any Communist messages in cinema. The next group included actors such as Ronald Reagan and Gary Cooper who were sympathetic to the goals of HUAC and provided the government body increased credibility in the public's eye. The nineteen "unfriendly" witnesses also received support from the Committee for the First Amendment (CFA) comprised largely of actors, for instance Humphrey Bogart, Frank Sinatra, Judy Garland, and Lena Horne.

When the time to testify came, all "friendly" witnesses were allowed to read from prepared statements, a courtesy that wasn't extended to the "unfriendly" witnesses. Before screenwriter John Howard Lawson could read his scathing critique of HUAC, committee chairman J. Parnell Thomas read the statement in advance and denied Lawson the opportunity to express his position. Subsequent witnesses followed the same twofold strategy outlined in Lawson's prepared remarks and famously debated between Lawson and Thomas: fall back on the First Amendment and when asked about group affiliation, refuse to answer without saying explicitly, "I refuse." This latter part proved to be a gross miscalculation on the part of the nineteen's legal team. As the gavel pounded over and over, the evasiveness of those that testified only hurt their cause in the eyes of the committee and the public. Moreover, the committee's decision to reject Lawson's statement preempted the overall strategy of the nineteen. Thomas eventually cited Lawson for contempt as he did nine subsequent witnesses, who along with Lawson became known as the Hollywood Ten.[16]

While the spectacle of the hearings damaged Hollywood's reputation, several newspapers spoke out against the insensitive manner in which HUAC conducted business. Consequently, HUAC suspended hearings temporarily—a pause that would last four years. Behind support in the press and with several more public events planned by the CFA, it appeared the Ten might emerge from the hearings relatively unscathed. However, from a producer's point of view, this sort of dark cloud over the movie industry was bad for business. After the House of Representatives voted to charge the Ten with contempt, the producers sounded the death knell in December 1947. After meeting at the Waldorf-Astoria Hotel in New York City, they fired the Hollywood Ten and stated they would not hire Communists, expressing their position in the famous Waldorf Statement, which began the blacklist.[17] This move by the producers silenced the support of the CFA and other support mechanisms in Hollywood. The actors, writers, and directors involved with CFA decided to save their careers and avoid the blacklist rather than form any sort of "anti-blacklist league." Humphrey Bogart's famous response entitled, "I'm No Communist,"[18] was typical of actors' efforts to distance themselves from their subversive colleagues. The careers of the Ten though were effectively ended for a long time. They were tried and convicted of contempt in 1948 and two years later, the Supreme Court—their perceived savior—refused to hear the case.

Several incidents (described above) transpired between November 1947 and HUAC's return to Hollywood in 1951. These domestic and world events caused the committee's sway over public opinion to be much greater and therefore their return was more feared than in 1947. The blacklist forced the public to realize that one could be reprimanded for political philosophies and associations. The 1951 hearings, while perhaps more vast in scope, were more concentrated in their targets. After the Hollywood executives turned their backs so easily on their Communist employees, but not their product, HUAC targeted individuals rather than the entire movie industry. Therefore, HUAC's goal was to eliminate radicalism from Hollywood itself, rather than from the movies. Beginning in March 1951 and intermittently for the next five years, 110 witnesses came to the stand and 58 decided to confess their subversive past and name their associates in the process.[19] Each person who was subpoenaed was encouraged by a HUAC investigator to follow the path of self-examination and confession that would lead to career salvation. In addition, committee members promoted the appearance of "sincerity" on the witness stand. For the television audience, the appearance of genuineness not only made the particular witness look good, but also shed a favorable light on the committee's reputation. It was the testimony of these cooperative witnesses, especially those who broke ranks and named former Communist associates, which gave HUAC its victory in this second round of testimony.

Why did so many actors, directors, and writers choose to testify? The answer most often given by them is that they had become disillusioned with the changing policies of the increasingly repressive Soviet Union. However, the real reason was set in motion in 1947: fear of the blacklist. Very few "informers" (outlined in Chapter 4, Elia Kazan was a notable exception, though much later) were forthright in admitting they were saving their careers by testifying. Despite the fear that compelled many to name names, there were many who refused to buckle under pressure and remained silent, but they too were blacklisted. The Hollywood Ten were the last important group of witnesses to rely on the First Amendment as legal protection. Shortly thereafter, witnesses began to invoke the Fifth Amendment's shield from self-incrimination. It was not clear how the courts would interpret the use of the amendment within the context of the congressional investigation, but since the First Amendment was routinely defeated in court, alternatives were few. Yet, the use of the Fifth Amendment by unfriendly witnesses also backfired in the eyes of the public. The committees conveyed to Americans that anyone who hid behind the Fifth Amendment was trying to conceal something in their past that might have proven their guilt. Consequently, in the court of public opinion, these so-called "Fifth Amendment Communists" were already guilty. The committees, therefore, had broad political implications beyond damaging the careers of innocent people not just in Hollywood, but in all professions. The Hollywood Communists and all other unfriendly witnesses were the most visible opposition to the policies and consequences of the Cold War. By silencing their criticism, the government was eliminating any political debate. As Hollywood director Joseph Losey lamented, "The most terrifying thing about the atmosphere was seeing the people succumb and seeing all protest disappear. Because if you did protest, you'd had it."[20]

Conformity and Suburbanization

The preceding discussion of anti-Communism amidst the Cold War explains one major facet of the fear so prevalent in society during the 1950s. Another societal cause of fear and anxiety, alluded to above by

Losey, concerns the pressures of conformity. As already suggested, any outward display of left-wing practices or associations would most likely have been branded as "Communism" or "Socialism." Therefore, the pressure to curtail such behavior in favor of more conservative values was immense. This sort of assimilation was at work in other aspects of daily life as well. As society became more technologically advanced and business grew in size, a higher level of social infrastructure was also necessary. In order to make these machines of commerce run smoothly, the parts had to work together. The crux of this new business ethic was the idea of "group-think" and "group-work." Consensus was the goal of this ideal and individualism was discouraged. Women were under the same pressure as well. Many corporations conducted classes in which wives were indoctrinated into the world of the executive and the goals of one's husband. Some companies would not hire or promote employees if their wife was deemed to be "unsuitable." The ideal wife was one who could market her husband to his colleagues. The goal of many young women was to get married, therefore avoiding outward intellectualism, individualism, or career aspirations in favor of her domestic roles and the importance of the company. As one executive lamented:

> We control a man's environment in business and we lose it entirely when he crosses the threshold of his home. . . . The younger generation of wives is the most cooperative the corporation has ever enlisted. Somehow they seem to give us so much less trouble than the older ones.[21]

What this created was an employee who looked for a long, secure, pleasant career with a company, but was not too ambitious to seek out a taxing executive position and thus sacrifice one's leisure time, exemplified in Sloan Wilson's *The Man in the Gray Flannel Suit* (1955). At one point in the novel the main character, Tom Rath, expresses reluctance when offered a more arduous executive position. His boss then reassures him, "There are plenty of good positions where it's not necessary for a man to put in an unusual amount of work."[22] In order to ensure corporate success, potentially combustible topics like politics and religion were off-limits in the work place. Apparently, athletes were afflicted with a similar malady. A *New York Times Magazine* article noted the respectability that crept into baseball:

> Baseball lately has been infiltrated by gentlemanly athletes, a tweedy brand of sportsmen who are polite to a fault, never chew tobacco, avoid late hours, eschew pinball machines and poker games, obey the scout laws, condone umpires, sing rotary, baby-sit, subscribe to *The*

> *Wall Street Journal* and who would not think of tripping their mothers, even if Mom were rounding third on her way home with the winning run.[23]

This pattern of conformity was so widespread that social scientist David Riesman sought to explain the developing phenomenon in his 1950 book, *The Lonely Crowd.* Riesman attempted to find a connection between the population growth of a society and the way that society treats conformity during different phases of population growth. To plot population change, Riesman used an S-curve that resulted from studies of developed nations and could be used to predict the future population growths of other less-mechanized cultures. This curve starts at the point in which the number of births and deaths are similar, resulting in high birth and death rates. The next phase was characterized by a population increase due to lowering of the death rate by various causes. The final stage is one in which the birth and death rates are again equal, but low. According to population theorists, the first phase carries with it "high growth potential." If some sudden technological or hygienic advance appeared, the population would change exponentially. The second period of development in which the death rate declines is known as "transitional growth." Lastly, when the curve balances out again, the period is called "incipient population decline."[24]

What Riesman discovered was that in each era on the curve, the particular society imposed conformity, thus shaping social character in a distinctive manner. The first phase of "high growth potential" finds its members conforming to family traditions, thus they are "tradition directed." This might be characteristic of more primitive populations in developing nations and in the West, or in peasant populations during the Middle Ages. Those societies in periods of "transitional growth" contain people who, at a young age, display a sense of individualism apart from tradition or any other social customs and are said to be "inner-directed." Riesman associates this period with the beginning of the Renaissance and just disappearing in the early twentieth century. In addition, a sense of expansion pervades this society, evidenced in the exploration and colonization of many parts of the world by Western Europe. With this development came expanded personal wealth due to brisk buildup of capital. The final phase of population growth is distinguished by the tendency to conform to the demands and choices of others. Appropriately, this group of people is called "other-directed." It is this final classification that Riesman equates to American society in the late 1940s and early 1950s.[25] This last phenomenon had already begun in Western Europe where less people were working in farming and manufacturing and increasingly in offices and executive positions.

Working hours became shorter while accumulation of material possessions grew as did leisure time.

In the United States of the 1950s, one finds the other-directed character type mainly in the middle to upper middle class of larger cities. While the phenomenon occurs in other highly industrialized cultures, the increasing other-direction found in the United States was in the 1950s, unlike other countries, the predominant method of conformity. The increased capacity for consumption of goods and services (both required and surplus) combined with a different road to success necessitates a society that is more wholly "socialized" where the peer group becomes the standard by which one measures success in all of these areas. As opposed to the inner-directed individual, the other-directed being receives his or her direction not from within, but from the peer group and more importantly, the mass media. Naturally, as the peer group shifts with age, so does the judgment of success and the level of influence by peers. The only things that remain constant for the other-directed are the level of concentration on the changes within the peer group and the persistent striving to maintain those standards, and thus approval of the group. In order to understand better the pressure—and resultant fear, anxiety, and alienation—of the other-directed individuals to conform to their society, one must examine the arenas in which their other-direction was manifested and by which they received their cultural signals.[26]

The place where other-directed individuals spent their leisure time and reinforced the importance of "fitting in" with their children was at home, usually in the suburbs. Of course, suburbanization and the desire to move away from the big city did not begin in the 1950s. The longing to own land and a home away from urban congestion, crime, and pollution goes back at least to the nineteenth century industrial revolution when romantic aspirations caused many to seek out the peacefulness of the countryside. However, until the 1920s, such pursuits were only available to the rich. Furthermore, when trains, trolleys, and automobiles made more widespread excursions possible, the Depression and World War II halted this progress. Through programs like the New Deal Federal Housing Administration (FHA) and a similar program sponsored by the Veteran's Administration called the Servicemen's Readjustment Act (1944), the postwar housing market experienced a boom following World War II.[27]

Perhaps no one benefited more from this surge in home ownership than Abraham Levitt and his "Levittowns" across the country. Before the war, Levitt and his sons built houses, mostly in New York State, that catered to the upper-middle class. In 1946, though, they acquired 4000 acres of land near Manhattan that was to be marketed towards new families created after the war. This was a massive undertaking, but the Levitts had honed their skills through government contracts for several hundred homes in places like Portsmouth, VA. For instance in Island Trees, NY, trucks dropped off building materials every sixty-feet and each home was built on concrete slabs. The Levitts controlled the process from every angle—materials, subcontractors, equipment, and lumber—all were owned and operated by the Levitts. When the subdivision was completed, it contained 17,400 homes and 82,000 residents and was renamed Levittown, NY.[28] So prevalent was the Levittown template that the homes provided the model for suburban developments throughout the country over the next thirty years. Such traits as location on the outskirts of a given city, low population density that resulted from larger lots and fully detached homes, little variety in architectural style, and most importantly, a uniformly aged, socioeconomic, and racial population, became commonplace in American suburbs. Because of such broad homogeneity within and between different suburbs, the residents themselves reflected this similarity to the point that individuals became seemingly interchangeable. As one writer observed:

> When the lady of the house hung out the wash, the awesome result was 17,500 pairs of shorts flapping in 17,500 backyards. The struggle for identity in these prefabricated circumstances reduced itself occasionally to a pretty fine point—like the tone of a door chime.[29]

William H. Whyte in his 1956 social critique, *The Organization Man*, suggested such a phenomenon. For his study, he researched suburban life in Park Forest, IL, during 1953 and discovered that the suburb mirrored the corporate axiom of individualism immersed in mass-produced sameness. As he states in his book, "an otherwise minor variation becomes blatant deviance; a man who paints his garage fire-engine red in a block where the rest of the garages are white has literally and psychologically made himself a marked man."[30] In such an environment, alienation was common for all members of the family. Societal pressures of conformity, peer acceptance, and job security had physical consequences as well:

> Life in growing suburbia, specifically in Englewood, N.J., is giving people ulcers, heart attacks, and other "tension-related psychosomatic disorders," according to a doctor [Richard E. Gordon] who practices there. He said that couples in suburbia felt they needed a new car every few years, that "there cannot be a blade of crab grass in the lawn, the house must be spotless and dustless, the children must be scrubbed clean. For the already overstrained couple conspicuous consumption can help cause bad tempers and high blood pressure."[31]

Many suburban residents cited the benefits for children as a chief reason for moving away from the city. In actuality, the suburbs created isolation from the outside world. The lack of ethnic diversity and other cultural benefits of the city demeaned the role the immediate environment played in education. In a world where parental models were mother as caregiver and house cleaner and father as corporate cog, children gleaned any external lessons from school and, to a greater extent, information was often atomized through the media, both of which further reinforced the corporate ideology of "fitting in." In one of a series of interviews conducted from 1948 to 1949, a preadolescent girl was asked to name her favorite comic book superhero. She listed the popular answer of Superman because he could perform tasks that no other character could. When asked if she would enjoy the ability to fly, she responded, "I would like to be able to fly if everybody else did, but otherwise it would be kind of conspicuous."[32] Clearly, the pressure to fit in the group and not "stand out" was a trademark of the mass media as well. Perhaps no single medium reflected this notion so pervasively and conveyed it so effectively to the American populace than television. In 1946, 7000 television sets were in operation. Four years later, 4.4 million households owned a television and a decade later that number rose to 50 million.[33]

Television was becoming a much more pervasive presence in the suburban home than the electric entertainment of the previous generation, the radio. In addition, television further eroded decaying family dynamics that had begun much earlier in the decade. Before radio and television, families depended on each other for their entertainment. Catalogs from the first decade of the 1900s contained advertisements for songbooks and collections of poetry, religious stories, and speeches. These products were arguably more enjoyable when conducted in collaboration with others. As the radio increased in popularity, families did not have to communicate verbally with one another, but could engage each other through eye contact. Further, television did not require any physical or mental exertion by the family, except through sight and hearing. The lack of contact between members of the family rendered the group dynamic to that of individuals sharing a physical space. In that sense, the "audience" was a mass of alienated viewers. The television is a microcosm of the suburban experience. As one is separated from the rest of humanity in the 1950s suburb, one can further isolate oneself in front of the television and not have to communicate with other people except at work. Lewis Mumford summarizes the ironic hopelessness of the experience:

> In the mass movement into suburban areas a new kind of community was produced, which caricatured both the historic city and the arche-

> typal suburban refuge: a multitude of uniform, unidentifiable houses, lined up inflexibly, at uniform distances, on uniform roads, in a treeless communal waste, inhabited by people of the same class, the same income, the same age group, witnessing the same television performances, eating the same tasteless pre-fabricated foods, from the same freezers, conforming in every outward and inward respect to a common mold, manufactured in the central metropolis.[34]

Waging the Peace: Postwar Atomic Proliferation

The escape to the suburbs to which Mumford refers, was primarily because of the often overwhelming realities of 1950s society. Beyond the aforementioned fear of Communism and the pressure to conform to an increasingly other-directed way of life, the threat of nuclear annihilation promoted a national anxiety equal to and perhaps greater than any other social/political issue. In the aftermath of the bombings of Hiroshima and Nagasaki, the atomic bomb changed the American way of life in many ways, perhaps none more noticeable than the nature of war. Instead, such power necessitated peace and so the United States began what was known as "waging peace."

In order to sell the Cold War and the subsequent military boost, the government employed a twofold strategy. The first, explained in the above discussion on anti-Communism, was to establish the enemy's identity and its subversive presence in every facet of society. Secondly, officials attempted to reassure an anxious public regarding the immense destructive power of nuclear weaponry. One way of executing this latter task, and the most popular one, was to persuade people to both fear and trust the power of the bomb; fearing Soviet missiles and trusting American weapons. As a 1955 issue of *Reader's Digest* conveyed, "It all adds up to this: whereas fallout from big bombs in wartime might become highly dangerous, there is no significant evidence that fallout from U.S. atomic tests now being carried out will be hazardous to people now or to future generations."[35] Another way the government attempted to ease the collective consciousness was to create a new jargon in order to make the whole experience seem more pleasant. For instance, levels of radioactive Strontium-90 were known as "sunshine units," or small nuclear weapons called "kitten bombs." The H-Bomb was at first known as the "humanitarian bomb" and casualties thrown about by blast impact became known as "displacement." *Look* magazine publicized it as, "One of the cheapest forms of destruction known to man."[36] Yet another approach taken by government officials played upon people's fears of nuclear attack. Given the increasing Communist menace, Truman warned Americans in the early 1950s that while he did not know when an attack would come or even if it would come, he maintained that one should be prepared nonetheless. Thus began a vigorous civil defense readiness program in which citizens learned how they could survive nuclear aftermath. A 1950 pamphlet entitled *Atomic Attack*, urged Americans to buy Geiger counters, replace their windows with Plexiglas or Lucite, and learn "atomic falling:"

> Fall flat. Fall face down, elbow stuck out in front, forehead on elbow, eyes closed. Junior will feel the wind go by, the dirt and pebbles blown with hurricane force against his head. But, his eyes and face protected, a few cuts on the arms and legs aren't important. . . . Can Junior fall instantly, face down, elbow out, forehead on elbow, eyes shut? Yes. With a little practice. Have him try it tonight as he gets into bed.[37]

The public responded positively to such marketing tactics, if for no other reason than to alleviate their fears. However, the consequences of such policies were as evident as the supposed public acceptance. For instance, residents were very protective of the fallout shelters they had built. Some placed machine guns in front of their compounds and armed themselves in other ways in order to protect against nuclear refugees. Despite the purpose of civil defense education to make citizens (especially children) accept the bomb and reassure them, they were discussing death and total destruction on a regular basis. For one to be upset and fearful at first was acceptable, but to maintain such feelings was considered immature. The only alternative was acceptance and rationalization of these irrational issues. Although children were expected to accept the possibility of nuclear holocaust like many other childhood truisms, fear of such a fate was equally prevalent. In order to deal with such a disturbing topic, they often followed the example of their parents and retreated from the delicate issues altogether. Adults put their trust in the military-industrial complex with the faith that all the spending would lead to a positive result.

Unfortunately, the acceptance of this gospel proved to be a naïve belief at best. While the government promoted the civil defense and civil readiness programs, the actual defense implemented was not designed to save lives. The first level of defense was a series of missile rings around cities equipped with early detection capabilities. The Strategic Air Command reinforced the missile rings by always being prepared to destroy the origin of attack. However, this plan had its problems as well. Concerning the SAC defense, one pilot stated that it was "not their policy to protect this country, for that . . . would interfere with our retaliatory capabilities."[38] Even the extensive civil defense network of shelters, education, and preparedness contained serious flaws. Congress backed away from its pledge to federally finance public fallout shelters, encouraging individuals to build their own accommodations. A final example of government-sponsored deception manifested itself in nuclear testing. In a 1958 *Life* magazine article one learns that from 1951-1958 the U.S. exploded 122 atomic bombs of various intensities, creating radioactive fallout that before the 1950s had not existed. The public knew about the fallout, but did not know how dangerous it was. To counteract this anxiety, the military reminded citizens that only fifteen percent of the 140,000 deaths at Hiroshima were the result of fallout, failing to state that this was from one bomb, not 122. The same article—hailed on the cover as "Dr. Teller refutes 9,000 scientists why nuclear bomb tests must go on," posited that tests must continue in order to develop a "clean" bomb. Teller's position was that the more bombs detonated in the desert, the less the level of radioactivity. Supplementary pictures showed smiling soldiers with a mushroom cloud in the background.[39]

Eventually, some citizens became disillusioned concerning the bomb and its "goodness." They also became disenchanted with the leaders who eased their fears and desired a prepared public. In most cases, however, those individuals were not elected government officials, but appointees, servicemen, or business contacts. As opposed to the other three branches of government, this fourth, nebulous group was never held accountable. Rarely were public fears converted into positive activism. Scientists like Linus Pauling and J. Robert Oppenheimer represented a vocal minority that was made even more obscure by lack of media coverage. Most Americans, however, ignored their feelings, followed the "official word," and became citizens of a "new normalcy." They felt quite helpless and anxious in the midst of such overwhelming factors. The Red menace, corporate demands on all aspects of daily life, and pressures to conform, all factored into this anxiety. However, the potential atomic peril was the gasoline that fed the fire. Citizens retreated from McCarthyism and the risk of war to the comforts of domesticity, material pleasures, and belonging. Their leaders returned the favor by assuring a nervous public that all was well.

Clearly, there were conflicting ideologies present throughout society during the 1950s. The Truman Doctrine attempted to halt the spread of Communism across the globe. However, at home, McCarthy, HUAC, and other virulent anti-Communist and anti-liberal groups suspended civil liberties in order to stop the movement in the United States, as well as silence any opposition. Citizens were told that atomic weapons were being produced to save lives and establish peace throughout the world. Yet, reports of fallout, widespread destruction, and potential genetic mutations did little to ease an anxious and fearful public. The promise of home ownership away from the crowded city dwellings drew many Americans to the ever-expanding suburbs. While the suburban lifestyle provided more space in which one could live, similar socioeconomic strata, age, and race forced many to conform or be branded an "individual," and thus undesirable. The convergence of these conflicting ideologies produced feelings associated with fear, anxiety, alienation, and isolation.

Film is a wonderful medium through which to examine a society's collective consciousness and is a primary example of popular culture. An important development following World War II was the production of films that explored relevant social problems, such as alienation caused by shifting postwar gender roles, alcoholism, and racial tensions. Hollywood also tackled political issues, for example, fear of atomic war, suspicion of Communism and Communist subversion, and class inequalities witnessed in corrupt labor organizations. *On the Waterfront* represents a wonderful example of a drama produced in the post-major studio era, but demonstrates incisive commentary that tends to be contrary to prevailing cultural values. In addition to its cinematic importance, *On the Waterfront* confronts several discordant political and social issues of the 1950s and their corresponding side effects. Chapter 4 attempts to explain how those issues are brought to bear in Budd Schulberg's screenplay, Elia Kazan's directorial vision, Leonard Bernstein's music, and their shared connection to many of the social and political issues mentioned above. Chapter 5 provides the reader a thorough understanding of how Leonard Bernstein was able to intensify the flimmakers' messages through his score.

4

THE HISTORICAL AND CRITICAL CONTEXT OF *ON THE WATERFRONT*: PART II

Hollywood in the 1950s

Following World War II and coinciding with HUAC's investigation of Communist subversion, Hollywood entered a period of transition in which the main issue for the movie industry was declining attendance. In 1948, ninety million people went to movies each week. However, that number dwindled to fifty-one million only four years later. As Americans grew wealthier, leisure time soared and with it the amount of activities in which one participated increased as well. One can attribute much of the decline in box office receipts to the coinciding growth in television sales and viewership. Before television though, two other factors had a profound effect on traditional Hollywood moviemaking as well. The anti-Communist investigations not only ostracized its more liberal representatives, but also forced studios to alter the product itself in order to correspond to the predominantly conservative, anti-Communist sentiment.[1] Thus, the demands that anti-Communists and conservative authorities made on studios at this time contributed to a higher level of overall mediocrity concerning plot types and subject material. Important socially and politically charged films such as *The Grapes of Wrath* (1940), *Citizen Kane* (1941), or *Meet John Doe* (1941) would have been less likely to be produced in the early 1950s. Production statistics demonstrate that in 1947, such "social problem" films comprised 28 percent of all movies released. By 1953-1954, that number had declined to 9 percent.[2]

The other development affecting the movie industry that preceded the flood of television viewers was the antitrust cases that led to the demise of the Hollywood studio system.[3] While this event was not as detrimental to the movie industry as the blacklisting and conservative trend in Hollywood, it did change dramatically the way movie studios conducted business and combined with the public relations nightmare of the blacklisting and the increasing popularity of television, could not have occurred at a worse time. Despite the dark cloud above Hollywood in the late 1940s and early 1950s, the destabilization of the major movie studios held promise for small independent companies like United Artists. While the number of films produced by the major studios fell by almost two-thirds over the course of the 1950s, independently produced pictures nearly doubled.[4] Consequently, large studios entered the business of financing and distributing the films of independent studios on an individual basis. In addition studio heads employed emerging technologies such as stereoscopic (3-D) film, Cinerama, and CinemaScope, and took advantage of relaxed MPAA Production Code guidelines in a broad effort to attract suburban audiences away from their televisions and back to a medium that offered a more entertaining viewing experience.

Despite the technological advances, greater dramatic possibilities resulting from loosening of censorship guidelines, and increased artistic freedom because of the decline of the major studio's influence, the majority of movies from the 1950s could not escape the increasingly pervasive conservative views towards religion, politics, foreign policy, and societal pressures to conform. In general, cinema, like other media, became guilty of reinforcing the image of suburban United States as a place where everyone was happy, no real problems existed, and material advancement and mass consumerism were paramount societal ideals. *On the Waterfront*—and by extension the artists who collaborated to make the film, most importantly for this study Elia Kazan and Leonard Bernstein—endures as a reminder that in a society encouraged constantly to "fit in," oftentimes the best way to make a difference is to "speak out."

Synopsis

On a dock in Hoboken, New Jersey, several men exit a small shack surrounded by large ships. Mobster Johnny Friendly tells ex-boxer Terry Malloy, "You take it from here slugger." Later, the audience sees Terry call up to Joey Doyle's apartment from the street below that he has recovered one of Doyle's pigeons and would like to return it to him on the roof. The camera pans up to thugs waiting on the rooftop and then back to Terry, who has just released the pigeon, followed shortly thereafter by Joey's cry as he is thrown off the roof. Terry, disturbed that Joey has been murdered, complains to his brother, Charley (Friendly's main assistant) because he was told only to "apply some muscle." Charley reassures his brother by saying that since Joey had informed waterfront investigators about illegal union activities perpetuated by Friendly, he deserved to die. Meanwhile, police interrogate those who have gathered around Doyle's body. Following the code of the waterfront, Joey's father, Pop, rebuffs the policemen and keeps silent about what he knows, wishing his son had done the same thing when approached by investigators. Joey's sister, Edie, is not so easily pacified and demands that Father Barry help her learn who killed her brother.

The next morning finds Terry on the rooftop with his pigeons. He laments to a young neighborhood boy named Tommy that the pigeons enjoy a carefree life. Later, workers gather at the dock to be considered for the day's work. Terry also arrives and is questioned by two members of the Waterfront Crime Commission about his knowledge of Doyle's death. At the "shape-up," the dock boss, Mac, hands out "brass checks" to those workers sympathetic to the corrupt union. As he comes to the last checks, he throws them in the air and the remaining longshoremen scramble to recover them. Malloy grabs one and attempts to keep it from Edie, who has come to the docks looking for answers. When a worker tells Malloy that Edie is Doyle's sister, he gives her the check, which she gives to her father. Also present that morning, Father Barry vows to help the longshoremen's cause and offers his church as a place where they can meet.

With Terry in the congregation as a Friendly spy, Barry again implores the workers to report the corrupt union officials to the authorities. After learning nothing, Kayo Dugan (a longshoreman and friend of Edie's father) explains to Barry that the workers are "D&D—deaf and dumb" when it comes to informing on co-workers and points to Joey as someone who did not follow the code. As Barry offers a benediction, a brick is thrown through the window and Friendly's henchmen intimidate the potential informants by beating pipes and bats on the ground outside. Malloy seeks out Edie in order to save her and they escape unharmed. Meanwhile, Dugan, badly beaten, pledges to Barry that he will testify before the commission.

Following the events at the church, Terry and Edie walk and talk together and Terry remarks that he remembers Edie from their youth and that she has matured quite nicely. Edie replies that she recognized Terry as well and they compare their current situations in life. Failing to heed her father's advice to stay away from Terry, Edie later seeks out Terry on the rooftop and finds him with Tommy where he explains to her the similarities between pigeons and people. The two begin to make a connection and Terry asks Edie if she would like to join him for a beer.

At the bar, the two talk and find that their philosophies on life conflict: Terry believes that everyone should look out for themselves and Edie thinks that humanity should take care of each other. The conversation turns to Joey's murder and Terry grows defensive; he wants to help her, but cannot. Distraught, Edie leaves and comes upon a wedding reception in the next room. Terry eventually calms Edie and pleads with her to dance when one of Friendly's men interrupts their quiet moment and tells Terry that Johnny is looking for him. Subsequently, the crime commission investigators issue Terry a subpoena, causing Edie to accuse him of being responsible for Joey's death. Terry then leaves the bar and is chased down by Friendly in order to confront him with the incriminating results of Dugan's waterfront commission testimony (given after the church meeting). Friendly then commands Terry to leave Edie and silence Dugan.

The next day, longshoremen load cases of Irish whisky to be taken on a sling out of the ship's hold when the crates are intentionally dropped on Dugan; although Terry tries to help Dugan, he is killed by the weight of the load. Barry arrives to give last rites to Dugan and proceeds to give a eulogy connecting his death to Christ's crucifixion. As he talks, Friendly's henchmen hurl insults and various objects at Barry and Terry does his best to defend the priest. Edie sees this and later that night, she meets Malloy on the rooftop and gives Dugan's jacket to him, after which their relationship intensifies when they share a kiss.

Following the experience at the dock, Terry seeks out Barry in order to confess his role in Doyle's death but does not know if he should do anything about it. Barry insists that he should tell Edie the extent of his role in her brother's death. Terry follows his advice and after a heart-rending scene, Edie leaves horrified while Malloy again retreats to the rooftop. Meanwhile, at a meeting of Friendly's men, the union boss orders Charley to ensure that his brother remains silent. Distraught at the prospect of hurting his brother, Charley leaves and later meets with Terry in a taxi. Terry does not know if he can help because there are too many variables now to consider. Charley then orders him at gunpoint to be silent at which Terry is perplexed and saddened. He then goes on to blame Charley for his failure as a boxer saying, "I could've had class. I could've been a contender. I could've been somebody . . ." and adds that instead of advancing himself in Friendly's organization, Charley should have been more concerned with Terry's well-being. Sorrowfully, Charley gives the gun to his brother, lets him go, and leaves in the taxi.

Terry then seeks out forgiveness from Edie, but after his confession, she wants nothing to do with him. Terry eventually breaks the door down and tries to kiss her, to which Edie resists initially, yet ultimately yields. They hear a voice calling to Terry from the street below to meet his brother in the same manner that he previously called Joey to the rooftop to meet his fate. Terry leaves with Edie close behind and after almost being struck by a pursuing truck, they see Charley's body hanging in an alley. While Edie believes they should leave the city, Terry seeks vengeance for his brother's death. At Friendly's Bar Father Barry accosts Terry and tries to convince him that the best way to get back at Friendly is not by murdering him, but by testifying at the crime commission hearings. Terry eventually acquiesces and implicates Friendly in Doyle's murder and several other crimes at the hearings the next day causing Johnny to banish Terry from the docks.

Malloy, with police protection, arrives back home to discover that he has been blacklisted for his violation of the waterfront code. Malloy again retreats to the rooftop where he finds Tommy in tears. The boy hurls a dead pigeon at him upon which Terry discovers that Tommy has killed all of his pigeons. Edie arrives to console him but unfazed, Malloy decides to go back down to the docks to work where Mac informs the workers that everyone could go to work except Terry. Eventually, Terry tires of waiting around and with all of the longshoremen following him, goes to Friendly's shack and calls him out. Terry taunts Johnny by saying that he is glad that he testified before the crime commission and that Friendly is nothing without his bodyguards. A fight breaks out between the two and when Terry appears to be getting the better of Friendly, the latter calls his goons to finish him off. Father Barry and Edie arrive at the scene and see that Malloy is badly beaten and learn that the longshoremen refuse to work unless Malloy is allowed into the warehouse. Friendly follows the shipping boss's order to get his men to work, but the longshoremen refuse and Pop Doyle shoves Johnny into the water. Barry eventually coaxes Malloy to get up and go to work by telling him that Friendly was "laying odds" that he would not get up. Terry struggles to his feet and slowly makes his way to the door of the loading area. He stops and the rest of the men follow him in, giving power back to the workers—for now.

From "Hook" to "Waterfront"

The original idea for a story about the waterfront crime activity came not from Kazan, but his friend, playwright Arthur Miller. Following the success of two plays, *All My Sons* (1947) and *Death of a Salesman*

(1949), Miller decided to turn his attention to the problems at the docks near his home in Brooklyn Heights. Miller was interested in ongoing media reports regarding exploitation of waterfront workers so he channeled this concern into a play entitled *The Hook* (*A Play for the Screen*). Miller based his story on a rebellious dockworker named Peter Panto who attempted to overthrow the corrupt mob bosses in the Red Hook district. According to Miller's research, Panto was killed by the mob because of the potential damage he could do to their organization. Miller began work on the screenplay in 1949 in which he renamed Panto "Marty Ferrara" and focused on the waterfront culture in exhaustive detail, especially the meetings among organized longshoremen that led to Ferrara's rise as a labor leader. In short, Miller refrained from painting Ferrara as a leader who organized the masses (i.e. Terry Malloy) and instead insinuated that the mobilization came first.[5]

After Miller finished an initial draft of the play he contacted Kazan for his opinion of the script and in the hopes that he might direct it as a film. Kazan was a natural choice to collaborate with Miller because he had directed Miller's aforementioned plays, the Broadway version of Tennessee Williams's *A Streetcar Named Desire* (1947), and was currently working on the film treatment of *Streetcar* (1951). Kazan aided Miller's treatment immensely through his removal of considerable amounts of dialogue that did not transfer well to cinema. He also felt that Miller should focus more on Ferrara and allow the audience to experience the story through him rather than a myriad of secondary characters. Miller heeded Kazan's advice and completed a workable script by January 1951 when the two traveled to Hollywood to solicit support for the project.[6]

When Kazan and Miller arrived they first looked to Kazan's studio, Twentieth-Century Fox. After failing there and at Warner Brothers, they discussed the project with Harry Cohn, head of Columbia Pictures.[7] Cohn—perhaps influenced by his desire to further partner with Kazan and Miller (Columbia distributed the film adaptation of *Death of a Salesman* [1951])—displayed initial fascination, yet because of the screenplay's focus on organized labor, consulted labor affairs expert Roy Brewer. Brewer headed several unions in Hollywood, served on the Motion Picture Alliance for the Preservation of American Ideals (a collection of conservative filmmakers who battled Communism alongside HUAC) and was the point person for anyone who wished to be cleared from the blacklist. Brewer was also friends with Joe Ryan, president of the International Longshoremen's Association, and adopted Ryan's opinion that Communists—rather than corrupt labor bosses and organized crime—were the force behind opposition to his union. Therefore, after much discussion, Brewer advised Cohn to endorse the project if Miller and Kazan portrayed Communists rather than racketeers as the true villains. Miller knew, after conducting extensive research, that the revision, as pitched by Cohn and Brewer, had no basis in reality. Consequently, Miller withdrew from the project and in February 1951, Columbia pulled out of the deal as well.[8]

While Kazan and Miller were busy collaborating on their version of the New York waterfront story, another writer was consumed with compiling his own rendition. Budd Schulberg first came to the New York docks in 1950 after reading a series of articles in the *New York Sun* by Malcolm Johnson (whose work was also known to Miller) entitled "*Crime on the Waterfront*." The Pulitzer Prize-winning articles, the first of which appeared in 1948, detailed the ruthless control of workers by the corrupt International Longshoremen's Association. Producer Joseph Curtis (Monticello Film Corporation) asked Schulberg to write a screenplay based upon Johnson's articles, which Schulberg called *The Bottom of the River*. Along with Schulberg, Curtis asked Robert Siodmak to direct the film. Schulberg finished the script just before his testimony before HUAC, but the project never materialized and in 1952, the rights to the story fell to Schulberg.[9]

Soon thereafter, Kazan contacted Schulberg and met the author at his home in Pennsylvania about ideas he had for doing a movie about corruption in an Eastern city (presumably the 1948 "Trenton Six" case). Given his previous work with Miller on waterfront corruption, he was intrigued to begin anew with Schulberg's version. While Kazan worked on other projects, Schulberg began in earnest on their venture and by November 1952 they began their new treatment, now set at the docks in Hoboken, New Jersey, which for filming purposes were much less crowded than the New York side.[10] The setting of the Hoboken docks witnessed assaults, beatings, bombings, and other illegal mob intimidation that occurred on a regular basis. The New York Crime Commission, spurred to action first by investigations by Governor Dewey (in 1951) and on a larger scale by Senator Estes Kefauver's committee on organized crime, began public hearings in December 1952. Witnesses were difficult to find because of the fear of retribution from the mob. For instance, Anthony "Tony Mike" de Vincenzo, on whom Terry Malloy was based, testified that Ed Florio, the chief of the I.L.A. in New Jersey, received payments from business executives for strikebreaking and controlling jobs.[11] Kazan remembers de Vincenzo's story:

> Tony Mike had not only seen the corruption, but had probably, at one time, benefited from it. Then apparently the injustice got too much for him. He resented being bullied as much as he scorned the dishonesty. . . . Then came the big step, one that may have even surprised Tony Mike. When he was subpoenaed to testify before the Water-

> front Crime Commission about the corruption he'd seen and how it worked, who "took" and how much, Tony Mike told the full truth and as no one had before. He named names. When he did that, he broke the hoodlum law of silence: If you want to live, don't talk. He was called a rat, a squealer and stoolie. He was ostracized, then threatened. Friends he'd had for years didn't talk to him. . . . Tony Mike told us about his experiences. He'd talked. He was still alive, but he knew that the last man who'd opened New York's waterfront rackets to view was found dead in a lime pit.[12]

The Crime Commission released its findings in May 1953 and the results did not surprise anyone: workers were compelled to take out oppressive loans for guaranteed work, illegal strikes elicited higher fees from shippers, and abuse of elections and accounting were rampant.[13] From this real-life drama of corrupt unions and individuals who decided to make a difference, Kazan and Schulberg obtained a wealth of material for their project. In addition, through the personal connection Kazan made with de Vincenzo, Kazan found the inspiration for the script's chief protagonist: Terry Malloy.

After taking the story to RKO, Kazan decided to go to Zanuck who he had always viewed as the most likely backer given his previous interest in socially conscious films like *The Grapes of Wrath* and the current Kazan/Zanuck project *Viva Zapata!* (1952). Following a lengthy deliberation with Zanuck the producer ultimately passed on the film for a variety of reasons, all of which added up to Zanuck's opinion that there was too much story and not enough star appeal.[14] After reading the script he felt that audiences would not be able to relate to longshoremen in the same way they connected with the Joads's cross-country migration more than a decade earlier. Some have claimed that in the new age of CinemaScope, which worked better for colorful film spectacles like the recent Fox success *The Robe* (1953), a film like *On the Waterfront* that was long on story and filmed in black and white was an outmoded format. Still others have noted that Zanuck would have made the movie if Kazan could have guaranteed him that Marlon Brando would play the lead role, but since Brando was unwilling to work with Kazan after the latter's HUAC testimony, such an arrangement could not be reached. Disillusioned but undeterred, Kazan and Schulberg went to United Artists, Warner Brothers, Paramount, and MGM, before they finally found support in May 1953.[15]

Staying on the same floor at the Beverly Hills Hotel, Schulberg explained the project to an independent producer named Sam Spiegel. Spiegel, who has arguably enjoyed more renown for his work on epic films like *The Bridge on the River Kwai* (1957) and *Lawrence of Arabia* (1962), decided to take a chance and agreed to all production duties for his Horizon Pictures (co-founded with John Huston) and negotiated distribution through Columbia Pictures. Spiegel had most recently produced Huston's *The African Queen* (1951) and perhaps was looking for something to reestablish his reputation after the recent failure of *Melba* (1953). Besides financial support and casting negotiations, Spiegel was heavily involved in creating the final shooting script. Spiegel encouraged Kazan and Schulberg to maintain an open mind regarding the script, even when it appeared they had a finished product. On one occasion Schulberg became particularly incensed at Spiegel when the latter changed his mind:[16]

> Schulberg got up one night, in the middle of the night—he was living in Pennsylvania then; and his second wife came in the bathroom at 3 a.m., [and found Schulberg] shaving, and she said: "What are you doing shaving at three in the morning?" He said: "I'm going to New York to kill Spiegel." He wanted to kill Spiegel because Spiegel kept saying: "It's [the script] very good now, I think we've got it. Let's start casting; all right." And then the next day he'd say: "Let's talk about this again, let's open it up again."[17]

Despite the frustrations that both Kazan and Schulberg experienced with Spiegel's constant revisions, they could not argue with the final product, which Kazan believed to be "a model script, a near perfect piece of work."[18] In addition to consistent revision of the script between the three collaborators, Spiegel contributed much to securing the eventual *Waterfront* cast.

Casting

Since Marlon Brando was unavailable for the lead role of Terry Malloy, the production team decided on Frank Sinatra, who had recently become a desired commodity after his award-winning role in *From Here to Eternity* (1953). Sinatra was born and raised in Hoboken and according to Kazan spoke "perfect Hobokenese."[19] Kazan had already discussed wardrobe possibilities with Sinatra when Spiegel approached him about casting Brando as Malloy instead. Kazan attempted to impress upon Spiegel the impossibility of his idea, but Spiegel insisted upon wooing the actor because he could secure a considerably higher budget with Brando as a cast member. Richard Schickel suggests that in order to lure Brando, Kazan asked friend and eventual *Waterfront* cast member Karl Malden (who was already serving as a *de facto* assistant director for the film) to cast an actor as an alternative to Sinatra. Malden eventually decided to choose a rising Actor's Studio star named Paul Newman and his wife, Joanne Woodward, as the love interest. Newman and Woodward performed for Spiegel, leaving the producer unimpressed, but achieving the effect Kazan and Spiegel had desired: Schickel reports when Brando heard that a young actor with a similar skill set was being considered for a coveted role, his agent contacted Malden immediately and by early fall of 1953, Brando agreed to play Terry Malloy.[20]

The character of Father Barry was based on Father John M. Corridan, associate director of the St. Xavier School in Manhattan, and a prominent figure in Johnson's articles about waterfront crime. Known as the "waterfront priest," he held meetings, gave homilies, advised longshoremen, and even urged workers to rise up against their oppressors. Kazan and Schulberg modeled Father Barry's eulogy/homily following Dugan's murder after one Corridan gave on the New Jersey docks. The sermon entitled, "A Catholic Looks at the Waterfront," was replicated in Malcolm Johnson's book *Crime on the Labor Front* (1950).

> You want to know what's wrong with the waterfront? It's love of a buck. . . . Christ also said, "If you do it to the least of mine, you do it to me." Christ is in the shape-up. . . . He stands in the shape-up knowing that all won't get work and maybe He won't. . . . What does Christ think of the man who picks up a longshoreman's brass check and takes 20 per cent interest at the end of the week? Christ goes to a union meeting . . . and sees a few with $150 suits and diamond rings on their fingers.[21]

Kazan wanted Father Barry to be different than most Catholic priests he encountered throughout life. Kazan was born into the Greek Orthodox faith and when his family moved to the United States and could not find a Greek Orthodox church, his father sent him to a Catholic school. After going to confession and learning Catholic dogma, he found the experience unfulfilling and the teachers somewhat insincere. In Father Barry, though, he wanted a man who possessed an unyielding moral character saying, "Priests are like that in those working-class communities." Of course, Kazan knew Karl Malden well from their previous collaborations and Kazan believed that the actor had in him a high ethical standard similar to that of Father Barry. As Kazan remembers, "When I got Karl, there wasn't much directing to do."[22]

The remainder of the major cast members was comprised, like Malden, of members of the Group Theater or Actor's Studio cofounded by Kazan. Eva Marie Saint, cast as Edie Doyle, belonged to the latter organization and had been on an early television soap opera, *One Man's Family* for approximately three years. In 1953, Kazan and

Spiegel witnessed Saint in her Broadway debut alongside Lillian Gish in *The Trip to Bountiful* (1953) and eventually decided on her over Elizabeth Montgomery. Kazan saw in Saint the innocence required to realize Edie's character and when he paired her with Brando in an improvisational exercise, Saint recalled the chemistry between the two was unmistakable.[23] With other cast members, Kazan made instinctual decisions. Regarding Rod Steiger as Charley Malloy, Kazan avowed that, "With Steiger you could just smell it. You could look at him and say, 'Here is a guy who is going to make it.' I just smell the soul and see what the hell is there."[24] Given his continued work from previous productions with actors like Brando and Malden, Kazan also returned to Lee J. Cobb as Johnny Friendly. Cobb created the role of Willy Loman in Kazan's production of *Death of a Salesman* and, like Malden, also appeared in *Boomerang!* (1947).

To inject an added sense of authenticity into the film, Kazan hired Tony Galento, Abe Simon, and Tami Mauriello, former prize-fighters, as Friendly's strongmen. Furthermore, most of the extras for the film were area longshoremen working on the Hoboken waterfront. When Schulberg conducted research on waterfront culture he immersed himself by talking to the workers, frequenting the same restaurants and bars, and spending time at the gym regaling the locals based on his encyclopedic knowledge of and connections with the boxing world. This latter talent proved to be a particularly useful way to gain acceptance among the longshoremen. By the time principal shooting began, the workers saw Schulberg as an advocate for their cause and the film as a voice for their plight, thus the longshoremen became more cooperative colleagues throughout shooting because of Schulberg's efforts.[25]

When Kazan set about designing the visual narrative of the film, he again turned to a previous collaborator. Kazan hired Richard Day, who worked with Kazan on *A Streetcar Named Desire*, as the art director and thus responsible for selecting the location and setting for each scene. Known for his evocations of both psychological and physical planes in his designs, Day viewed the American urban experience as intimidating and constraining. For instance, in *On the Waterfront* following the taxi scene and up until Terry and Edie find Charley's body, prominent are closed, confined spaces, dark alleyways, and underground garages that seem to consume unsuspecting citizens. Throughout the film, the distant, ominous skyline of Manhattan surrounds the action and contributes to a feeling of imminent threat. Kazan chose freelance cinematographer Boris Kaufman to realize the gloomy landscapes chosen by Day. Kaufman learned his craft from his brother, the renowned Dziga Vertov, who was part of the Soviet Kino-Pravda film group, and later was the favored cameraman of French director Jean

Vigo. The style he learned from his brother and utilized for Vigo's films approximated documentary method, which he applied to *On the Waterfront*. Kaufman preferred black and white photography because he believed that the potential range of emotional and psychological contrast was much greater than in color films. Kaufman wanted to maintain consistent lighting patterns as much as possible and the shooting schedules that occurred at different times during the day made this a problem. To make the best of the situation, Kaufman burned trash fires that allowed light to disperse evenly. These trash fires were also functional within the narrative as unemployed longshoremen gathered around the fires to keep warm during the cold, winter days. Furthermore, the misty atmosphere obscured the lines of the aforementioned closed spaces and echoed the moral uncertainty surrounding the characters' actions.[26]

The final piecc added to this collaborative puzzle was Leonard Bernstein's music. As filming drew to a close, Kazan, Schulberg, and especially Spiegel, were worried that people would not go to view the finished product. There was also concern that Columbia would shelve the film so that it would not compete with what the studio considered its main candidate for Best Picture Oscar, *The Caine Mutiny* (1954). Spiegel decided that *On the Waterfront* needed one more big name to increase box office drawing potential. It was Bernstein's achievement and renown as a conductor and composer in both "serious" and popular musical arenas that made him so attractive to Spiegel.[27]

Bernstein had been offered film projects before, but demurred because he could not bring himself to compose music, which to him, when it was written well, should be unnoticed. After a few unsuccessful attempts by Spiegel to lure Bernstein's talent early in 1954, the composer finally succumbed and watched a "rough cut" of the film with the producer, Brando, and Kazan present.[28] Bernstein was not the first composer Kazan would have chosen for this project. Alex North, who scored Kazan's *A Streetcar Named Desire* and *Viva Zapata!*, was a more likely choice, but since Kazan's testimony before HUAC, their collaboration ceased. Bernstein's familiarity with the Group Theater/Actor's Studio through Copland and Blitzstein (and the fact that he had met Kazan previously) in addition to his prestige in the musical world, made him a suitable alternative. In an effort to plead his case and convey the impression that the film was in desperate need of Bernstein's services, Spiegel apologized to Bernstein for the crude state of the film during the screening. Apparently Kazan took umbrage at what he considered Spiegel's overindulging of Bernstein's talent and told Spiegel that he believed it to be a fine effort. Bernstein agreed and remembered being "swept by my enthusiasm into accepting the commission to write the score. . . . I heard music as I watched: that was enough."[29] Bernstein signed a contract for $15,000 with Spiegel's independent group, which was the standard rate for an established film composer. In addition to being given the option of conducting the score (something most Hollywood composers did), he was granted the sole financial rights to arrange the music into a suite. While other composers were given this privilege, the fact that Bernstein was the only financial beneficiary was a rarity in Hollywood.[30]

Beginning in February 1954, Bernstein screened the film countless times on a Moviola in order to determine when to incorporate music. Since Bernstein was new to the mechanical aspects of film composition, he was forced to learn them on his own.

> Nobody told me I was supposed to be supplied with cue sheets, a cutter, and a converter table. I just did it all by myself. . . . Day after day I sat at a Moviola, running the print back and forth, measuring in feet the sequences I had chosen for music, converting the feet into seconds by mathematical formula.[31]

The fact that Bernstein spent so much time completing these more tedious tasks of film music composition probably helped lead to Columbia's hiring of orchestrators for the project. Furthermore, it was not unusual for Bernstein to work with orchestrators as he collaborated with them on Broadway and in some concert music projects. Recording of the score was to transpire late in April 1954, and music director Morris Stoloff found two orchestrators, Gil Grau and Marlin Skiles. Bernstein's sketches demonstrate that he made decisions regarding instrumentation and orchestration and copied them down in a shorthand notation. Beyond being copyists, there is conflicting anecdotal evidence as to Grau's and Skiles's other roles. Some have suggested that the orchestrators corrected several timing errors Bernstein had made while compiling his cue sheets. However, Jon Burlingame points to a *Los Angeles Times* article that stated only a few errors occurred as a result of Bernstein's lack of experience in the mechanical side of film composition.[32]

Given the detail of Bernstein's short score sketches (discussed more in Chapter 5) and the degree to which his instructions were followed by Grau and Skiles (evidenced by the conductor parts housed at Sony Music Division) their efforts were almost certainly channeled towards correcting the aforementioned mechanical considerations and ensuring that the orchestration progressed smoothly such that all deadlines were maintained. There were times when Bernstein trusted their expertise, for instance in one of the source music cues when Edie and Terry dance together to the Love theme, Bernstein noted on his sketch to "Give to Marlin Skiles" because of Skiles's expertise as a dance band arranger going back to his days as a pianist with the Jean Goldkette Orchestra in the 1920s.[33]

The score was recorded on 24, 27, and 28 April 1954. Naturally (and contractually), Bernstein could have conducted the sessions, but declined citing his unfamiliarity with simultaneously conducting an orchestra and synchronizing with the film images. Thus Stoloff conducted the entire score (a position in which he was quite capable as head of Columbia's music division) except for the opening scene of the film in which Terry and Johnny emerge together from Friendly's dockside shack, which Bernstein conducted himself due to the complex cross rhythms that were integral to the composer's stylistic idiom.[34] Forty-seven musicians were involved in the event, with one extra pianist—Bernstein—who performed a bluesy piece of music on the piano for a scene in which Malloy and Edie are meeting at a bar. The recording, which was well publicized, attracted many musicians, including André Previn, who commented (along with others) that while Bernstein disagreed with Stoloff regarding sound balance and a couple of cues, the session transpired quite smoothly.[35]

Following the recording of the soundtrack, Bernstein stayed in Los Angeles to participate in the dubbing process in which engineers mix dialogue, music, and sound effects. The dubbing occurred on the third floor of Columbia's Sound Department, which Bernstein referred to as "Upper Dubbing" in a 30 May 1954 *New York Times* article entitled, "Notes Struck at Upper Dubbing, California: Tyro Film Composer Leonard Bernstein Lauds Sound Technicians' Marvels." The article mainly recounted Bernstein's aggravation with how his music was sliced and manipulated in order to integrate well with the other filmic aspects. Bernstein's chief frustration concerned a scene in which the music, during its emotional climax, was "dialed down" in order to hear dialogue between Terry and Edie.

> For example, there is, in *On the Waterfront*, a tender, hesitant love scene on the roof between the inarticulate hero and the inhibited heroine surrounded by cooing pigeons. It was deliberately underwritten, and there were long, Kazan-like pauses between the lines—an ideal spot, it would seem for the composer to take over. I suggested that here I should write love music that was shy at first and then, with growing, *Tristanish* intensity, come to a great climax which swamps the scene and screen, even drowning out the last prosaic bits of dialogue, which went something like this, "Have a beer with me?" (Very long pause) "Uh-huh." The music here was to do the real storytelling, and Kazan and company agreed enthusiastically, deciding to do it this way before even one note was written. So it was written, so orchestrated, so recorded. But then in Upper Dubbing, Kazan decided he

> just couldn't give up that ineffably sacred grunt which Brando emits at the end; it was, he thought, the two most eloquent syllables the actor had delivered in the whole script. And what happened to the music? As it mounts to its great climax, as the theme goes higher and higher and brasses and percussion join in with the strings and woodwinds, the all-powerful control dials are turned, and the sound fades out in a slow *diminuendo*. Musically ridiculous, of course; and to save a grunt, the tension on the screen lessened in precisely the proportion that it mounts in my own pummeled psyche. *Uh-huh*.[36]

While Bernstein may have lost the battle regarding this cue, most of his score ended up in the film. The cue, as Bernstein described it remains in the film, and is perhaps more effective because of the job done by the engineers in "Upper Dubbing." Had the cue been allowed to progress as Bernstein wished, all dialogue would have been obscured and the dramatic importance of the crucial encounter between Terry and Edie would have been diminished. Furthermore, there is no "grunt" as Bernstein laments and the vast majority of what he wrote for the cue survives in the film. Perhaps a more accurate account of Bernstein's experience in the sound department can be gleaned from the closing statement that, "It was a glorious experience: I wouldn't have missed it for anything."[37]

Despite his complaints about his experience in the sound booth, Bernstein did write in a letter to his teacher and confidante, Helen Coates, that, "I've made millions of good new friends and I find I actually like it here for the very reasons Hollywood is usually attacked: namely, that there is nothing to do but see people."[38] In a sense, Bernstein did get the last laugh as he received equal billing with Spiegel, Kazan, and Schulberg on the publicity poster of the Astor Theatre in New York when the film premiered on 28 July 1954. As is the case with current Academy Award politics, the winners are not always the ones who create the best artistic rendition. Rather, the award often goes to the person who campaigned the hardest. Spiegel was not alone in this Hollywood tradition and on 9 March 1955, placed a full-page ad in the *Hollywood Reporter*, praising his cast's accomplishment, highlighting that of Bernstein. The Academy did not listen and gave the award to Dimitri Tiomkin, a favorite among the organization, for his score to *The High and the Mighty*.[39]

Soon after, Bernstein began in earnest the compiling of his score into a symphonic suite. The work premiered on 11 August 1955 with the Boston Symphony Orchestra and Bernstein later recorded it with the New York Philharmonic on 16 May 1960. The reasons why Bernstein never composed another film score are most often related to his experience in "Upper Dubbing." As close friend Charlie Harmon surmises, "He always claimed that he didn't do another film because he was so upset at the cutting and editing process over which he had no control."[40] While Harmon may be correct, Bernstein was simply too busy with his rigorous schedule of composition, conducting, and teaching over the next thirty-five years to devote considerable time to film composition. Regardless, Bernstein's recruitment to the project put the finishing touches on a memorable collaborative team that had more in common with each other than solely working on this film.

HUAC, Informing, and Critical Reception

As important as the issue of waterfront crime was to *On the Waterfront*, another event that contributed to the impact of the film was the degree to which HUAC impacted many of the creative personnel involved in making the film, best exemplified in both Kazan's and Bernstein's shared political beliefs and their separate experiences with anti-Communism leading up to their involvement in *On the Waterfront*. Throughout the 1940s and through success on Broadway and in films like *A Tree Grows in Brooklyn* (1945) and *Gentleman's Agreement* (1947), Kazan reflected upon his meteoric rise from a young Greek immigrant, through the Group Theater, and to Hollywood, and believed that he was capable of telling stories that might help enact real social change. The populist message espoused in *Viva Zapata!* and his "Waterfront" corruption treatment with his friend Arthur Miller would seem to indicate he was serious about continuing to make socially conscious films. Yet, given Miller's abrupt decision to abandon their "Waterfront" project, Kazan was also well aware of the cost involved in being labeled a Communist. In addition, Kazan knew that his activity in Communist cells within the Group Theater was certainly making its way through government channels to HUAC. So when Kazan was first called before a private session with the committee on 10 January 1952 he was forthcoming regarding his Communist association within the Group Theater, but refused to name any names, even though he was encouraged to do so (and despite the fact he was provided with transcripts from previous cooperative testimony, including that of Budd Schulberg, who he hadn't met at this time).[41]

Brian Neve asserts that the committee cited Kazan with contempt for his refusal to fully cooperate, but that he was ultimately dismissed and apparently free from any further testimony until an article appeared in the *Hollywood Reporter* in March about his first appearance and his decision to refrain from naming names. Following the article and under increasing pressure from his bosses at Twentieth-Century Fox, it became clear to Kazan that he needed to be fully transparent with the committee when he was called again in April 1952. Kazan read his statement before the committee and restated his membership in a cell within the Group Theater. He then went on to describe his orders from the party, which consisted of learning Marxist doctrine and ultimately making the Group Theater an instrument of the party. He inferred that he left the party because he insisted his artistic beliefs were being smothered. Kazan listed several associates including Clifford Odets (who as agreed upon between the two, named Kazan at his session) and defended questionable items in his filmography as fully supportive of the anti-Communist cause and genuinely American in spirit.[42]

Following Kazan's confession, he published a notice in the *New York Times* encouraging others to testify and exercise what he considered a civic duty to stop Communism's threat against the American way of life. Someone who certainly read this article but who as of yet had not been officially exposed for past and present political connections was Leonard Bernstein. As suggested in Chapter 2, Bernstein was familiar with the Group Theater, its actors, and its political persuasions and it must have struck a personal blow to see an artistic acquaintance like Kazan buckle to HUAC's pressure. Throughout the 1940s, Bernstein attended numerous events and supported several causes that in the early 1950s were being questioned as Communist front organizations. For instance, through Group Theater member Stella Adler, Bernstein appeared at a function for an organization the FBI considered a precursor to the Young Communist League. He dined in support of the Joint Anti-Fascist Refugee Committee, which was eventually subpoenaed by HUAC in 1946 to relinquish its membership directory. Shortly after Hollywood studio heads released their Waldorf Statement that established the blacklist late in 1947, Bernstein revisited Blitzstein's agit-prop *The Cradle Will Rock* for his final concert with the New York City Symphony.[43]

In the 1950s Bernstein continued to identify with more liberal lines of inquiry through works that questioned mass commercialization (*Trouble in Tahiti*) and gender roles (*Tahiti* and *Wonderful Town*) as functions of the new suburban frontier and criticized the blacklist and the pervasive culture of fear (*Candide*). In addition he inaugurated the Brandeis Arts Festival in 1952 in which he stated:

> This is a moment . . . when civilization looks at itself appraisingly, seeking a key to the future. . . . The art of an era is a reflection of the society in which it was produced and . . . the intellectual and emotional climate of the era. Through (the arts) the patterns of thought and expression which characterize each generation can be analyzed.[44]

In the same way that Kazan saw film as vehicle for social change, so too did Bernstein view music possessing the same power and by extension, his role as a musician and conductor. Given Bernstein's concern for liberal causes and his increasing prominence in American culture, it was not long before Bernstein too was touched by anti-Communist hysteria. Of course, fueling this fire was an FBI file on Bernstein begun in 1943 that would eventually comprise 700 pages.[45] Shortly after his longtime collaborator Jerome Robbins became a friendly witness before HUAC in May 1953, Bernstein discovered that his passport application had been denied by the State Department. Bernstein already enjoyed much success in Europe so the potential closing of that creative avenue for him, as well as the black mark of the passport trouble, put him in a precarious scenario. In order to renew both his application and reputation, Bernstein was compelled to disavow himself of any previous activity that might be construed as Communist or supporting Communism. Afterwards he was granted a temporary pass to conduct in South America in September and Italy in December, but it was not until 20 May 1954—ten days before Bernstein's famous "Upper Dubbing" article appeared in the *New York Times*—that he was ultimately cleared and treated like a normal citizen again.[46]

Much of the immediate critical reception of the film was extremely positive[47] and the profound success at the Academy Awards ceremony the following year would seem to indicate that Kazan's testimony was no longer an issue to many within the film industry. Yet, Terry Malloy's decision to speak out against the waterfront culture of silence has since been connected with Kazan's HUAC testimony and thus criticism of the film since 1954 has been predominantly based on what scholars have viewed as a justification for informing. Kazan himself has done much to fuel this critical fire with statements like:

> When people said that there are some parallels to what I had done, I couldn't and wouldn't deny it. It does have some parallels. But I wasn't concerned with them nor did I play on them. They were not my reason for making the film. I had wanted to do a picture about the waterfront long before any of the HUAC business came up.[48]

Kazan's multivalent yet agonizing decision to confess his previous Communist ties and implicate former associates aside, one can see the congruence. Kazan pointed out in his remarks before HUAC that the Communist Party's influence on the Group Theater had become too intense, such that Kazan felt creatively shackled. In the two decades that separated Kazan's Group Theater membership and his HUAC testimony, the director used his films as the vehicle through which he developed an individual voice. However, because he remained silent about past Communist activities he was always under suspicion by the authorities and his studio bosses. So in order to finally establish his identity and ensure his creativity remained free, he felt compelled to speak out.

Interestingly, scholars have latched onto the film's final scene in which Terry leads the longshoremen to work past a defeated Johnny Friendly as the site of the most heated debate. Lindsay Anderson decried the message of the sequence as "fascist" because the workers merely transferred their loyalty from one "leader" to another before being called to work by a well-dressed "overseer."[49] Peter Biskind, in a more reasonable and convincing analysis, viewed the film and its ending as demonstrative of what Arthur Schlesinger, Jr. termed in 1949, "The Vital Center." In other words, rather than decrying the state as leftists had in the 1930s, cold war liberals saw the state, church, and family as the means through which society could advance. Thus, with Father Barry (church) and Edie (family) looking on, Terry mobilizes the masses and leads them to a better life.[50] Further, Kenneth Hey posits that the final scene is but one of many examples of ambivalence displayed throughout the film.[51]

Another way to view this scene would be through the lens of contemporaneous social theory. Clearly Terry is an individual at odds with his environment, perhaps the result of an inner-directed personality at odds with an increasingly other-directed society. However, Terry's actions do not reflect the way society brings its members to conformity, but rather how these individuals deal with their imposed social character. Rather, Terry more closely approximates David Riesman's autonomous individual. Riesman distinguishes between adjusted, anomic (from the French *anomique*), and autonomous social roles. In addition, Riesman suggests that each of the social roles can be found in tradition, inner, and other-directed societies. For instance, during the nineteenth century when inner-direction was the norm, the Romantics would have been considered autonomous, as opposed to the adjusted "Philistines." Those that are adjusted to a given social character are archetypal examples of that character. Anomic individuals are the opposite, or as Riesman calls them, "maladjusted." Autonomous citizens are "capable of conforming to the behavioral norms of their society—a capacity the anomics usually lack—but who are free to choose whether to conform or not."[52] Moreover, this concept of autonomy is directly related to one's ability to "work on one's self" and is only possible through an evolution of the self akin to that experienced by Terry Malloy.

For much of 1951 Bernstein spent his time composing in Cuernavaca, Mexico, at various residences, including that of Martha Gellhorn. There he learned the fate of several prominent Hollywood personalities including John Garfield. Of Garfield's plight Bernstein remarked, "I suppose there is nothing to be done when your life and career are attacked but strike back with the truth and go honestly to jail if you have to. . . . I hope I'm as brave as I sound from this distance when it catches up to me."[53] It is easy to view this comment as ironic given Bernstein's confession two years later, yet it also offers further insight into how Brando's performance motivated the composer to accept work on the film. Throughout his life Bernstein never abandoned his romantic spirit and in 1951 conveyed an attitude of confidence that was tempered through the passport incident. When "it" did finally catch up with him, Bernstein chose to preserve his career—and thus his identity—by confessing to his liberal past. Thus as the waning passport misfortune coincided with his work on *On the Waterfront*, it is very likely that in addition to the music Bernstein "heard" while screening the film, he also viewed Terry's vindication in the context of a new beginning in his own life. Following the fallout from his testimony Kazan had also experienced a series of defeats at the box office (most recently with *Man on a Tightrope*) and on Broadway (notably *Camino Real*), so *On the Waterfront* represented a turning point for Kazan as well and propelled him to successes with *East of Eden* (1955) and *A Face in the Crowd* (1957). Bernstein entered arguably the most successful era in his career with a slate of television appearances that began later in 1954, continued conducting opportunities and the New York Philharmonic directorship in 1958, while *Candide* (1956) and *West Side Story* (1957) followed shortly thereafter. Through Terry's journey and eventual triumph both Kazan and Bernstein renewed their careers and collaborated to create one of the most enduring cinematic works in film history. Chapter 5 examines thoroughly the music's contribution to this masterpiece and argues that in the same way that *On The Waterfront* stands as an example of a new way of filmmaking, Leonard Bernstein's first and only film score contributes mightily to post–World War II film scoring and the manner in which we consider film music today.

5

AN ANALYSIS OF THE SCORE

Just as the longshoremen unified and went with Terry to work at the close of *On the Waterfront*, so the triumph of this film results from the collaboration of the cast and crew united under Kazan's singular vision. Schulberg compares the creation of the ideal motion picture with a horse race where all the participants cross the finish line in a "dead heat."[1] Schulberg and Kazan's story of redemption to which all people can relate, the depth of character portrayal by Brando, Saint, Steiger, and Malden, the documentary style of Kaufman's photography, and the dual nature of the Hoboken docks—both idyllic and dangerous—make this film a photo finish. Furthermore, the movie is one of those rare art works that not only portrays the cultural *Zeitgeist*, but also allows viewers of subsequent generations to apply it to their particular place in history. Upon twenty years of reflection about the movie, Elia Kazan stated that, "the love scenes are the best thing in the film."[2] While Bernstein's music enhances those love scenes quite well, the following analysis concentrates not only on "love" music but also on those musical cues that escaped critical acclaim, but, arguably, were written more effectively.

The Leonard Bernstein Collection in the Music Division of the Library of Congress is the home of Bernstein's manuscripts pertaining to *On the Waterfront*, notably the short score manuscript for the film score, an inventory of which can be found in Appendix I. This manuscript would have been given to orchestrators Skiles and Grau to produce the full score. Two of the cues in Appendix I, "Accident" and "The Challenge" were composed and recorded, but not included in the score. The former was intended to accompany Kayo Dugan's death scene and the latter was to enhance Terry's verbal taunting of Friendly before their climactic fight. In the first substantial study of the score, William Hamilton suggested the cues were deleted because "the soundtrack was already too full of dialogue and ambient noise to accommodate any music at all."[3] In addition to the Library of Congress, the Music Division at Sony Pictures houses a variety of materials related to the film score and with the manuscripts at the Library of Congress comprise the chief source of the examples in this document because they reflect best what appears on the soundtrack.[4] While musical cues were organized by reel/part number they also bore Bernstein's titles for each cue as well and because the latter nomenclature makes more direct reference to the appropriate scene, the analysis below is organized by Bernstein's cue titles (which appear on both his short score sketches and the corresponding conductor parts).[5] Dating back to Hamilton's analysis of the score in 1954 the following culminates the most thorough examination of Bernstein's first and only film score.[6]

"Main Title"

During the opening credits, Bernstein sets the mood for the subsequent drama and introduces themes that will recur throughout the movie. He presents one of the main musical themes of the film as a solo in the French horn, displayed in Ex. 5.1. This melody is filled with a sense of grim, stoic determination. The horn sounds the opening motive centered on *f'*, which sinks down, then rises again to its original place. It falls a second time, then ascends even higher to its peak in measure four. The theme then descends and reaches resolution.

Ex. 5.1. *On the Waterfront*, Conductor Part. "Main Title." Opening solo in French horn, mm. 1-6.

The opening of *On the Waterfront* is but one of many compositions in which Bernstein began the piece with a solo instrument. Jack Gottlieb noted several works in which Bernstein follows this "theatrical impulse . . . [that] demands the attention of an audience since the listener must be particularly alert and sensitive to intimate or exposed sounds."[7] In addition the steadily rising, arpeggiated melody gives the feeling of attaining a goal. Although m. 6 outlines a D minor triad, the A-natural (after five measures of A-flat) creates a sense of resolution, later emphasized by the same F-natural that opened the excerpt. As mentioned in Chapter 2 the opening pentatonicism and flatted fifth in measure five lends much to the vernacular nature of the film's drama, but there is more to this opening material than melody. The six measures encompass two smaller three-measure units in which the rhythms and meters (4/4, 4/4, 3/4) within each unit are identical. In addition the arched melodic contour, enhanced by the forte in m. 4, lends an added sense of antecedent/consequent balance to the overall phrase. Yet there is a sense of imbalance as well. The insertion of the triple meter into measures 3 and 6 interrupts the more confident duple progression, thus mitigating its gait. Moreover as asserted in Chapter 2, the sudden modulation from a pentatonic rendering of F natural minor to D dorian, centered on the C-flat—F tritone in measure 5, creates a rather unexpected turn in the theme.

After viewing the film (as Bernstein had before writing any music), this unanticipated modulation and its resolution foreshadows the redemption of Terry Malloy—in this instance, the reclaiming of his dignity—and the theme serves as a microcosm of Terry's journey.[8] Joanna E. Rapf, in her study of Kazan's production notebook for the film, notes that the idea of dignity was foremost on the director's mind as he worked on this project. One of the first instructions Kazan wrote was, "He [Terry] wants his dignity back. He wants his self-respect back. He's not going to be cowed anymore. . . . He wants his dignity back. . . . He testifies!" Later he notes under the heading, "Theme [underline Kazan's]" that, "This Motion Picture is about one thing only: a Young man who has let his dignity slip away, and regains it!"[9] In a broader sense, Terry's journey speaks to the risks involved when one attempts to stand up against a highly conformist group. Terry is continuously at odds with his surroundings and the people he encounters; it is not easy to be an individual in such a setting. Accordingly, Bernstein presents the opening material—from this point referred to as the Dignity theme—in the hero's instrument (the horn). Even more interesting is Bernstein's suggestion of opposing forces through competing harmonic areas. Bernstein insinuates Terry's conflict between the workers/folk and the establishment through the pentatonic version of F minor. Eventually the masses triumph through modality as the passage ends in D Dorian and on F-natural as the excerpt began; Terry is still Terry, but musically and dramatically he has changed.

That this melody pertains to Terry's journey seems also to be borne out in some of his sketches at the Library of Congress. Bernstein typed the following lyrics on a yellow legal pad:

> I got two arms
> And a man's back
> And a hook and a glove:
> Two fists
> And a mean aim
> And a woman I love.

Oh you can't set
Worlds on Fire
With a hook and a glove:
Only make a day's pay
For the woman you love.

One guy is nobody special:
Me, there's thousands like me.
Thousands and millions like me
Will keep us free. . . .

Free to work hard
For a day's pay
With a hook and a glove:
Hard work and a day's pay
For the woman I love.[10]

On another page Bernstein set these same lyrics to the melody of the Dignity theme in a handwritten vocal score.[11] The song is in a conventional AABA form in which the A sections are each set to the material in Ex. 5.1, although Bernstein added an additional eighth-note pairing between C-natural and E-flat (to precede the F-natural that begins the Dignity theme in m. 1) presumably to make the lyrics fit. Bernstein modulates to F major for the bridge section (Ex. 5.2), which highlights the collective action to work that culminates the film. The passage then ends on an E-flat and sends the song back into F minor.

Ex. 5.2. Leonard Bernstein. "Waterfront Song." Bridge melody and lyrics, mm. 9-15.

Besides the sense of *esprit de corps* that embodies the bridge, most notable is the degree to which the song's protagonist relies on the love of a woman for his motivation. Moreover, these lyrics supply the opening theme of the film with renewed meaning. Love is the end game and plays a crucial role in both this song and Terry's journey (see "Glove Scene" and "Walk and End Title" below for more detail) while the opening measures coincide with the humdrum of daily life and the recognition that the status quo—"Oh you can't set worlds on fire with a hook and a glove"—will no longer suffice and that a change must be made.

Following the theme in Ex. 5.1 Bernstein imitates the melody between the first trombone and flutes and similar to its implementation on Broadway, such counterpoint in the opening moments, and even more effectively throughout this film score, was uncommon even in 1954. As Keller noted as early as 1955:

> [I]t is indeed the largely contrapuntal texture of the Waterfront score that constitutes a momentous historical event in the realm of the most modern of all arts which, on the musical side, has hitherto shown a predilection for the most outmoded homophony. From the single thematic line with which the title music opens and the ensuing two-part canon at the octave, it is clear that Bernstein is determined to subject the Hollywoodian sound track to a radical spring cleaning.[12]

Bernstein restates the second half of the Dignity theme—and thus its most crucial portion—twice in the trumpets accompanied by the harp, bass clarinet, and clarinets playing a pedal point on F-natural, seen in Ex. 5.3.

Ex. 5.3. *On the Waterfront*, Conductor Part. "Main Title." Second half of Dignity theme repeated in trumpets, mm. 13-17.

As the main credits wind down one notices that the theme concludes in an interrogatory manner, thus questioning what might come after the visual dissolve. In a subtle acknowledgment of the waterfront setting, Bernstein places the accompanying winds in octaves played sub tone (Ex. 5.4) and reminiscent of foghorns, ship whistles, and other waterfront machinery.

Ex. 5.4. *On the Waterfront*, Conductor Part. "Main Title." Winds in subtone to suggest ships and other waterfront machinery, mm. 18-19.

"Opening Shot to Scream"

In the opening scene, Bernstein creates a dramatic shift in mood from the music of the opening credits. One sees a large ship in the background and in the foreground the docks. As a group of men leaves a small shack, the audience witnesses Johnny Friendly patting Terry Malloy on the back saying, "You take it from here, slugger." Accompanying the action, we hear a highly rhythmic, violent theme, first in the second timpani, then imitated in the first timpani, and finally in the drums (Ex. 5.5), creating a thunderous polyphonic texture that forces the viewer to focus on the men on the dock and not the overall view.

Ex. 5.5. *On the Waterfront*, Conductor Part. "Opening Shot to Scream." Percussion entrances of Violence theme, mm. 1-19.[13]

Above this ostinato a second theme—played "dirty-close to mike" according to the conductor part—in the alto saxophone sounds; a lament that serves as the Pain theme shown in Ex. 5.6.[14]

Ex. 5.6. *On the Waterfront*, Conductor Part. "Opening Shot to Scream." Pain Theme in alto saxophone, mm. 23-33.

The relentless energy of the Violence ostinato suggests a primitive, unrelenting force that is not in tune with this seemingly innocuous scene of men walking away from the docks. In addition, the irregularity of the percussion polyrhythms and shifting meters within the low register of the timpani establishes a sense of unease that creates tension with the serene view of the docks. Further, the music reveals not only the inner violence of Johnny Friendly's gang, but also the pressure under which Terry reluctantly follows his orders and conforms to the will of the group. In addition, the extreme metric dissonance between the ostinato layers and the Pain theme further underlines the pain caused by this violence and pressure on Terry. It is clear from the expression on Terry's face and his sloppy gait that he is not excited about whatever it is that he is going to do. His face suggests a person struggling with a moral dilemma. As Kazan puts it:

> Watch the way Brando walks—he did it himself—in sort of an abashed way, his head down. . . . The feeling that he's not himself, a feeling that he belongs to somebody else, a feeling that he wants his boss's approval, a feeling that he's tied up in a situation that he has no choice about.[15]

The action moves to a street outside of an apartment where Terry yells up to his friend, Joey Doyle, and underneath this dialogue, one hears development of the first four notes of the aforementioned Pain theme (Ex. 5.6) in the cellos and basses of Ex. 5.7. In addition, Bernstein alternates repetition of the last three notes of the Pain theme with its retrograde in the violins. From a practical point of view Bernstein also thins out the instrumentation by removing the percussion, thus allowing the audience to hear the dialogue clearly while providing enough pertinent thematic material to comment on the narrative. Much negative criticism involved Bernstein's perceived obscuring of dialogue with music, but this scene demonstrates the contrary was true and that Bernstein was sensitive to the dialogue. Given the recent meeting between Terry and Friendly's men, the dissonance of the first four notes of the Pain theme in the low strings—semitone followed by tritone counterbalanced by the more consonant major seconds and thirds in the violins—suggests to the listener that there is much conflict between Terry's words and Terry's intentions.[16]

Ex. 5.7. ***On the Waterfront*****, Conductor Part. "Opening Shot to Scream." Pain motive in low strings against final Pain theme notes in original and retrograde forms, mm. 46-50.**

As the camera pans up to show men on the roof, the audience realizes that this is a set-up. In this scene between Terry and Joey, Bernstein presents the "Violence" theme *tutti* (Ex. 5.8), and offers a striking contrast with the force of the entire orchestra. Bernstein asks the audience here to consider not only the nature of these same men, but also the brutality of the murder they are about to commit. The first four measures comprise an oscillation between a G-minor/F-sharp minor bichord, followed by another bichord between A-flat minor/E-flat major. The dense orchestral context, the louder dynamics, and the increased level of intervallic tension as a result of the polytonal harmonies within this presentation of the "Violence" theme helps to realize more fully the musicodramatic implications of the opening timpani figure.

Ex. 5.8. *On the Waterfront*, Conductor Part. Violence theme *tutti*, mm. 69-74.

"Roof Morning"

Bernstein achieves yet another stark contrast between musical cues as the audience gets its first view of the rooftops. In the film, the action takes place in two main locations: on the ground (the church, the waterfront, the bar, the streets) and on the rooftop. Kazan has created two worlds from Terry's point of view: the dirty, hard reality of the ground and the more peaceful, ideal world on the rooftop. It is on the rooftop that Terry contemplates his fate in life while caring for pigeons. It is on the rooftop where Terry and Edie fall in love and have their first kiss. Later, it is on the rooftop where, after his testimony, Terry decides that he must go to the waterfront and confront Johnny Friendly. The first time we see the rooftop, it is the morning after Joey's murder. There is a haze in the air and life appears to be fine in the aftermath of the previous night. A boat whistle softens the visual dissolve between the previous scene (recall Bernstein's sub tone boat whistle in Ex. 5.4) and that of a local boy (Tommy) running to meet his idol, Terry, who is considering the events of the previous night. Kazan presents the boy as a metaphor of innocence and Terry's potential as a child. Tommy confronts the adult Terry, who is clearly guilt-ridden, a self-proclaimed bum, and embodying a wasted potential. To accompany this scene,

Bernstein wrote a dreamlike, rather pensive piece of music. Bernstein scored the passage for flutes, solo oboe, harp, muted strings, and vibraphone (Ex. 5.9). The harp presents a near whole-tone, impressionistic-sounding arpeggio answered by sustained vibraphone and muted strings.

Ex. 5.9. *On the Waterfront*, Conductor Part. "Roof Morning." Dual ostinato in harp, strings, vibraphone, and flutes, mm. 3-8.

Above this accompanimental material is an oscillating passage between A-flat and E-flat in the flutes. The dual ostinato serves as the foundation for a melancholy solo based on the Pain motive, here in the oboe (Ex. 5.10).

Ex. 5.10. *On the Waterfront*, Conductor Part. "Roof Morning." Melody in oboe based on Pain motive, mm. 10-29.

The harmonic stasis and searching, soulful melody create a mood of solitary reflection—isolated from the real world. The scene, though tranquil, conveys a sense of profound sadness—Terry's sorrow regarding his actions and the unfortunate course his life has taken since *he* was that innocent, little boy. Bernstein also evokes a sense of unease in this passage, veiled by the outwardly serene quality of the cue. In his contemplation, Terry is afraid of the unknown consequences that certainly await him in the real world below. Bernstein displays this melodically with the characteristic minor second between flatted-fifth and fourth scale degrees (in F-minor) of the Pain motive in Ex. 5.10, m. 10. Furthermore, two descending passages in the oboe (between E-double flat and A-flat in mm. 18-20 and between F-flat and B-flat in mm. 24-26) outline tritones and therefore contribute to the melancholy of the melodic component. An additional sense of harmonic uncertainty is created through the presence of a tritone-related chord between tonic and lowered dominant triads centered on F-natural and C-flat in the strings (m. 4; the figure is repeated in m. 6). The tension between the lamenting, dissonant melody and the tonally ambiguous accompanying material underlines the conflict between Terry's ideal world and his reality; between his potential and what he is. The music of this scene is in stark contrast to the most recent theme—the aggressive, pulsating rhythms of the Violence theme. In addition, Bernstein's use of the Pain theme in a different context adds a sense of continuity to both the drama and the score.

In addition to the relationship with Britten's *Peter Grimes* (see Chapter 2), Bernstein once again calls upon a more general sense of his affective memory of the concert music tradition in order to comment even more subtly on the dramatic implications of this scene. With the oboe Bernstein refers to the instrument's place as the favored instrument of the pastoral or idyllic, witnessed in Beethoven's Symphony No. 6 "Pastoral" (second movement), Berlioz's *Symphonie fantastique* (third movement), or Grieg's "Morning Mood" from the *Peer Gynt* Suite No. 1. In each of these pieces the composer employs the oboe to suggest a scene from nature or the countryside. Moreover, the practice made its way into the early development of film music as Joseph Carl Breil used similar instrumentation in *The Birth of a Nation* (1915) to underscore the bucolic "Love Valley" sequence in which the Stoneman and Cameron families walk peacefully amongst slaves picking cotton in a utopic vision of the antebellum south.[17] One could draw interesting parallels between the oboe's connotations of the pastoral and depictions of shepherds with Terry's guardianship over a flock of pigeons and his ultimate leadership of a flock of men to work at the film's conclusion.

"Scramble"

As the action moves to the docks (again elided by ship noise in the diegetic background), the audience hears yet another striking shift in Bernstein's music. Dozens of longshoremen await the "shape-up" in which the hiring boss walks among them and decides who works and who does not. According to the district attorney in Johnson's book, the poor standard of living in the dock area could be traced directly to the "shape-up" system. This particular scene in the film came from Johnson's account of the docks:

> The scene is any pier along New York's waterfront. At a designated hour, the longshoremen gather in a semicircle at the entrance to the pier. They are the men who load and unload the ships. They are looking for jobs, and as they stand there in a semicircle their eyes are fastened on one man. He is the hiring stevedore, and he stands alone, surveying the waiting men. At this crucial moment he possesses the power of economic life or death over them, and the men know it. Their faces betray that knowledge in tense anxiety, eagerness and fear. They know that the hiring boss, a union man like themselves, can accept them or reject them at will. . . . Now the hiring boss moves among them, choosing the man he wants, passing over the others. He nods or points to the favored ones or calls out their names, indicating that they are hired. For those accepted, relief and joy. The pinched faces of the others reflect bleak disappointment, despair. Still they linger. Others will wander off inconsolately [*sic*] to wait another chance.[18]

Just as Johnson describes, Mac picks for work those in the crowd he knows, or is sympathetic to in Friendly's gang. As he states that all positions have been filled, several men close in on Mac begging for work. When the pressure becomes too great, Mac throws the remaining brass "checks" into the air and out of the melee that ensues as the workers scramble for the chance to work, one hears the material in Ex. 5.11.

Ex. 5.11. *On the Waterfront,* Conductor Part. "Scramble." Alteration of Pain motive to create Scramble music theme, mm. 6-10.

The highly energetic quality of the music enhances the frenzied action of the dockworkers quite effectively. The camera angles also contribute to the success of the scene. The camera is near the ground to follow the scrambling workers. All movement is downwards as if to enhance the distinction between oppressors and oppressed and allows the viewer to experience the chaos as well. As the confusion intensifies, Bernstein varies the figure in 5.11 by repeating each note of the theme in a staccato, sixteenth-note passage, but continues to harmonize with the dissonant, mostly descending passage: D-natural, C-natural, B-flat, B-natural.

The fight for survival that transpires on the docks is indicative of the fear workers experience each day. To help convey this reality more clearly to the audience and maintain dramatic and thematic continuity, Bernstein again incorporates the Pain motive in this section but obscures it through inversion. Bernstein employs an ascending minor second followed by an ascending perfect fourth (E; F-sharp; D; G) rather than the usual descending minor second and perfect fourth. Furthermore, the placement of the theme in irregular, syncopated rhythms establishes increased tension and underscores the unpredictability of the scramble for the brass checks. To emphasize further the importance of the Pain motive in this section, Bernstein uses the material in the trombones and violas as a sort of countersubject between presentations of the Scramble theme (Ex. 5.12). The presence and insistence of the theme throughout the orchestra, within irregular, yet invigorating rhythms and dissonant harmonies, is a further reminder of the angst and frustration involved when one is forced to conform to Friendly's system in order to make a living.

Ex. 5.12. *On the Waterfront*, Conductor Part. "Scramble." Interjection of Pain theme in trombones and strings, mm. 12 and 14, mm. 12-15.

The "Scramble" cue is also another notable example of the sort of score excision that Bernstein lamented in his "Upper Dubbing" diatribe. As Terry shoves Pop Doyle out of the way to grab one of the last brass checks, Edie confronts him—even hitting him—in order to retrieve the check for her father. One of Terry's colleagues points out to him that the girl with whom he is fighting is Joey's sister and when Edie finally yells, "You give me that!" Terry relents and turns over the check. In the film, upon Edie's demand and Terry's recognition, the cue ends with a unison presentation in the orchestra of a three-note rising figure (Ex. 5.13) that will eventually form the beginning of the Love theme (see below).

Ex. 5.13. *On the Waterfront.* Conductor Part. "Scramble." End of "Scramble" cue with Edie's command, mm. 40-42.

Yet in Bernstein's short score and in the conductor part the cue extends for eleven more measures and continues with a presentation of the first half of the Love theme in the low strings and low winds with a lighter version of the "Scramble" material on top (5.14). At m. 47 Bernstein cadences the passage and allows the accompanimental filigree to taper off, closing the cue.[19]

Ex. 5.14. *On the Waterfront.* Conductor Part. "Scramble." Bernstein's unused extension of "Scramble" cue, mm. 43-47.

Had the conductor part version of the score been allowed to continue, it would have ended as Terry calls back to Edie, "Well, it's been nice wrestling with you." It is unclear when exactly this material was removed from the score, but since the conductor part indicates that the material was revised on 20 April 1954 and because acetate disks of the scoring session one week later preserve the material, one must conclude that the passage was removed during postproduction editing. While the ending of the cue as presented in the film arrives a bit awkwardly, continuing the music—given its ultimate identity as the Love theme—underneath the following dialogue would have been pointless:

> TERRY: You Joey Doyle's sister?
> EDIE: Yes I am.
> TERRY (to co-worker): You don't want to go to work anyhow. (To Edie) Well it's been nice wrestling with you.

Moreover, the music coincided with the furious scuffle to obtain the brass tabs so when the fight ended, sensibly the music ended too. With the edit, the first three notes serve only to close the scene and can be connected with the Love theme only after hearing its more delicate presentation later in "Glove Scene" (see below). An oft-cited criticism of this score was that in places the music continued underneath the dialogue for too long and using the original version of the cue would certainly have added fuel to that fire. Yet, the preserved cue as the source of the Love theme in "Glove Scene" would have provided an interesting musical juxtaposition between the two cues as well as an interesting commentary on the "beginning" of their love. In addition, because Bernstein employs a similarly forceful version of the Love theme when Terry goes to apologize to Edie in "Cab and Bedroom" (see below), one could have argued convincingly to retain this similarly dynamic evocation of the same material in "Scramble." Regardless, while this cue was not mentioned in the "Upper Dubbing" article, it likely contributed to Bernstein's consternation with the editing expressed therein.

"Riot in Church"

The next important thematic area in the score occurs during a scene in which there is a fight at the church. As the "congregation" begins to leave, hired men from Johnny Friendly's gang throw rocks through windows and bang clubs outside the church in order to intimidate those inside. As this violence ensues, Bernstein presents a vigorous ostinato in the violas and clarinets beneath a dissonant theme in the flutes, oboes, and horns, seen in Ex. 5.15. Bernstein makes the theme more dissonant by adding dyads separated by a major second to the notes of the theme (top notes), tightly grouping the three note chords. As the scene increases in intensity, the orchestration becomes denser.

Ex. 5.15. *On the Waterfront*, Conductor Part. "Riot in Church." Riot music heard as violence ensues at the church, mm. 4-6.

As demonstrated in Chapter 2 above, the cue comprises a reconfiguration of the musical materials associated with the Pain motive. The harmonic basis, in both "Opening Shot to Scream" and "Riot in Church," is a rapidly moving ostinato to highlight the unyielding brutality of Friendly and his supporters; an alternation of thirds, primarily in the timpani and piano for the Violence theme (Ex. 5.5), and a repetitive stepwise pattern in the strings and woodwinds for the Riot ostinato above. Secondly, the ideas both conclude in a similar manner—fast, descending three-note patterns marked by stepwise motion followed by a large leap (see Ex. 2.8 and 2.9 above). Furthermore, the melody of the Riot theme, like the Scramble music above, is a rhythmic alteration of the opening Pain motive. Beginning in Ex. 5.15, m. 5 above, the lowest notes in each chord cluster coincide note-for-note with the original Pain motive (see Ex. 5.6), while the upper notes multiply the dissonant effect. In addition, when treating the tonic of the passage as G-centered, Bernstein places the initial semitone of the Pain motive on scale degrees flat-5 and 4, disrupting our aural expectations inherent in the diatonic scale and suggesting jazz or modal scalar collections. Finally, one hears the opening notes of the Pain motive in their original form interjected throughout this passage, thus reinforcing the link between the two thematic areas.

This multi-faceted thematic integration is also evidence of Bernstein's consideration of dramatic continuity. When the audience first heard the Pain theme, it accompanied the events leading up to and including the murder of Joey Doyle (Edie's brother). In this most recent scene, the music complements the brutal acts carried out at the church. In each instance, the music reminds the audience of violence perpetuated on the workers and their loved ones in order to keep them in line. Furthermore, Bernstein comments upon the struggle endured by those who desire to break free from the grasp of Friendly's gang and stand as individuals. As the intimidating presence of Friendly's goons suggests, there is a great price to pay for going against the group. Bernstein recognizes this and writes music whose melodic and harmonic dissonance, rhythmic syncopation, and urgent ostinato all combine to create aural instability, thus capturing the feeling of fear induced by violence.

"Glove Scene"

Amidst the melee inside the church, Terry grabs Edie and they leave unnoticed and untouched by Friendly's men. The couple walks down the street together and engages in small talk. The conversation turns to a discussion of why a gentle person like Edie would want to hang around the docks and where she was before she came back to Hoboken. Edie drops her glove and Terry puts it delicately on his hand, commenting to Edie that she has changed much since they were in school together. Terry, a former boxer, tries on a different pair of gloves as if, Hey remarks, "he were about to 'try out' her moral values."[20] Eventually the viewer notices a delicate theme (Ex. 5.16) in the flutes as Edie confirms that she remembered Terry from their youth.

Ex. 5.16. *On the Waterfront.* Conductor Part. "Glove Scene." Full presentation of Love theme as Terry and Edie reminisce, mm. 2-8.

Generally, whenever there is a tender moment or a passionate kiss shared between Terry and Edie, one hears the Love theme. Yet Bernstein also employs the theme prominently in the culminating scenes when Terry and Edie are separated physically. In addition, as suggested in Chapter 2, Bernstein's derivation of the Love theme from the final notes of the Pain theme underscores a multifaceted thematic relationship. The last musical cue heard before the Love theme was the ending of the Riot theme. Therefore, the violent events at the church brought the two together and led to their first meaningful conversation together. Besides the obvious relationship between Terry and Edie, the love of Father Barry for his parishioners and for justice on the docks informed his decision to hold the secret meeting and summoned Friendly's subsequent ire. It was also Father Barry's words that began to change the way Terry perceived his situation. When viewed in this way the Riot theme that accompanied the meeting at church becomes even more effective because it not only allowed the love between Terry and Edie to develop, but it also triggered a series of events that led to Terry's eventual redemption.

On a deeper psychological level, Terry and Edie's love evolved out of their separate connections to Joey Doyle's life and tragic death. Edie, in her determination to learn who killed her brother, has put her trust in the one person whom she should not trust. Her love for Terry, then, grew out of a need to ease her pain. Bernstein recognized this dramatic conflict and designed themes that are in opposition, yet related to each other. Not only is the ending of the Pain theme and the beginning of the Love theme an almost exact retrograde in intervallic design, but also the harmonic contrasts are much different. The passages that employ the Love theme are the most diatonic and lyrical in the score. However, those sections associated with the Pain theme are dissonant and distinguished by their vigorous rhythms.

The idea of love was a central issue to both Kazan and Schulberg as they tried to depict Terry Malloy as a rough individual with a tender side, witnessed in his caring for pigeons and the gentle manner with which he toys with Edie's glove. The theme also appeared important enough to Bernstein and his orchestrators that some materials in the Sony Music Library refer to it as the "Waterfront Theme." For instance, on a duplicate copy of the conductor part for "Glove Scene," marked in pencil in all caps is "Waterfront Theme entire cue." In other cues the same markings occur with references to specific measure numbers as well as bracketing marking those measures in the score as "Waterfront theme." Thus it appears that someone involved with the scoring viewed the theme with enough esteem that they equated it with the title of the film.[21]

Bernstein, along with Spiegel perhaps, must also have believed that the theme would have some traction outside the film as well. The theme most closely resonates with Bernstein's gifted lyrical ability, witnessed in its prefiguring of material in *West Side Story* (see Chapter 2) and its frequent appearances on film scoring compilation recordings since the film's release. Moreover, enthusiasts of Bernstein's musical theater works might recognize in the theme's second gesture (beginning on the last beat of the second full measure in Ex. 5.16) the chorus of "A Quiet Girl" from *Wonderful Town*.[22] In addition to the "Waterfront Song" described above in "Main Title," Bernstein's sketches at the Library of Congress also include a handwritten vocal score of a song entitled "With All My Heart" (with lyrics by Mitchell Parish) whose chorus and introduction use the Love theme for its source melody. The song is again in AABB form with the following lyrics:

> VERSE: My cup of love is overflowing; the skies are showing their brightest blue.
>
> VERSE: My love can be no halfway measure, because I treasure each thought of you.
>
> CHORUS (Repeated): I love you with all my heart, with all my soul and all my heart; together or far apart, I want you with all my heart. As roses need summertime, so my heart needs you; for you are my summertime. The one I love with all my heart is you.[23]

Bernstein signed the score on 7 June 1954, which was about halfway between the time when the score was recorded and the film released. Given the timing one could surmise that Spiegel or a representative at Columbia considered using the song as a marketing tool similar to Dimitri Tiomkin and Ned Washington's "Ballad of High Noon" in *High Noon* (1952). Though this song was never published, Columbia Pictures did capitalize on Bernstein's talents when it released "On the Waterfront" (with lyrics by Bernstein's initial *Candide* collaborator, John LaTouche) through J.J. Robbins, also in 1954. The published song's cover featured Terry and Edie in each other's arms and credited the principal players in the Columbia Pictures production.[24] While the lyrics of both songs do not factor into the film's plot to the degree that the ballad does in *High Noon*, clearly Bernstein and others believed the melody possessed much commercial appeal and while there is no evidence that "With All My Heart" was published or recorded, aspects of the Love theme found new life in *West Side Story* three years later.

"Pigeons and Beer"

After this most recent encounter with Terry and being ordered by her father to stay away from him, Edie remains steadfast in her mission to learn the identity of her brother's killer. She goes up to the roof—the scene of the crime—hoping to find answers. To accompany this transitional scene, Bernstein presents the Pain motive in high, shrill strings accompanied by a searching, questioning line in the piano (Ex. 5.17). The piano line contains ascending sevenths, which seem to be taken from the preceding Love theme. Moreover, the piano excerpt in m. 4 is a near retrograde of the antecedent piano passage in m. 3. Another possible source for this interrogatory figure in the piano is the Pain motive, presented boldly at the beginning of the cue. For instance, the opening E-flat, D-natural, A-natural piano gesture in m. 3, by inverting the initial M7 one creates a minor second followed by a perfect fourth, the same as the Pain motive. One could apply the same procedure throughout the excerpt in Ex. 5.17 to create similar intervallic shapes. Regardless, this new musical material that appears to obscure both the Love and Pain themes insinuates that the beginnings of Edie's love for Terry might be developing, but that she is cautiously keeping her emotions under control as she searches for answers about her brother's recent death.

Ex. 5.17. *On the Waterfront.* Conductor Part. "Pigeons and Beer." Edie searches for answers on the rooftop, mm. 1-7.

The use of the Pain motive is appropriate where a coop with Joey's name on it, pigeons flying around, and other signs of Joey's life surround Edie and make it an emotional experience. As Edie looks across the rooftop, she sees Terry and in this instance the Pain motive seems to foreshadow the grief the couple will experience when Terry finally confesses to Edie. Further, the ambiguous quality of the piano melody echoes Edie's quiet search for answers. The thematic material that Bernstein uses in this cue is doubly important when one considers its relevance to current events because it also speaks to Edie's paranoia at the moment. It is not clear what lies around the corner, even in daylight. Throughout the film, Kazan and Kaufman use various enclosed spaces as contexts for action. In some instances, this suggests intimacy. More often though, the restricted settings hint at entrapment or confinement. As Edie bends down to look at pigeons in a cage one is reminded that the image parallels the way of life for the dockworkers. There are no answers, only questions and everyone is a suspect, including Terry. The piercing quality of the high strings coupled with the dissonance of the minor second once again suggests that fear and apprehension lie beneath Edie's search. Furthermore, the theme reminds the audience of what can happen when a person chooses to speak out against the mob; when one chooses individuality over conformity on the docks.

The first half of the cue ends as Edie sees Terry across the rooftop signaling to his pigeons. "Pigeons and Beer" is comprised of two small cues that act as one unit in the film, even though several minutes pass between the two parts. The second part of the cue culminates with a grand presentation of the Love theme to which, as detailed above, Bernstein protested. Yet, the cue was never intended to be divided and similar to the edits imposed on the "Scramble" cue above, the connecting material in "Pigeons and Beer" was removed in postproduction. In the film, the music ends initially when Edie calls out to Terry and he asks her why she is on the roof and returns later with the Love theme when Terry invites Edie to see his pigeons. In the interim, Terry explains to Edie that he started the Golden Warriors after which Tommy—Terry's shadow—begins to box Terry and the two engage in a playful bout. At first Bernstein continues the piano gesture in Ex. 5.17 into the flutes and clarinets with a solo violin playing the first three notes of the Love theme above a sustained string texture (Ex. 5.18).

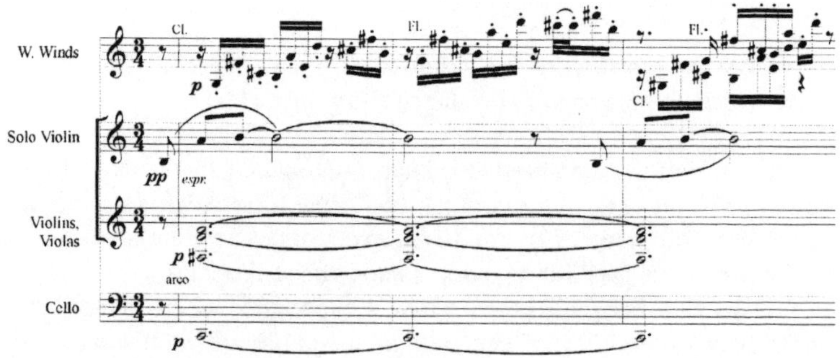

Ex. 5.18. *On the Waterfront.* Conductor Part. "Pigeons and Beer." Continuation of piano theme (Ex. 5.17) cut from score, mm. 15-18.

The excision of the Love theme from this cue was an unfortunate decision because the ascending, questioning, yet incomplete gesture says much about the current state of Terry and Edie's relationship. Yet the edit is understandable given the prominent place of the Love theme that culminates the cue. Bernstein softens the ominous quality of the piano by placing the theme in the clarinets and flutes, which leads nicely into the more playful music written to accompany the "bout" between Terry and Tommy (Ex. 5.19).

Ex. 5.19. *On the Waterfront.* Conductor Part. "Pigeons and Beer." Terry and Tommy spar, music cut from film, mm. 24-30.

Most regrettable about this cut is the way that the Pain motive in m. 30 (had it been left in) halted Terry and Tommy's roughhousing and immediately caught Terry's attention. The playful material for winds helps to evoke a softer side to Terry's personality and perhaps better explains why Edie is so willing to go have a beer with Terry in the subsequent scene. Yet the music would have distracted from much of Terry's story of the Golden Warriors and its very lightheartedness is at odds with virtually the entire score and seems more suitable for a dance sequence (especially since the material is reminiscent of the lighter textures in the "Somewhere Ballet" from *West Side Story*).

Untouched though is Bernstein's extended statement of the Love theme, which he famously lamented in the "Upper Dubbing" article. As many scholars have noted, what separates Terry from previous virile protagonists (especially Stanley Kowalski) is his tenderness. Terry often exudes toughness and machismo, but throughout the film his tenderness—fostered by Edie and Father Barry—is what compels him to do better and go farther than his ugly surroundings. Terry's compassion always seems to shine brightest when he is on the rooftop with his pigeons. On one of the sunnier days depicted in the film, Bernstein sought to underscore the rapid, intense development of the relationship between Terry and Edie that results in large part from the tenderness Edie witnesses as Terry cares for his pigeons. As the composer indicated in his "Upper Dubbing" article, Bernstein expanded the Love theme contrapuntally through the strings and harp, and increased the polyphonic intensity by adding the trumpet exactly halfway through the 42-measure passage. What one discovers after viewing this section of the film is that Bernstein protested too much in his "Hollywood memoir" and unintentionally gave critics of his scoring considerable ammunition. Contrary to Bernstein's account, the gradual crescendo is audible on the soundtrack—beginning with a *mezzo piano* at m. 41 (conductor part) and reaching a *fortissimo* and modulation to D major by m. 73—that only gets stronger as the cue ends (Ex. 5.20) and moves *attacca* to Bernstein's boogie-woogie piano playing in the subsequent cuc.

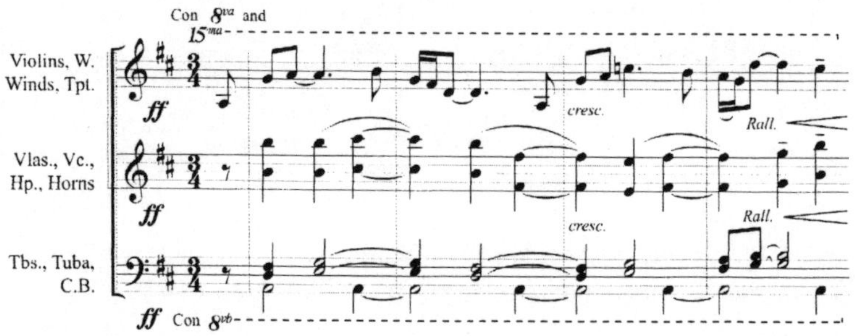

Ex. 5.20. On the Waterfront. Conductor Part. "Pigeons and Beer." Tutti crescendo culminating the cue, mm. 78-82.

"Juke Box"

After much coaxing from Terry, Edie agrees to go have a drink with him and the two go to a bar for conversation. As the scene shifts to the bar, one hears piano music emanating from a jukebox. While many have claimed that Bernstein improvised the music heard in the cue, in fact, sketches in the Library of Congress collection demonstrate he composed the piece marked "Slow drag" for jazz piano trio. Initially he most likely improvised a figure based on a blues progression, but ultimately notated the excerpt, down to the swirling patterns in the right hand (Ex. 5.21).

Ex. 5.21. *On the Waterfront.* Short Score. "Juke Box." Bernstein's piano source music as dissolve between roof and bar, mm. 4-6 (Piano only).

This example of source music in the score begins a sequence in which five of the next six cues are diegetic. Some of the cues, like the piano improvisation, are not related to the score thematically and serve to create mood, or in this instance as a dissolve between the emotional scene on the rooftop and the "real world" down on the street in a bar.

"Saloon Love"

Beginning with "Saloon Love" Bernstein based the next two cues on the Love theme. Terry tries to loosen the tension with Edie by ordering some drinks and offering his philosophy on life: "Do it to him before he does it to you." After Edie comments on the callous and unfeeling manner of his comments, Terry interprets her remarks as a personal affront and lumps Edie with Father Barry and others who he believes are singling him out for his role in Joey's death. Terry then realizes he has offended Edie after which he denies her plea for help. Terry claims that he "would like to help," but insists that there is nothing that he could do, under which Bernstein offers the Love theme against sustained tones throughout the orchestra (Ex. 5.22).

Ex. 5.22. *On the Waterfront.* Conductor Part. "Saloon Love." Terry tells Edie that he'd like to help, but cannot, mm. 1-3.

As Edie turns to leave, Terry encourages her to stay and apologizes for not doing more. Edie then caresses Terry and understands that he "would do more if he could." As a sense of warmth returns to the scene, Bernstein removes the sustained texture and allows the Love theme to continue amidst an equally warm string texture (Ex. 5.23).

Ex. 5.23. *On the Waterfront.* Conductor Score. "Saloon Love." Terry asks to Edie to stay, mm. 5-9.

Throughout, Bernstein recalls the Love theme as employed in "Pigeons and Beer" and seems to endanger and encroach upon the theme through the initial dissonant, sustained tones. Later as the Love theme gains in intensity, Bernstein restricts the harmonic movement to a few pedal tones. Yes there is a sense of mutual attraction and genuine affection between the couple, but given Terry's unwillingness to help, Bernstein suggests that there is too much uncertainty (both musically and dramatically) for the theme—and their relationship—to develop more fully.

"Waterfront Love Theme (Sentimental Fox)"

Edie eventually leaves the table and, seeking a way out of the bar, she runs into a wedding celebration accompanied by Gil Grau's polka arrangement of Wagner's wedding march (marked "raucously").[25] Eventually Terry finds Edie and escorts her past the mob of wedding revelers to another room where the source band plays a slow "fox trot" arrangement of the Love theme called "Waterfront Love Theme" in the conductor part, but marked wittily "Sentimental Fox" by Bernstein in his short score (Ex. 5.24).

Ex. 5.24. *On the Waterfront.* Conductor Part. "Waterfront Love Theme." Terry rescues Edie and they both dance, mm. 1-8.

Edie comments, "That's a pretty tune" and begins to dance with Terry for the remainder of the song. Bernstein emphasizes the growing relationship between Terry and Edie by again using the Love theme, but integrates it more fully into the narrative by placing it into a source music cue within a contemporaneous vernacular style. By dissolving the boundary between diegetic and non-diegetic spheres, Bernstein elevates his level of participation in the drama from narration to intimate interaction. In other words, when Edie notices the same pretty tune that we in the audience have enjoyed for the last several minutes, not only does Bernstein suggest that something very intense is growing between Terry and Edie, but he brings us more fully into contact with their world such that we too drown out the noise of the wedding party, focus on Terry and Edie, and share collectively in their romantic moment.

"Blue Goon Blues"

While in Terry's arms, Edie calms down until a dance band arrangement of a sea chanty ends. Then, Barney (one of Friendly's goons) approaches Terry and tells him that something has gone wrong and that

Friendly wants to see him immediately. As Terry receives the message, one hears a bluesy arrangement of the Pain theme in the trumpet displayed in Ex. 5.25, beginning in m. 3.

Ex. 5.25. *On the Waterfront.* Short Score. "Blue Goon Blues." Terry receives and order from Johnny Friendly, mm. 1-6.

The presence of the Pain motive, whose characteristic semitone here is between scale degrees flat-3 and 2, in this diegetic context speaks to the fact that Terry cannot escape Friendly's reach and his role in Doyle's death, even when he is trying to enjoy himself. Like "Sentimental Fox" above, we feel Terry's agony more intensely as the line between diegetic and non-diegetic worlds remains blurred. Later, and before Terry has a chance to go see Friendly, the two crime commission agents who interrogated Terry earlier at the docks discover him at the dance. They give him a subpoena to appear before the commission, an offer that for the moment, Terry refuses. As Edie witnesses the exchange she too begins to question Terry more vigorously and as she stings him by repeatedly insisting he is still a bum, one notices the Pain motive presented with renewed vigor. Edie becomes so disgusted with Terry's refusal to help the authorities that, completely distraught, she runs away from Terry, leaving him alone.

Bernstein appears to suggest that because Terry is concerned about his role in Joey's death, is afraid of what lies ahead, and remains disgusted at his place in life, his "pain" manifests itself as music. In his paranoia, a slow blues piece at a wedding becomes a reminder of all that is wrong in his life outside those doors. Earlier in his conversation with Edie (immediately before "Saloon Love" begins), he complained that everyone was against him and he did not like the way Father Barry looked at him in the church. Edie reminded Terry that "he was looking at everyone the same." One finds further evidence of this paranoia as Terry leaves the bar and walks down the street in the dark whistling the Pain theme. Often, when a person walks down a dark street alone, whistling can be a calming device. Not for Terry, who only has his fear and pain to comfort him as he becomes increasingly isolated from the world around him.[26]

"Accident"

Shortly thereafter both Johnny and Terry's brother Charley confront Terry with news that Kayo Dugan agreed to testify following the church riot, and suggest this happened because Terry failed as a spy at the church meeting. Johnny and Charley also believe that Dugan must be silenced and Terry should stop associating with Edie, punctuated with a command to, "Wise up!" from Charley to his brother. At this moment the music from "Opening Shot to Scream" was supposed to commence, but as reported above, the "Accident" cue never made it to the final cinematic version. That said, the cue was recorded and notes in Bernstein's score at the Library of Congress indicate that he planned to underscore the setup and realization of Kayo Dugan's murder almost exactly like he enhanced Joey Doyle's execution. According to his notes and the recording from the scoring session, Bernstein again used the percussive Violence music but instead of the alto saxophone, he called upon a muted trumpet to convey the Pain theme. In addition, the dynamics begin *piano* instead of *fortissimo* and do not move much beyond *mezzo forte* until the Violence theme *tutti*. In addition, when compared to "Opening Shot to Scream" the Pain theme is not repeated in the winds and some of the material presented in Ex. 5.7 was lengthened considerably.

As Hamilton indicated in an early analysis of the film, there was presumably too much dialogue to keep the music in the film and when placing the music against the scene as realized in the film, one sees his point. In addition, because the "Accident" material was so similar to "Opening Shot to Scream"—the substitution of the muted trumpet for alto sax representing the most notable change—the surprising impact of the whisky cases falling on Dugan might have been lessened by the portentous clue provided by the music. In addition the parallels between the two scenes—both open with a long view of the docks and a large ship in the background and follow the camera to Johnny and his gang setting a plot in motion, culminated in the silencing of a whistle blower—are so apparent that music could have rendered the scene less potent. Regardless, it appears that Bernstein saw the connection between the two scenes dramatically and musically, desired the cue to remain in the scene, but suggested that it might be a moot point evidenced in the last two words of his notes: "Use I-B [the reel and part title for "Opening Shot to Scream"] exactly, but begin *p* instead of *ff*. Sax solo played by muted tpt., *mp*. WW (woodwinds) repeat *mf*. (B). Cresc. to C. Thereafter as is. *I hope* [italics mine]."[27] Despite this speculation, the most compelling reason that "Accident" was cut in post-production might have been Bernstein's effective musical treatment following Dugan's murder.

"After Sermon"

After Dugan's "accident" Father Barry arrived to perform last rites and proceeded to make an impassioned speech equating Dugan's murder with Christ's crucifixion—reminding those responsible that Christ was indeed on the docks watching them all. Much like the camera angles in the shape-up scene, the dichotomy between oppressor and oppressed is made clear. Furthermore, the constrained framing within the darkened bowels of the ship enhances the feeling of paranoia. However, as Father Barry and Pop Doyle ride up with Dugan's body on the sling, the action is reversed to an upward motion, as opposed to the downward movement during "Scramble." When Father Barry says "Amen," Bernstein presents a plaintive lament in the upper strings (Ex. 5.26) accompanied by a pedal tone in the low strings and percussion.

Ex. 5.26. *On the Waterfront.* Conductor Part. "After Sermon." Plaintive theme following Kayo Dugan's death, mm. 1-6.

For this melancholic theme, Bernstein reinterprets the Violence theme, displayed *tutti* above in Ex. 5.8. The original version (Ex. 5.5) of this theme was much more vigorous, scored mainly for percussion, and served as an ostinato accompaniment to the Pain theme. Within its new context, Bernstein completely changes the Violence theme's affect. The motive ceases to be an accompanimental idea and moves to a primary, melodic role. In addition, the tempo is slowed considerably and the passage is re-scored for strings, thus distancing it from its more primitive-sounding predecessor. Furthermore, Bernstein avoids a traditional resolution in the statement of the revised Violence theme, made more dissonant by the pedal tones on F-natural in the bass.

This harmonic ambiguity echoes the sense of uncertainty inherent in the drama at this point. After hearing Father Barry's compelling sermon, Terry's battle with his conscience has intensified. His developing feelings for Edie, combined with witnessing Dugan's murder, has made it more difficult to remain loyal to his brother and Johnny. The night before he had immediately discarded a subpoena to testify for the Waterfront Crime Commission, yet less than a day later he struck one of Friendly's men (Tillio) for disrupting and dishonoring Father Barry during his speech. Clearly the tension between conforming to this group and emerging as an individual is powerful. The opposition between the two elements is enhanced by the ambiguity in Bernstein's reflective, yet tragic-sounding music and the theme's metamorphosis calls attention to Terry's ongoing character development.

Even though the Pain theme (which originally was accompanied by the Violence ostinato) is absent here, the melodic minor second on beat 1 in m. 5, while obscured in its original context above timpani and piano, here seems to carry out the Pain theme's emotional function. In fact, Lias notes that the Pain theme, though hidden, is present in the resolution in m. 2. The tetrachord D-natural, E-natural, F-natural, G-natural is a reordering of the same collection as the Pain theme transposed up a perfect fifth (F-natural, E-natural, G-natural, D-natural).[28] While one does not hear the Pain motive on the soundtrack, Bernstein wrote the cell as an inner voice in mm. 15-16 of the short score and conductor part (Ex. 5.27). What one hears on the soundtrack is mm. 11-12 repeated and mm. 13-14 replacing mm. 15-16 (Ex. 5.28) before the cue culminates as written. Interestingly, when this passage is incorporated into the Symphonic Suite, the Pain motive does appear, marked *lontano*, perhaps intended as an echo.[29]

Ex. 5.27. *On the Waterfront*, Conductor Part. "After Sermon." Bernstein's excised inclusion of the Pain motive, mm. 15-16.

Ex. 5.28. *On the Waterfront.* Conductor Part. "After Sermon." Excerpt as realized on the film soundtrack, mm. 11-14.

The omission of such an important motive from a context in which it would be appropriate is puzzling. Yet because the excerpt exists in both Bernstein's short score and the conductor part, and because the film soundtrack and scoring acetates reflect the treatment in Ex. 5.28, the decision to go against Bernstein's wishes likely occurred at the recording session. Lacking any notes to explain why the motive was removed from the full conductor score (and lacking the score itself), perhaps Stoloff (the conductor), or Skiles (the cue's orchestrator) or (much less likely) Bernstein did not want to disturb the effect of the recasting of the Violence theme in order to further highlight the contrast between it and the Pain theme, as well as the difference between the two musical passages in "After Sermon" and "Opening Shot to Scream."

Regardless of who omitted the Pain motive from the cue (or why), the excerpt as a whole makes very good musicodramatic sense. The original Violence theme is associated with events leading up to murder. However, the modification of the theme is related to actions following murder. The latter manifestation evokes a feeling of painful reflection after terrible events, while the former lends a sense of anticipation of evil. Rather than use themes that are polar opposites (for example, the Love and Pain themes) to indicate these differing emotional states, Bernstein *modifies* the harmonic and rhythmic contexts to emphasize their respective relationships to acts of violence. Furthermore, it reminds the audience of yet another tragedy that has occurred at the hands of Johnny Friendly, making Terry's eventual redemption at Friendly's hands even more satisfying.

"Roof 3"

Following Dugan's death, Edie seeks out Terry to give him Joey's jacket. She finds him alone and wrestling with his thoughts. Kazan draws another parallel between the dockworkers/mobsters and pigeons/hawks when Terry tells Edie that the pigeons are nervous because there was a hawk in the area recently. Kazan perhaps draws a further comparison between Joey Doyle's jacket and virtue. Earlier in the film Pop presented Dugan with Joey's jacket. Here, the jacket went from one whistle blower to another. Now, Edie offers the jacket to Terry, "I brought you Joey's jacket. Yours is coming apart." It is as if Edie is saying, "Here. Try on Joey's true sense of right and wrong. Your moral fabric is wearing thin." By accepting this gift from Edie, Terry bears a heavy burden. Throughout the scene one hears a clear presentation of the Love theme, most noticeably as a solo in the flute. This exchange also leads to a culmination of their intensifying emotions towards each other with their first kiss. At the moment the couple engages one another (m. 22) one hears the following musical passage (Ex. 5.29).

Ex. 5.29. *On the Waterfront.* Conductor Part. "Roof 3." Terry and Edie kiss, mm. 20-23.

Instead of the expected harmonization of E-minor in m. 22, Bernstein uses an E-flat chord that creates a tritone on beat 1 with the descending melodic cell, beginning on A-natural, creating an even more unexpected cadential phrase than the usual deceptive cadence the listener has grown accustomed to hearing.

As if recalling another moment on the rooftop in which Terry was in a reflective mood ("Roof Morning"), and reinforcing the presence of E-flat, Bernstein recalls the harp arpeggio used in "Roof Morning," here comprised solely of E-flat. The harmonic tension, made stronger by the tritone relationship between E-flat and A-natural, establishes a striking contrast with the relatively simple melodic and harmonic material that precedes it. In addition, the measure contains the densest orchestral texture as well. This musical material synchronized with the kiss highlights the dramatic implications of the embrace. Edie has fallen in love with the man who helped murder her brother and Terry is hiding that secret from the woman he loves. Through Bernstein's harmonic variation, the kiss carries with it a bittersweet feeling. Because the audience knows the painful connection between the two lovers, one feels a sense of uneasiness—joy for the couple and sadness for their unfortunate situation. From Terry's point of view, the conflict between love for Edie and devotion to "family" has increased significantly. The continual pressure to conform to this group, made manifest in the next scene, is wearing on Terry and Bernstein underscores this fact with the music to accompany the tender, yet tragic kiss.

While the Love theme exists outside of the film in the "On the Waterfront" song it also finds its place in Columbia Pictures films whose scores are not credited to Bernstein. Mischa Bakaleinikoff was a composer and conductor for Columbia and a musician with a reputation for "track jobs" in which he compiled existing cues from other composers and bridged the material with his own work. For instance in *Gunmen from Laredo* (1959) the hero (Gil, played by Robert Knapp) and the exotic Rosita (Maureen Hingert) evade a marauding band of Apache by hiding out in a cave. The close quarters apparently enhance their growing attraction and one notices a portion of Bernstein's Love theme from "Roof 3" to underscore their romance.[30] Interestingly the bittersweet connotations in m. 22 of "Roof 3" are mimicked in *Gunmen* as the kiss occurs at precisely the same point. In fact, there exists in the *On the Waterfront* materials at Sony Pictures a duplicate copy of the "Roof 3" conductor part in which the Love theme is marked in pencil as the "Waterfront Theme," a marking consistent with other cues in the collection that also contain the Love theme. While difficult to prove, it is possible that these markings reflect Bakaleinikoff's edits for use in other films.[31]

"Confession Scene"

The next morning, because of his growing love for Edie and the encouragement of the conscientious Father Barry, Terry decides that he will confess to Edie his role in her brother's death. As Terry makes his case to Edie, the noise of dock machinery and a steam whistle renders the dialogue inaudible. Kazan instead allows the audience to see Edie's horrified look and the expression of guilt and regret on Terry's face. Here the facial expressions speak louder than words or music ever could. As Edie flees the confrontation in horror, Terry remains overcome with guilt and remorse. At this point Bernstein recalls the Pain motive in the high strings creating a sense of heightened tension and distress (further recalling the texture from Britten above). In an extraordinary instance of integration between drama and music, Bernstein synchronizes the rhythm of the Pain motive with that of the distant dock machinery (Ex. 5.30).

Ex. 5.30. *On the Waterfront.* Short Score. "Confession Scene." Pain motive synchronized with sound of dock machinery as Terry confesses to Edie, mm. 1-4.[32]

Again Bernstein employs the Pain motive to comment upon an action of Terry motivated by his guilt and its effectiveness is again enhanced by Bernstein's harmonization and scoring. On the first note of the cell, the composer places an A-natural against the B-natural, creating a clash whose resolution moves in contrary motion by semitone to B-flat. Because the Pain motive does not clearly resolve (Bernstein reiterates the opening minor second) the closest Bernstein comes to resolution is the B-flat in the opening measure above. Analyzed in this way, Bernstein exploits the tension between scale degrees 1 and flat-2 (here respelled as B-natural) thus undercutting the expected whole step between those same notes in the diatonic collection. For the third note of the motive, the composer employs a G-natural, creating a tritone with the D-flat, which then resolves down to the A-flat by perfect fifth and up from the G-natural by semitone. Moreover, the placement of the melodic material in the high strings and with accents on the semitone and tritone further intensifies the dissonance through the instruments' shrill tones against the background machinery. Bernstein maintains this scoring throughout the cue to echo the feeling of unease. As the noise of the piledriver fades away, Bernstein replaces it with an echo of the Pain motive in the lower strings (placed extremely high in their ranges) with marimba. When the action moves to the rooftops to find the Waterfront Crime Commission investigator searching for Terry, the music seems to suggest that this confrontation might also be particularly "painful" since Bernstein culminates the cue with the opening two notes of the motive accompanied by a sustained string cluster (Ex. 5.31) just before Terry begins to talk to Detective Glover.

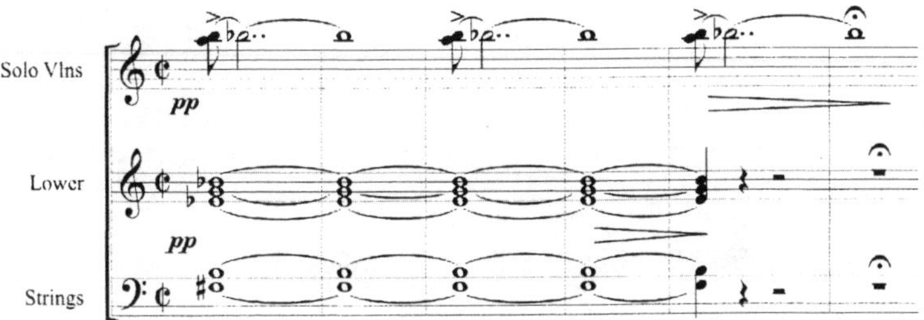

Ex. 5.31. *On the Waterfront.* Conductor Part. "Confession Scene." Terry considers his fate after confessing to Edie, mm. 25-30.

Terry's courage to confess and rid himself of this burden has been growing, along with his love for Edie. Naturally, the main problem in confessing to Edie is the potential of destroying the relationship forever. The thematic material in Ex. 5.30 enhances Terry's fear of losing Edie as well as Edie's realization that she has fallen in love with a person integrally responsible for her brother's death. Furthermore, the overwhelming presence of the dock machinery suggests to the listener that the great, corrupt mechanism—Friendly's organization—is the main agent of evil in the characters' lives. The dominance of the noise on the soundtrack insinuates that Terry's quest to break free from the machine's grip on his life is truly daunting. As he retreats to the rooftop once again, the sustained textures suggest a cessation of the background chaos, but the pain still remains.

"Kangaroo Court"

One of the most complex and dramatically convincing sequences in the movie begins during the famous taxi scene between Terry and his brother Charley. Charley is Johnny Friendly's most trusted associate but due to Terry's increasingly close connection with Edie, Friendly decides that he must deal with him before he testifies in front of the Waterfront Crime Commission. Johnny makes it clear that Charley must persuade Terry to remain silent or face certain death. As Charley leaves to negotiate with his brother, Bernstein introduces a new theme (Ex. 5.32).

Ex. 5.32. *On the Waterfront.* Conductor Part. "Kangaroo Court." Charley theme, mm. 1-4.

Charley must convince his brother not to betray his "friends" by any means necessary. This foreboding theme matches Charley's emotions exquisitely. The presence of three interlocking tritones in the arpeggiated chord (F-natural—B-natural; E-flat—A-natural; and F-sharp—C-natural)[33] in mm. 1-2 and the same chord (the Charley chord) in m. 3 lend much to the sense of unease felt by Charley as he must now conform to the will of the group, or face dire consequences. However, the way that the chord is voiced hides the triadic derivation of embedded tritones. The rapid repetition of the block chords in mm. 3-4 enhances the sense of urgency in Charley's orders while the use of brass *fortissimo*, especially the low brass, seems to convey a darker, more ominous feeling than the same notes played in the strings. This cue recalls modernist works of Schoenberg and Berg and may have influenced Leonard Rosenman, among others, to use a similar texture in *East of Eden* (1955).[34]

Finally, the excerpt has much in common with the "Dirge" from Bernstein's Symphony No. 2 "The Age of Anxiety" (1949, 1965). Each excerpt opens with a slowly unfolding, disjunct progression, loud dynamics, and occurs at a crucial moment in the respective narratives. In the same way that Bernstein heightens the dissonant nature of the layered tritones through arpeggiation and loud sustained tones in "Kangaroo Court," the composer presents the twelve-tone row that opens the "Dirge" mainly as a series of thirds and because he spreads the row over such a wide range (like "Kangaroo Court") one experiences more profoundly the impact of twelve tones sounding simultaneously.[35]

"Cab and Bedroom"

In the ensuing scene, Terry gets into a taxi to talk to his brother. Charley begins with small talk before discussing the true reason for the meeting. He offers Terry a high-paying job at another dock where he could get away from his present surroundings, provided he holds true to the D&D code. Unfortunately, Terry's refusal compels Charley to pull out a gun, rendering Terry shocked and saddened. Charley puts the gun away and is profoundly discouraged. At the beginning of the cue we hear the Charley theme in reduced orchestration. As Charley begins to reminisce about Terry's former career as a boxer, the Charley theme repeats and the Pain motive sounds as a solo in the alto saxophone (mm. 8-9, Ex. 5.33).

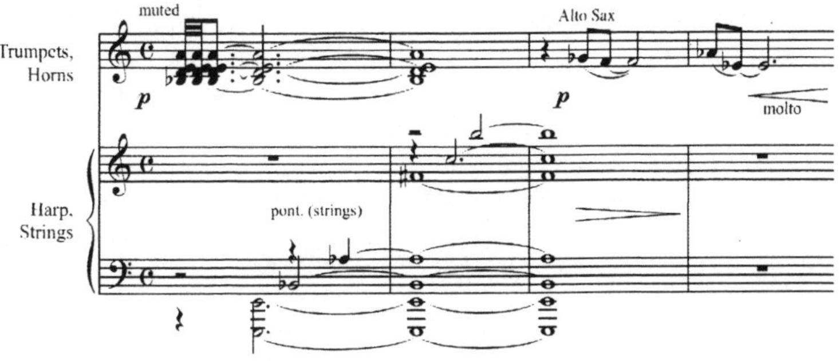

Ex. 5.33. *On the Waterfront*, Conductor Part. "Cab and Bedroom." Charley chord sustained against opening motive of Pain motive, mm. 6-9.

Bernstein creates added tension by sustaining the dissonant chord from the Charley theme in m. 8. Although the Charley chord is stacked similarly, the B-natural is now the highest note of the chord and the A-flat replaces the A-natural. In addition, the held notes of the Pain motive (F-natural and E-flat) generate tension between roots (F-sharp and E-natural) of the bichord. The tritones between E-natural and B-flat and from F-sharp to C-natural help convey a sense of tonal ambiguity, which echoes the sense of unease felt in the drama as the audience does not know what Charley will do. However, there is one less tritone in this collection than in the previous example. Perhaps Charley is beginning to waver in his loyalty towards Friendly as he reflects upon his betrayal of Terry in the name of duty.

Given the material in Ex. 5.32 and 5.33 as it pertains to Bernstein's Second Symphony, and based on where Bernstein placed the cues in the film (immediately preceding and during the iconic scene between Terry and Charley in a cab), it is worth recalling Bernstein's program note describing the "Dirge":

> *The Dirge* is sung by the four [see Chapter 1] as they sit in a cab en route to the girl's apartment for a nightcap. They mourn the loss of the "colossal Dad," the great leader who can always give the right orders, find the right solution, shoulder the mass responsibility, and satisfy the universal need for a father-symbol.[36]

One could extend the idea of the "colossal Dad" in *On the Waterfront* to a "colossal family" comprised of Johnny, Charley, and the entire Friendly organization. As Terry and Charley meet together in the cab (after which he ends up at Edie's apartment), Terry has increasingly gone against the wishes of the only real family he has ever known in the form of Johnny Friendly. In addition, Charley has long been Friendly's right hand and embarks upon his plea to Terry motivated by preserving the relationship he has with that "Dad." Yet as we learn in "Cab and Bedroom," Charley will disobey Friendly to save his brother and forever alienate his "father" in business and life. In fact, when Charley first realizes he cannot follow through and execute his brother, Bernstein presents a reprise of the "Kangaroo Court" material from Ex. 5.32 as a reminder of Friendly's final order. In order for Terry to reclaim his dignity he must ultimately denounce his father and family, both literally and figuratively.

As Terry reminds Charley that he was ultimately responsible for his current situation, one notices a transformed, Brahmsian[37] version of the Pain motive in Ex. 5.34 that recalls the melancholy of the oboe solo from Ex. 5.10. In m. 14, a major second replaces the characteristic minor second of the Pain motive, but as Bernstein does throughout the score, he maintains the basic shape of the original material when varying it. By using the major second in this instance, Bernstein preserves the opening figure of m. 10 and the mostly whole step motion of the melody, while still incorporating the Pain theme material. Furthermore, Bernstein gives the familiar theme an additional sense of anguish with the doubled tritone in the bass of m. 14, beat 3 and m. 15, beat 1, which clashes with the perfect fourth of the Pain motive in each instance.

Ex. 5.34. *On the Waterfront.* Conductor Part. "Cab and Bedroom." Variation of Pain motive (mm. 14-17) as Charley reminisces about Terry's former career as a boxer, mm. 10-17.

As Terry famously laments to his brother, "You don't understand. I could've had class. I could've been a contender. I could've been somebody instead of a bum, which is what I am, let's face it," Bernstein repeats the material begun in Ex. 5.34, m. 10, with violins doubled and played *fortissimo* (Ex. 5.35).

Ex. 5.35. *On the Waterfront.* Conductor Part. "Cab and Bedroom." Terry complains to Charley about his failed potential as a human, mm. 18-23.

We discover that Charley bet against his brother in a title contender bout. Terry threw the fight and ruined any chances of earning a shot at the title. The irony in this scene is that Terry's journey to become his own man has precedent: he has always wanted to achieve his own identity. However, just as Friendly controls his life now, Friendly, with Charley's help, forced Terry to submit to what the gang wanted and quelled his dreams of becoming a great fighter—a "contender." As Kazan remembers, "What I wanted [in this scene] was to show the moment when a man suddenly thinks of what he could have been, like everybody does at some point in their lives."[38] One senses the guilt and remorse in Charley's voice as he realizes that by following orders, he held his thumb on Terry's ambitions and this mood is enhanced through Bernstein's sorrowful rendition of the Pain motive. At the same time, the music highlights Terry's contemplation of what might have happened had he decided on that fateful night to follow his conscience.

In retrospect, the synthesis of the Charley material and the Pain motive in Ex. 5.33, when analyzed with the sequence that follows it, provides a fitting transitional passage both musically and dramatically. At the beginning of the scene, Charley's attempt to silence his brother and the pressure to remain in Friendly's good graces was the focal point, thus the presence of the Charley theme. After the gun is pulled and we begin to learn more about Terry, it is appropriate that the thematic material was based upon the Pain theme. In examining Ex. 5.33, one notices a dissonant combination of the two themes, suggesting the opposition between the brothers and their separate problems, as well as a shared frustration with conforming to Friendly's terms.

In an important moment, Charley decides not to press Terry further and gives him the gun. In this action of defiance against the family,

Charley hopes to atone in some small way for the harm he has caused his brother. As he gets out of the taxi, the camera pans to the taxi driver's face and we see the vehicle drive into an underground garage and then Johnny Friendly through a window above. As this action transpires, one hears the more turbulent music of the Riot music first encountered during the frenzied acts of violence at Father Barry's meeting in the church (Ex. 5.15). As established above, it derives from the Pain motive through rhythmic alteration and in this case, as in the latter instance, the music suggests a sense of imminent violence. In the former example, the potential agitators were reminded of what happens to those who attempt to weaken the organization's grip on the workers. Charley knows that there is only one possible consequence for his defiance and the thematic material perhaps suggests the fear he feels as the underground garage seemingly swallows the taxi whole.

The action shifts to Edie's apartment where Terry pounds on the door to see her. The furious Riot music from the preceding action lingers, reinforcing the sense that a confrontation between Edie and Terry is inevitable and, perhaps, imminent violence. As Edie goes to the door one notices the Love theme once again, but with a more urgent and harsh-sounding orchestration played *fff* in the strings and brass and with jarring interjections by the percussion (Ex. 5.36). Unlike previous iterations of the theme, Bernstein maintains the orchestration from the preceding Riot music and casts a grittiness to the Love theme that echoes virtuous Edie in her white slip (recall her white gloves) juxtaposed against discolored white walls and obscured in shadow. When Edie hears Terry at the door she fixes her hair, goes to the door, but tells Terry to "Go away!" Terry breaks the door down and pleads with Edie to listen.

Ex. 5.36. ***On the Waterfront*****, Conductor Part. "Cab and Bedroom." Love theme in different orchestral context, mm. 53-61.**

Edie is obviously disturbed and does not want to see Terry, yet her actions indicate differently. The placement of the Love theme in this more abrasive scoring seems to comment on the dualistic nature of the exchange between Terry and Edie and recalls music used (and unused) to accompany a similar struggle during the "Scramble" (see Ex. 5.13 and 5.14 above). Terry exclaims to her, "Edie! You love me!" To which Edie clarifies, "I didn't say I didn't love you. I said stay away from me!" Under the impression that Terry has come for consolation, she tells him to "let your conscience tell you what to do." During that exchange, the Riot music returns briefly and reminds the listener yet again what happens on the docks when a person follows his conscience.

"Coda—Accident"

The previous cue ends abruptly as Terry and Edie kiss, but their embrace is interrupted by a voice shouting to Terry from the street that Charley wants to see his brother. The parallel to the beginning of the movie when Terry calls to Joey from the street is obvious and Bernstein seems to have been conscious of Kazan's dramatic framing. In addition, it was Edie's brother in danger in the beginning of the movie and now it is Terry's brother who is in trouble. To enhance this symmetry in the drama, Bernstein used the same material—the Violence and Pain themes (Ex. 5.5 and 5.6)—that he used in the opening sequence of the movie. Thus, based on the cue's title (and the presence of the muted trumpet instead of alto saxophone for the Pain theme), the music originally planned to accompany the events leading up to and including Kayo Dugan's murder in "Accident" was used instead to highlight Terry's role reversal and connect more directly with the material encountered in "Opening Shot to Scream."[39]

Terry walks down the street to look for Charley and Edie runs after him pleading with him to return to her apartment. The camera cuts to a pair of headlights and one hears the fierce Violence theme throughout the orchestra (see Ex. 5.8). The way the entrance of the Violence theme *tutti* corresponds with the headlights in this scene, perhaps even more so than the beginning of the movie, lends more to the dramatic intensity than the visual component of the film. The headlights belong to a truck that is moving towards Terry and Edie with increasing speed. Within a dark alley and seemingly no escape, the feeling of entrapment is arguably never more apparent. Terry is then able to break open a door, saving Edie and himself, and in a superb example of camera work, the passing truck blocks the nearby streetlight and after it passes the streetlight reveals across the alley Charley's body hanging from a hook. The moment that Terry realizes it is Charley's body before him, we hear the same variation of the Pain motive from the taxi sequence, seen above in Ex. 5.34 and 5.35. The use of that specific theme is particularly poignant in this instance. Shortly before Charley's death, the two brothers were in a taxi (together for the last time) and the theme suggested the guilt and remorse Charley felt for his neglect of Terry. Now, it represents Terry's guilt and remorse for not coming to Charley's aid in time to help him. Accordingly, Bernstein captures the anguish of this latest catastrophe with the restated plaintive chords of the modified Pain motive.

The final musical passage of this long sequence is a reharmonization of the Violence theme (Ex. 5.37) as it was heard after Father Barry's speech in "After Sermon" (Ex. 5.26). In this most recent setting (here in 7/8 subdivided into 4+3 rather than alternating measures of 4/4 and 3/4 above), Bernstein places the material in muted trombones surrounded by sustained strings, a steady pedal tone in the timpani, and a foreboding tone in the lowest part of the orchestra and seems to strike a more ominous, anticipatory tone.[40] Bernstein, once again, maintains dramatic continuity by incorporating the same musical material in these two scenes. As already mentioned, this music suggests painful reflection after a tragedy. In these two sequences, it also marks distinct, changing moments in Terry's development as an individual. Following Father Barry's speech about caring for one's fellow workers on the docks, Terry was inspired to go to the priest and confess his role in Joey's death. Barry suggested he confess instead to Edie, which ultimately helped their relationship. Because of this most recent event, Terry's thoughts of exacting revenge for his brother's death will, as the next sequence demonstrates, lead eventually to his testimony in front of the crime commission, thus damaging Friendly's influence on the docks. In each case the tragedies emboldened Terry to take control of the situation and change his life.

Ex. 5.37. *On the Waterfront.* Conductor Part. "Coda—Accident." Reharmonization of Violence theme in "After Sermon" as Terry resolves to avenge Charley's death, mm. 16-17.

"Throwing the Gun"

Terry then goes to Friendly's Bar, hoping to kill the man responsible for his brother's death. Father Barry enters the bar as well, intent on calming Terry and helping him think more rationally in the aftermath of Charley's murder. Father Barry advises Terry that if he really wants to make a difference, then testifying before the crime commission "armed with the truth," not killing Friendly and becoming like him, is the best way to exact vengeance on his nemesis. As Terry wrestles with this idea, the listener notices a contrapuntal setting of the Pain motive beginning in the low strings and bass clarinet and answered at the octave with augmented note values in the violas and horns. The texture is striking as this stricter, imitative counterpoint has been mostly absent from the score since the "Main Title" music. In order to do what Father Barry asks of Terry he would have to deny his past and obey the law like the rest of society despite the painful feelings of revenge. Bernstein comments upon this dilemma by casting the Pain motive in the orderly, canonical texture seen below in Ex. 5.38. Through the compositional technique employed here, Bernstein not only recognizes the strict rules that govern imitative canon, but also acknowledges the multivalent nature of the word "canon" as it pertains to both law, and perhaps more to the point given Father Barry's role in Terry's decision, church law.

Ex. 5.38. *On the Waterfront*, Conductor Part. "Throwing the Gun." Contrapuntal setting of the Pain motive, mm. 1-12.

As Terry considers Father Barry's challenge, Bernstein seems to capture the conflict in Terry's conscience between the two methods of revenge and their implications in addition to the fear he must feel in confronting the one person who would most certainly hurt him. This is the ultimate step for Terry, and the layering of the Pain motive in this cue also indicates the weight it has on his psyche. In order to further intensify the effect of the thematic material in this instance, Bernstein alters the repetition of the usual complementary perfect fourth of the Pain motive and makes it a tritone, seen above in m. 3 and 10. It is as if Terry is considering all the tragic events that have occurred thus far, all represented by the increasingly dense entrances of the motive in "Throwing the Gun." Moreover, as the successively louder entrances of the Pain motive each adhere to the laws of counterpoint, Terry seems to be surer that the high road of virtue is the correct path to take in defeating Friendly.

The musical counterpoint builds to include the entire orchestra as Terry realizes that Father Barry is right. The two share a beer and for Terry this action indicates his acceptance of Father Barry's request to depose Friendly in court, accompanied by the Pain material in full orchestration, accented by chime strokes (Ex. 5.39). Bernstein makes the opening minor second of the Pain motive even more dissonant as it is accompanied by another minor second moving in contrary motion (both involving the raised fourth and fifth scale degrees in F-minor, B-natural, and C-natural), seen in m. 19. The music emphasizes the dual nature of the scene in that while fear and doubt surround Terry's decision, the chimes perhaps suggest that this could be a potentially triumphant moment for those attempting to break free of Friendly's control. The cue ends as Terry hurls Charley's gun at a picture of Friendly and a supporter on the wall of Friendly's Bar, possibly foreshadowing the weakening of Friendly's power. Yet, the lack of a conclusive resolution and the tonal instability throughout the cue causes one to ponder whether Terry is satisfied both with the decision he has made and his new role within waterfront society.

Ex. 5.39. *On the Waterfront*, Conductor Part. "Throwing the Gun." Grand presentation of Pain motive accompanied by chimes, mm. 19-24.

"Dead Pigeons"

Terry then appears before the crime commission and tells them everything he knows, implicating Friendly in the corruption for which he is responsible and causing Johnny to assure Terry that he will never work another day on the docks. The scene shifts back to Edie's apartment, where Terry has been escorted by two policemen. Terry acknowledges one of his co-workers, who walks past him as if he were invisible. Since Terry broke the sacred longshoremen oath of D&D, he will have to enjoy his victory alone. As he is rebuffed by his friend, one hears another, elegiac rendition of the Pain theme as a solo in the violas with sparse accompaniment (Ex. 5.40).

Ex. 5.40. *On the Waterfront*, Short Score. "Dead Pigeons." Terry treated as *persona non grata* following his testimony, mm. 1-6.[41]

This particular variation of the Pain theme is the most distantly related to the original in the score, but the general shape of the motive is still clear. In m. 1, a major second replaces the characteristic minor second and the complementary perfect fourth is substituted for a major sixth. Later in mm. 4-5, the minor second returns, but the corresponding figure is replaced with a minor third. Bernstein's harmonization adds tension to the relatively consonant intervals of this modified Pain material. In addition, the sparse string scoring helps to convey the poignancy of the scene while the timbral contrast between violins and violas reminds the listener of Charley and Terry's scene in the cab. While contrasting in texture with the previous cue, "Throwing the Gun," Bernstein does employ similar voice leading characteristics. In Ex. 5.39, m. 19, in the trumpets and trombones, and Ex. 5.40, m. 2, in the first and second violas the minor ninth resolves to a major seventh disguised as dissonant voice exchanges. Up to this point, the Pain motive enhanced the struggle when someone, usually Terry, was attempting to break free from the control of the group. In the aftermath of his bittersweet victory over Friendly, Bernstein seems to suggest that while the old fear may have subsided, new-found individuality carries with it a different set of challenges. Terry is now alone in his life as a longshoreman and now that he has distanced himself from the protection of the Friendly organization, a new fear sets in—that of being alone. One of the risks of becoming an individual in a highly conformist setting, like the mob, is sudden isolation from the former group. Bernstein's music enhances this idea quite effectively, both in this variation of the Pain motive and the solemn manner in which it is set.

Terry continues upstairs to Edie's apartment where she attempts to console him. The theme continues as they talk, freely varied, and repeats an octave higher in the violin. Edie's soothing words do not aid

Terry and he retreats once again to the rooftop. As mentioned above, Kazan juxtaposes the idealism of the rooftop against the realism of the streets and docks. Furthermore, when Terry goes to the roof, he most often seeks refuge in or around the pigeon coop. When the audience first viewed the rooftop, Terry was situated just outside of the cage. When Edie first found Terry on the rooftop, much of the conversation took place while Terry was within the coop; a pigeon talking about other pigeons. Later, when the Crime Commission investigator, Glover, looked for Terry on the roof, the latter sensed danger and retreated to the confines of the enclosure to answer questions from Glover who remained on the outside.

The coop, then, is where Terry seems to go when he desires to be alone with his thoughts. In this scene it is not an intimidating place of confinement, but a sanctuary of the familiar; perhaps, maintaining the many animal metaphors throughout the film, a natural habitat. Now that he really is alone, he goes to the coop and greets his protégé, Tommy. The boy runs away and before Terry can follow him, he throws a dead pigeon at Terry screaming, "A pigeon for a pigeon." The revised Pain motive, which had been playing through this dialogue, repeats in strings, woodwinds, and brass (Ex. 5.41) as Terry is struck by the dead pigeon. In case the reference to the original Pain theme was not clear, Bernstein precedes the restatement of this variation with a sequential statement of the opening notes of the theme in mm. 15-16. Terry then goes to the coop and discovers that Tommy killed his entire flock of pigeons whereupon Edie comes over to comfort Terry, wondering if it would be best if they left the waterfront altogether. Now that Terry's last bastion of privacy has been violated, it would seem that Edie was correct in her suggestion. The music, after reaching a climax at m. 17 in Ex. 5.41, subsides by m. 22 and the spare string scoring from earlier in the cue returns.

Ex. 5.41. *On the Waterfront*, Short Score. "Dead Pigeons." Original Pain motive (mm. 15-16) and variation presented throughout orchestra as Terry is struck by the dead pigeon, mm. 15-22.

Thus far in "Dead Pigeons," the music has served to emphasize the fact that there is much that is uncertain in this new life as an autonomous individual. However, despite Edie's pleading, Tommy's brutal act, and the death of his brother, something in the distance catches Terry's eye. The camera pans to the imposing skyline of Manhattan and a large ship that is leaving the port. As Terry sees the vessel and ignores Edie's pleas, for the first time since the opening credits, one hears the Dignity theme (Ex. 5.42), marked "nobile" by Bernstein, and in the hero's key of E-flat major.[42]

Ex. 5.42. *On the Waterfront,* Conductor Part. "Dead Pigeons." Return of Dignity theme as Terry looks to the distant waterfront, mm. 35-40.

As Edie continues to explain why she thinks they both should leave the waterfront, Terry takes his longshoreman's hook and sets off to work. As the exchange between Edie and Terry continues, Bernstein reprises the Love theme and in order to demonstrate the conflict between both sides of the dialogue—Terry's quest for dignity and Edie's love for Terry—Bernstein sets the Dignity theme (now taken up in the horn, its original instrument) in counterpoint against the Love theme in the flute (its usual instrumentation), bassoon, and bass clarinet (orchestrated to suggest a ship's whistle in a similar manner to Ex. 5.4).[43] When Terry states, "They always said I was a bum. Well I ain't a bum, Edie." one hears the section of the Dignity theme on which the Pain theme was based (Ex. 5.43, mm. 44-45).

Ex. 5.43. *On the Waterfront,* Conductor Part. "Dead Pigeons." Dignity theme in counterpoint with Love theme, mm. 40-45.

Returning to the aforementioned idea of the Dignity theme as a narrative of Terry's journey, the placement of this motivic cell (mm. 44-45), marked by the tritone between the lowered dominant and tonic scale degrees, serves as a microcosm of Terry's actions when he was that bum. He did many terrible things, most of which were out of fear of being ousted from his comfortable standing in the group. Finally,

Bernstein separates the "blue" notes from both themes (the D-flat on beat 1 in m. 44 for the Love theme and the B-double flat on beat 1 in m. 45) by just one measure, perhaps further suggesting the close relationships between Terry's journey and the role of love in that journey. The cue closes with a solo presentation of the "resolving" triadic figure from the end of the Dignity theme (see Ex. 5.42, m. 40) as Terry arrives for work, his "friends" distanced from this traitor according to the group code. As Bernstein brings back the Dignity theme in conjunction with Terry's decision to go back to the docks to "get [his] rights" he begins to fulfill the prophesying nature of the Dignity theme at the film's opening and allows the listener to become reacquainted with the material before he uses it to culminate the film.

"Wild Phrases/The Challenge"

Mac then informs all the workers gathered at the dock that everyone will work that day except Terry. When Terry informs Mac that he is "one man short in the hatch," Mac chooses the same homeless man that Terry accosted earlier in the film. Alone again, Terry decides that the only way he can win back the respect of the workers and reclaim his dignity is to confront Friendly himself. In a cue entitled "Wild Phrases," one hears three short segments of the Dignity theme in the French horn as Terry makes his way down to Friendly's shack and calls the mobster out (Ex. 5.44). As if to suggest that Terry still had something to accomplish, Bernstein concludes "Wild Phrases" on a C-natural and just before the distinctive major second-augmented fourth passage would normally sound. In addition, the half-cadence on C-natural after an interrogatory, ascending passage, leaves the viewer feeling as if a question has been posed, but not answered.

Ex. 5.44. *On the Waterfront*, Short Score. "Wild Phrases." Terry is rebuffed by Mac and makes his way to confront Friendly, m. 1-6.

Another more functional reason that the passage ends on a half-cadence is because Bernstein planned to resolve the figure in a cue called, "The Challenge." However, as indicated in the introduction to this analysis, "The Challenge" is one of two cues that was notated and recorded, but not included in the film score. The material was intended to underscore Terry's walk towards the gangplank and verbal taunting of Friendly. However, a comparison between the short score, conductor part (Ex. 5.45), and Bernstein's Symphonic Suite demonstrates that the cue does survive in the suite.[44] The music that follows "The Challenge" in both the short score and the Symphonic Suite is identical and is described below. In the cue, Bernstein develops the Dignity theme in contrapuntal fashion first between brass (Ex. 5.45), then strings, then woodwinds and strings. Further, the musical intensity increases upon each successive entrance and in the change in meter between 4/4, 3/4, and 5/4.

Ex. 5.45. *On the Waterfront.* Conductor Part. "The Challenge." Cue omitted as Terry goes to confront Johnny Friendly, mm. 1-9.

The most obvious explanation for the cue's omission from the soundtrack is that the music would have obscured Terry's speech to Friendly—a crucially important piece of the narrative whose effect would have been diminished by the inclusion of music. Another possible explanation is that such a development of the Dignity theme might have detracted from the theme's important role in highlighting Terry's final redemption. Moreover, the music would have rendered inaudible the excited murmurs of Terry's co-workers as they followed him to the confrontation. The dull thud of Terry's hook thrown against the door to Friendly's shack—akin to a slave throwing down his tool in protest of the master—would also have been muffled. So too would have been the far-away moan of a ship's steam whistle, perhaps a further reminder of who is really boss on the waterfront—commerce.[45] Yet, knowing that Bernstein intended a significant development of the Dignity theme to accompany Terry's challenge of Johnny lends further credence to the theme's role—established in "Main Title"—as a microcosm of Terry's redemptive journey.

As emotions reach a fevered pitch, one notices a reprise of the Scramble music (see "Scramble," Ex. 5.11), preceded by some sustained material that calls attention to the boiling emotions between Terry and Johnny, relieved only when the two combat in "The Fight" (see below). The brief introduction to "The Fight" represents the only part of "The Challenge" that made its way into the score. The dissonant chord in the strings and winds (Ex. 5.46) is made more strikingly discordant by the rising line in the trumpets and creates an aural manifestation of two opposing forces that have reached the breaking point.

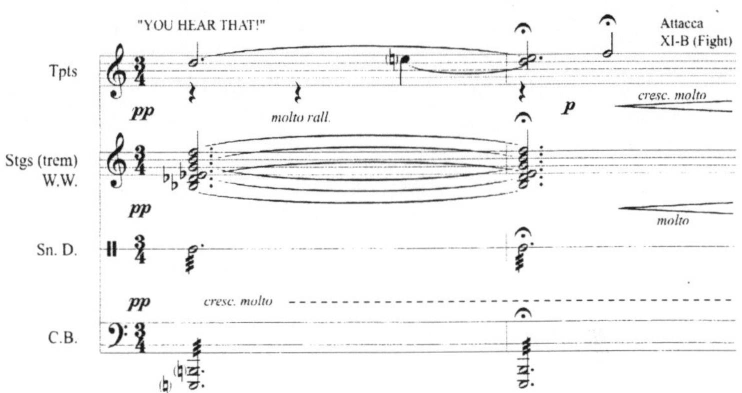

Ex. 5.46. *On the Waterfront.* Conductor Part. "The Challenge." Intact excerpt from "The Challenge" as intro to "The Fight," mm. 30-31.

"The Fight"

Beginning with m. 6 (see Ex. 5.11) from "Scramble," Bernstein employs the next twenty-three measures from that cue, before repeating mm. 17-24 from "Scramble," to serve as the music for "The Fight" between Terry and Johnny. Bernstein's reuse of this theme is both dramatically consistent and captures the visceral intensity of the fight between Terry and Friendly. The first time this theme was heard, it also accompanied a fight on the docks, albeit between workers fighting each other for precious brass checks and a chance to work. Now, as those same workers look on, Terry is struggling with Friendly not only for a chance to work, but also for personal vindication. Earlier during Terry and Edie's "date" in the bar, he explained that Friendly "bought a piece" of him when he demonstrated potential as a boxer. Now, in a sense, Terry is realizing that potential as he attempts to "buy back" his life from Friendly.

While much of "The Fight" is reprised verbatim from its appearance in "Scramble," there are some important differences. Because there is more dialogue interspersed between the action in "The Fight" than there is in "Scramble," Bernstein employs thinner textures and sudden dynamic contrasts to coincide with similarly stark diegetic juxtapositions between dialogue, sound effects, and visuals. For instance, as two of Friendly's goons (Tillio and Slim) attempt to hold back workers from helping Terry, Bernstein drops the low strings and percussion and uses *piano* dynamics so that we can hear Jimmy state, "They'll kill him" answered by Luke's observation, "It's a massacre" (Ex. 5.47). As the camera pans back to the fight, *subito fortissimo* dynamics and brass punctuate accordingly. As Jimmy and Luke decide to help, Bernstein again recognizes their exchange with a sudden shift in musical texture. Throughout this sequence, and in other important places throughout the score, Bernstein demonstrates—despite criticism to the contrary—that his scoring is sensitive to dialogue, especially for a first time scorer.

Later, after a few measures in which the material from Ex. 5.47, m. 40 is repeated, Bernstein added a somber coda comprised of the thematic material from the Scramble theme in the strings, but slowed in tempo and with more sustained notes throughout (Ex. 5.48).[46] When Terry starts to get the better of Friendly, he calls in his goons to help finish the former boxer off. A flurry of violence ensues and Friendly says off camera, "Just let 'em lay there."

Ex. 5.47. *On the Waterfront.* Conductor Part. "The Fight." Dynamic contrasts to accompany similar juxtapositions between action and dialogue, mm. 34-40.

Ex. 5.48. *On the Waterfront*, Conductor Part. "The Fight." Coda derived from Scramble music as workers suspect the worst about Terry, mm. 44-50.

Because the audience has not seen the worst of the fight, they along with the workers are left to wonder if Terry is alive or dead. The altered Pain motive within this context of harmonic dissonance, tonal ambiguity, and whose melodic cadence on A-sharp lacks clear resolution, enhances the feeling of doubt and distress. Although the cadence on A-sharp sounds inconclusive here, it forms the fifth of an expectant D-sharp minor chord—heard that way because Bernstein de-emphasizes the F-sharp octaves in the xylophone and piccolo in favor of the bottom-heavy open fifth between D-sharp and A-sharp—that serves as the "resolution" before the next section begins. As the music suggests, uncertainty creeps in on several levels. First, there is concern that the main protagonist of the film has been murdered, thus damaging the workers' hopes for better conditions on the docks. Secondly, since Friendly appears to have defeated this challenge to his authority, one might expect that the working environment could one day worsen for the other workers as a demonstration of Friendly's absolute power. Finally, there is most likely a feeling that one missed an opportunity. Their standard of living and working might have improved immeasurably had they too broken their code of conformity and aided Terry. In the aftermath of Terry's beating, Kazan focuses on the faces of the men on the docks. As Kazan put it, "He was the first one to do what they in their hearts knew they should do but didn't have the guts to do."[47] In this simple setting of the Pain motive, Bernstein's music describes effectively the pain and regret they now feel.

"Terry Unconscious"

Father Barry and Edie arrive on the scene and inquire as to what happened, but the workers still maintain their code of saying nothing. Badly beaten himself, Friendly ascends the plank and a shipping boss orders him to get his men inside to work and when Friendly obliges, his men do not listen. The workers tell Johnny that if Terry is not allowed to work, then no one will work. As Friendly physically forces his men inside, Pop Doyle, after years of maltreatment, pushes Friendly from high off a dock into the cold river below and attains a measure of vengeance against the man responsible for his son's death after falling from the rooftop. Subsequently, the workers come to tell Terry that if he worked, they would follow behind him. However, as they see his condition, their hopes are quickly dashed. As the audience witnesses the true extent of Terry's condition, one hears material in the strings similar to that heard in the opening measures of the coda material from "The Fight" (Ex. 5.48, mm. 44-47).

Father Barry, sensing the powerful effect Terry's leading the men to work would have, attempts to convince him that he should get up and finish what he started, despite his physical state. This dialogue is accompanied by a rendition of the Pain motive in the bassoons in "Terry Unconscious," (Ex. 5.49). In encouraging Terry to "win the war," he is asking him not to forget all the pain and anguish he has expended thus far in exposing Friendly and breaking free from the mob's control. Bernstein seems to underscore that fact with yet another rendition of the Pain motive. The use of the minor seventh leap up to the first note of the motive keeps it consistent with its presentation in the previous cue as the altered Scramble theme while also emphasizing the first note (A-flat) of the Pain motive even more. Moreover, the dialogue between bassoons helps here in conveying the intimacy of the theme. When Terry came back down to the docks to work again, surrounded by his co-workers, he was considered an outsider in his redefined role within the waterfront culture. Now as he has defeated Friendly, his colleagues encircle him as friends intent on helping him to his feet and walking to work alongside him.

Ex. 5.49. *On the Waterfront*, Conductor Part. "Terry Unconscious." Rendition of Pain motive in bassoons as Terry regains consciousness, mm. 3-5.

The workers follow Father Barry's example and encourage Terry to get up as well. Terry's redemption cannot be complete until he leads the men to work. However, after Terry refuses Barry's challenge, he attempts to coax him by telling him (falsely) that Friendly was "laying odds" that he would not do it. Bernstein echoes the effect this challenge has on Terry by repeating the minor second of the Pain motive in the flutes (Ex. 5.50), but not finishing the thought, perhaps indicating that a change in Terry's demeanor is transpiring and that his fear might be diminishing.

Ex. 5.50. *On the Waterfront*, Conductor Part. "Terry Unconscious." Incomplete presentation of the Pain motive as Terry begins to consider Father Barry's challenge, mm. 8-9.

As Terry slowly begins to get up, one detects the Dignity theme, again as a horn solo, begin to emerge in slow, long tones against sustained octaves in the winds and harp (Ex. 5.51). Slowly and subtly, Bernstein builds the theme *attacca* into the next cue and what will become a rousing musical and cinematic climax.

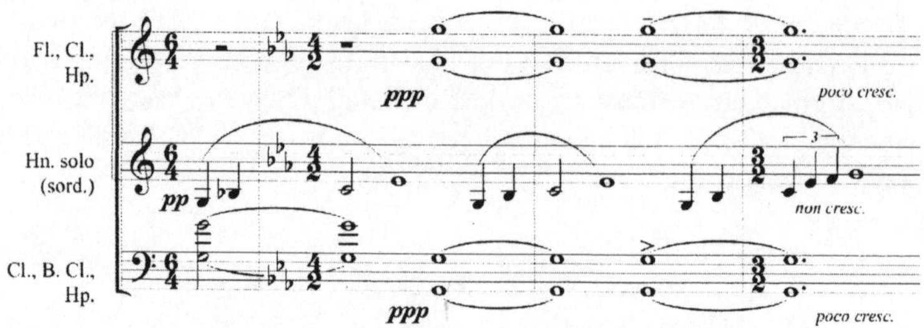

Ex. 5.51. *On the Waterfront.* Conductor Part. "Terry Unconscious." Dignity theme in horn, mm. 9-12.

"Walk and End Title"

Terry's final, triumphant march, after humiliating Johnny Friendly in front of his fellow workers, is one of the great closing scenes in cinema. Musically, the score exhibits a culmination of themes encountered throughout the drama. As Terry rises to his feet, we recognize the Dignity theme in a different orchestral context. As Terry struggles to walk, one can see that he is disoriented and half-conscious. To accompany this action, Bernstein moves the Dignity theme from the horn and sets it as a solo in the vibraphone, evoking a dreamlike quality echoing Terry's semi-coherent state (Ex. 5.52). Bernstein accompanies this figure with a repetitive passage in the strings and percussion. The alternation between F-natural and C-natural, within this slow tempo, suggests a slow, deliberate walk similar to the pace with which Terry makes his way to work.

Ex. 5.52. *On the Waterfront*, Conductor Part. "Walk and End Title." Re-orchestrated Dignity theme as Terry rises to go to work, mm. 1-4.

Upon closer examination, one notices that the secondary material in Ex. 5.52 also derives from previous materials. The passage in the violas is a staggered version of the opening notes of the Pain theme where a major second substitutes for the characteristic minor second of the Pain motive; the familiar perfect fourth lies in the cellos, basses, and percussion. In using this altered setting of the Pain motive to accompany the Dignity theme, Bernstein reminds us of the agony Terry has experienced thus far, as well as the physical pain he endures presently. However, after encouragement by Father Barry and his co-workers that in getting up and going to work he will finally defeat Johnny Friendly, this disjunct manifestation of the Pain motive fades to the aural background and suggests that both the physical pain and the scars on his psyche still exist, but are beginning to subside even more as he realizes his redemption. In addition, Bernstein gives the theme more prominence as it moves from the vibraphones first to the trumpets and woodwinds, and finally to the entire orchestra. Finally, in previous renditions of the Dignity theme, Bernstein maintained the inherent shifts in meter (See Ex. 5.1) and preserved the theme's somewhat jerky rhythmic component. Ironically as Terry struggles mightily on his way to work, Bernstein places the cue in triple meter that does not give way even as the cue (and score) ends. Despite Terry's outward appearance, the unrelenting triple meter suggests a determination that only gains momentum—dramatically and musically—and that was missing in previous versions of the theme.

As Terry nears the door to the warehouse, he stops before the shipping boss who commands all the workers, "Alright, let's go to work!" At that moment, we hear a brass fanfare that sets the Dignity theme in the horns and third trumpet, in counterpoint with the Love theme presented in the first trumpet, displayed in Ex. 5.53. Counterpoint—ranging from strict imitative canon to freely treated dense polyphony—has been a chief facet of Bernstein's musical language evidenced throughout this score. In these final measures, one witnesses not only a summary of prominent themes, but in a fashion that calls attention to the dizzying contrapuntal cinematography that alternates between omniscient and subjective point of view shots of Terry's bloodied face, his staggered yet determined gait, the gathered longshoremen, and the warehouse. In his compositional treatment here and elsewhere in the score, Bernstein demonstrates to audiences and future film scorers that an effective way in which to enhance visual counterpoint is through similarly nuanced musical counterpoint.

Ex. 5.53. *On the Waterfront*, Conductor Part. "Walk and End Title." Brass fanfare juxtaposing Dignity and Love themes, mm. 20-24.

As the journey towards Terry's redemption is complete, Bernstein reminds us that Terry's triumph would not have been possible without the love of both Edie and Father Barry. Bernstein's combination of the themes echoes Kazan's alternation between shots of the workers walking in and Father Barry and Edie standing in admiration of what Terry has accomplished; the former represented by the Dignity theme and the latter distinguished by the Love theme. For the moment and for one of the first times since the opening scene of the film, the Pain theme is absent, suggesting that perhaps Terry has finally conquered his fear and is confident as the leader of a better way of life for the longshoremen. Yet, as the screen darkens and the audience views the Columbia Pictures logo, the music of the Dignity theme subsides and one hears a dialogue between motives throughout the orchestra. The opening motive of the Love theme is audible in the horns and strings. This material is contrasted with the familiar minor second of the Pain theme, sounded in the piccolos, flutes, and first trumpets, and answered by the perfect fourth in the bass clarinets, bassoons, contrabassoons, second trombone, and tubas (Ex. 5.54), thus breaking our brief respite from the theme.

Also evident in Ex. 5.54, the final appearance of the Pain motive occurs in the penultimate measure and is resolved in the final measure. This contrasts with the two previous statements, which are both answered within the same measure. In this final, brief epilogue to the music heard thus far, Bernstein does not appease the listener by providing a triumphant, Hollywood cadence. This was a story about a self-proclaimed bum who attained redemption through the love of a young woman, thus the presence of the Love theme. However, the dissonant exclamations of the Pain motive remind the audience that this was also a very violent story and several tragic events marred the hero's path to victory. The repeated statements of the Pain theme's characteristic semitone leave the listener with a lingering sense of unease. In addition, the ascending minor second in the clarinets and trombones clashes with the descending half step of the Pain theme. Bernstein achieves further dissonance as the A-natural in the trumpets and high woodwinds is discordant with each of the notes in the E-flat major triad on beat 1 of mm. 30-32. Bernstein's music enhances the fact that there seem to be more questions than real answers as the steel "curtain"—in the form of the warehouse door—comes down. Furthermore, Bernstein's music echoes what Neve states that "The last shot of the film is not of Father Barry and Edie—plainly satisfied with the resolution, Edie incomprehensibly so—but of the shutters coming down, adding to doubts about how much has changed."[48]

Ex. 5.54. *On the Waterfront*, Conductor Part. "Walk and End Title." Pain motive combined with Love theme at closing of the score, mm. 29-33.

However, the final chord also seems to comment about the way things have been and perhaps always will be. Through the various intervallic relationships that Bernstein employs in this final chord, the composer recalls one last time various motives from throughout the score and supplies the chord with an added musicodramatic meaning. The predominant tonal center throughout these last several measures is E-flat. In the flutes and trumpets lies an A-natural in the chord and used as a decorative note. The raised fourth in E-flat recalls the tritone that is central to the Dignity theme. The flatted seventh on D-flat in the horns and strings harkens back to the opening of the Love theme as well as the peak of the melody on the "blue" flatted seventh. The figure in the timpani both functions as the consequent perfect fourth of the Pain theme and also recalls the percussion ostinato that served as the Violence theme. In addition to its melodic presence in the preceding measures, the initial semitone of the Pain theme is represented harmonically with the presence of B-flat in the timpani and trombones.

This compositional endeavor aside, Bernstein's brilliance is realized in the way he voices the chord. The way in which Bernstein builds the chord from bottom to top represents a very close approximation to the natural overtone series on E-flat. For instance, the bass contains octaves and perfect fifths, going up there are tighter triads in the lower brass and woodwinds, and the flatted seventh and sharped fourth reside in the upper woodwinds and brass. Bernstein perhaps philosophizes in this final chord—which culminates a keen sense of thematic integration throughout—that pain, love, violence, and dignity are all part of a natural order of humanity. Whether that natural order favors (or will favor) the workers or the mobsters is not clear. Perhaps all that one can do is go forward armed with dignity and compassion.

AFTERWORD

Like the score's final chord, the closing shot of the film is another example of the type of dramatic duality seen throughout the narrative. It is not known who Friendly's boss really was. The character was only briefly alluded to in the film. Most think that the "Mr. Upstairs" was I.L.A. president Joseph P. Ryan, who remained in control of the waterfront in 1954. When Friendly promises, "I'll be back," he is correct. Nothing will have changed for the workers. Kenneth Hey echoes Neve by stating:

> As the warehouse door closes behind the victorious workers in the last shots of *On the Waterfront*, the image of the caged pigeons should return to the viewer's mind. The warehouse symbolizes both protection and entrapment. The workers, having for the moment regained control of their union, must face the problem which originally brought unions into existence: how can the laborer maintain autonomy and dignity in a capitalist society? . . . With its ambivalent ending, the film suggests that the challenges require constant vigilance. The structural argument blamed corrupt individuals for the failure of a workable institutional structure; the ambivalent ending with its suggestion of continued corruption posited the idea that oppression is inherent in the institutional system. The two positions—the viability of liberal institutions and ambivalence toward individual action—contradict each other. Thus, the film is a curious mixture of assertions favoring social reform and suggestions as to the futility of such reforms.[1]

In his article, cited frequently in Chapters 4 and 5, Hey examines each aspect—directing, acting, cinematography, and music—of the making of *On the Waterfront* and how the various artists involved in the film's production contributed to its success. Hey argues that one overarching idea connects the efforts of the film's collaborators—ambivalence. Ambivalence in this sense refers to the simultaneously conflicting positions and ideas that the film proposes. For instance, Hey points out that the clash between the divergent personalities of Johnny Friendly and Father Barry results in an amalgamation of the two in Terry Malloy.

The latter fuses equal parts "selfishness and selflessness, but as an individual staggering beneath the burden of moral decisions, he remains unconvinced of the rightness of either extreme."[2]

Using ambivalence as the focus of his analysis, Hey employs an idea that appears to be prevalent throughout much of society during the 1950s. Attempts for social progress, such as rights of the poor, the emerging civil rights movement, peace efforts, and intellectualism, were all combated, treated, and labeled by right-wing groups as Communism, and therefore attempts to undermine the traditional American way of life. U.S. foreign policy sought to fight for freedom across the globe in the hopes of halting the spread of Communism. Conversely, in battling the spread of Communism at home, liberties were sacrificed, loyalties called into question, and promising careers extinguished. While there was much expansion during the 1950s in which the standard of living rose for many, the military/industrial/corporate complex developed exponentially at the expense of education, improved urban housing, and other social programs. The Cold War dictum of "waging the peace" through nuclear proliferation—thus making the threat of nuclear war so terrible one would not wage it—led to much fear and anxiety for many U.S. citizens as they built fallout shelters, bought Geiger counters, and worried about a war that hopefully would never come.

The portrayal of the suburban lifestyle as the ideal place to raise a family lured many young families from apartments in the cities to a home and security in the suburbs. However, the homogeneity of race and social class in the suburbs, the repressive expectations of gender roles, and cultural isolation left many suburbanites searching for domestic utopia. Furthermore, the increasing predominance of the other-directed personality in the late 1940s and early 1950s, as described by Riesman, conflicted with the simultaneous decline of the inner-directed individuals, who still clung to their mode of societal conformity.

Such conflicting ideologies are also present in *On the Waterfront* both on the screen and behind the camera. Terry Malloy wants to be somebody, but while he chafes under the burden of the Friendly organization, Terry knows he will always be a bum. However, when offered a different way of viewing life through the eyes of Edie Doyle, he ridicules her for being a "fruitcake." One is either a pigeon or a hawk in Malloy's world, and to him, only the hawks fly free; the pigeons end up in coops. Father Barry's promise of redemption through confession and self-examination sounds hollow to workers in an environment where one is "deaf and dumb." Barry reminds the longshoremen that the path to liberation lies in alerting the proper authorities, but the workers know that they will live longer if they remain silent in their coops.

For his first and only venture into film music composition, Leonard Bernstein relied upon his considerable talent for composing beautiful melodies and driving rhythms for his score to *On the Waterfront*. In addition, he displayed his knowledge of the Western canon in the way that he developed key motives throughout the score. Moreover he was able to call upon his vast knowledge of that same canon, as well as his personal experience with vernacular styles (and their assimilation into his musical language) to further inform the rich stylistic diversity that comprised the *On the Waterfront* score. The opening melody contains both the solemn determination and sense of anguish that is at the heart of the drama. The minor second and the tritone form the basis for the primary motives found in the score, beginning with their place in the pivotal interval of the Dignity theme. Furthermore, that cell serves as the basis for the most important motive in the score, the Pain theme, whose characteristic opening minor second enhances the feeling of angst and loss in Terry's journey towards freedom. In addition, the placement of the motive in various orchestral contexts—harmonized by a semitone in contrary motion in the high strings, rhythmically altered presentations in the "Scramble" and "Riot in Church" scenes, synchronized with diegetic machinery noise, and in a slow, bluesy boogie-woogie for piano, trumpet, and tenor saxophone—intensified the painful emotions involved in Terry's struggle for redemption. Bernstein also employed ostinatos effectively as the accompaniment for the Pain and Riot themes. Finally, the derivation of themes (for instance, Pain from Dignity, Love from Pain) reflects the interdependency of these emotions in conveying the narrative as well as enhancing the tension amidst the conflicting feelings that complement Terry's conversion.

So what then is this score's legacy? Despite some aforementioned criticism, some composers considered it "one of the great scores ever written in Hollywood."[3] Moreover, besides Aaron Copland and Bernard Herrmann, Bernstein represents an important influence on more contemporary composers like John Williams who have combined a fondness for the Golden Age sound of composers like Erich Wolfgang Korngold and Max Steiner with a more integrated sense of motivic development across themes exhibited by Bernstein.[4] Perhaps the biggest compliment the score can be paid is, as suggested earlier, the important role it played in creating *West Side Story*.

Based on the shared musical characteristics between the excerpts in Chapters 2 and 5 and the respective dramatic situations, it would seem the initial comparison between *On the Waterfront*'s Love theme and *West Side Story*'s "Somewhere," and "Something's Coming" in Chapter 2 was 1) not coincidental and 2) but the most obvious in a host of musicodramatic connections between the two works. Yet, what is perhaps most fascinating is the significance of these striking similarities. Like the final chords and scenes of both *On the Waterfront* and *West Side Story*, this significance is appropriately ambiguous—somewhere. For example take the original point of departure: in each instance—the Love theme, "Somewhere," and "Something's Coming"—the protagonist yearns for things that are both real and ideal. Tony speaks of Maria, but ultimately a better life away from gangs, the street, peace between ethnic groups and oppressive authority figures. Terry refers to Edie but also his attempt to reclaim his dignity in an environment where such a quest went against the code of the longshoremen. In addition, consider the famous lyrics from "Somewhere": "There's a place for us, somewhere a place for us. Peace and quiet and open air wait for us somewhere."[5] Three years earlier, similar sentiments were voiced by Terry and Edie before Terry left on his own to confront Johnny Friendly:

> EDIE: Terry, there's no place that's safe for you now on the waterfront. Maybe inland . . . out west some place . . . a farm?
> TERRY: A farm.
> EDIE: You could do lots of things ... anything as long as you're away from Johnny Friendly.[6]

Recalling Riesman's concept of the autonomous individual (see Chapter 4), ultimately Terry—and Tony, Elia Kazan, and Leonard Bernstein—did what was best for him despite the pressures from the community of peers. The poet e.e. cummings captures this spirit of autonomy—and thus the challenge of becoming someone, somewhere—in an excerpt from his *A Poet's Advice to Students*, "To be nobody but yourself in a world which is doing its best, night and day, to make you everybody else—means to fight the hardest battle which any human being can fight; and never stop fighting."[7]

NOTES

Introduction

1. Roy M. Prendergast, *Film Music: A Neglected Art, A Critical Study of Music in Films*, 2nd ed. (New York: Norton, 1992), 130.
2. Edward Murray, *Ten Film Classics: A Re-Viewing* (New York: Frederick Ungar, 1978), 93.
3. William Baer, ed., *Elia Kazan: Interviews* (Jackson: University Press of Mississippi, 2000), 179.
4. Aaron Copland, "Film Music" in *What to Listen for in Music*, rev. ed. (New York: McGraw-Hill, 1957), 256.
5. Copland, 256-57.

Chapter 1

1. Humphrey Burton, *Leonard Bernstein* (New York: Doubleday, 1994), 35.
2. Burton, 7.
3. Burton, 9.
4. Burton, 10.
5. Burton, 17.
6. Ron Gwiazda, "Leonard Bernstein at Boston Latin School" in *Leonard Bernstein: The Harvard Years 1935-1939*, ed. Claudia Swan (New York: Eos Orchestra, 1999), 41, 44.
7. Carol J. Oja and Kay Kaufman Shelemay, "Leonard Bernstein's Jewish Boston: Cross-Disciplinary Research in the Classroom," *Journal of the Society for American Music* 3:1 (February 2009), 14.
8. Burton, 24.
9. Burton, 28.
10. Leonard Bernstein, "The Occult" in *Findings* (New York: Simon & Schuster, 1982), 32.

11. Bernstein, 30.

12. Leonard Bernstein, "Aaron Copland at 70: An Intimate Sketch," in *Findings* (New York: Simon & Schuster, 1982), 284-85.

13. Bernstein, 286.

14. For insight into Bernstein's eclectic spirit, see Paul R. Laird, *Leonard Bernstein: A Guide to Research* (New York: Routledge, 2002), 13-15. In addition, Barry Seldes quotes a speech Bernstein gave at the Curtis Institute in 1975 in which he stated, "Our sense of truth must be interdisciplinary, and our sense of beauty must be expansive, even eclectic." (Barry Seldes, *Leonard Bernstein: The Political Life of an American Musician* [Berkeley: University of California Press, 2009], 200n13.) Regarding Prall's aesthetic classes, Seldes reports that Bernstein and others were drawn to Prall's deconstruction of prevailing positivistic norms for evaluating beauty in favor of Prall's preference for judging art based on "experience and feeling" evidenced in his *Aesthetic Judgment* (1929). Further, Prall employed form and feeling equally—against conventional aesthetic judging criteria—thus as Seldes puts it, Prall "dignified feeling and legitimized innovation (Seldes, 13-14, 199n12).

15. Quoted in Timothy W. Boyd and Carolyn Higbie, "Not So Much New Deal as Old Howard: Leonard Bernstein and Aristophanes' *The Birds*," in *Leonard Bernstein: The Harvard Years 1935-1939*, ed. Claudia Swan (New York: Eos Orchestra, 1999), 85.

16. Bernadette A. Meyler, "Composing (for a) Philosophical Comedy," in *Leonard Bernstein: The Harvard Years 1935-1939*, ed. Claudia Swan (New York: Eos Orchestra, 1999), 75-77.

17. For more on the Union's role in producing *The Cradle Will Rock*, see Drew Massey, "Leonard Bernstein and the Harvard Student Union: In Search of Political Origins," *Journal of the Society for American Music* 3:1 (February 2009), 67-84.

18. Seldes, 24.

19. Barbara P. Heyman, *Samuel Barber: The Composer and His Music* (New York: Oxford University Press, 1992), 34.

20. Burton, 69.

21. Burton, 80.

22. Howard Shanet, *Philharmonic: A History of New York's Orchestra* (New York: Doubleday, 1975), 506-19.

23. Paul R. Laird, "The Influence of Aaron Copland on Leonard Bernstein" (M.A. thesis, Ohio State University, 1982), 7.

24. Laird (1982), 8-9.

25. Burton, 179.

26. Leonard Bernstein, Symphony No. 1 "Jeremiah" (New York: Boosey and Hawkes, 1943, 1992).

27. Leonard Bernstein, Symphony No. 2 "Age of Anxiety" (New York: Boosey and Hawkes, 1965, 1993).

28. Bernstein (1965, 1993).

29. For instance, Neil Butterworth, *The American Symphony* (Brookfield, VT: Ashgate, 1998), 169.

30. For instance, in Copland's Sonata for Piano.

31. Laird (2002), 32.

32. Laird (2002), 35.

33. The *tresillo* rhythm is a 3+3+2 pattern characteristic of the rumba and is found throughout Latin American music. In addition, Copland used the rhythm in *El Salón México* (1936; and for which Bernstein published a piano reduction in 1939) and Bernstein employed it to great length in *West Side Story* (1957).

34. Burton, 129. For a more detailed account of Abbott's contribution to *On the Town*, including the significant cuts he made, see Helen Smith, *There's a Place for Us: The Musical Theatre Works of Leonard Bernstein* (Burlington, VT: Ashgate, 2011), 7-42.

35. Burton, 130.

36. Burton, 198, 208-9.

37. Both of which were made into critically acclaimed films in 1956 and 2008 respectively.

38. *Mad Men* premiered in 2007 and as of this writing is in the midst of its fifth season.

39. Incidentally, Aaron Copland composed the score for *The City*.

40. Quoted in Smith, 48.

41. For a more detailed discussion of *Trouble in Tahiti*'s connection to Blitzstein and Brecht, see Smith, 44-47.

42. Junior is unseen in the opera but is shown briefly in a 2003 BBC/Opus Arte DVD adaptation. See Carol Oja, "Leonard Bernstein: *Trouble in Tahiti* (Review)," *American Music* 23:4 (Winter 2005), 526-28.

43. In fact, Burton points out that in an early draft of the opera, Sam's wife was named "Jennie" after Bernstein's own mother and was changed to "Dinah" because the latter was more singable (Burton, 223).

44. Smith, 49.

45. For more on Bernstein's use of pastiche to suggest New York in the 1930s, see Smith, 79-90.

46. Katherine Baber, "Leonard Bernstein's Jazz: Musical Topic and Cultural Resonance" (Ph.D. diss., Indiana University, 2011), 177. For more on the political implications of both *Trouble in Tahiti* and *Wonderful Town*, see Baber, 171-87.

Chapter 2

1. Leonard Bernstein, "Statement: Conducting Versus Composing," in *Findings* (New York: Simon & Schuster, 1982), 103.

2. Paul Laird, *Leonard Bernstein: A Guide to Research* (New York: Routledge, 2002), 39n4.

3. Laird, 13-14.

4. Bernstein, 50.

5. For a concise, yet very useful summary of Bernstein's musical language, see Laird, 13-44.

6. The latter of whom went on to compose incidental music for several plays including Tennessee Williams's *The Glass Menagerie* (1944).

7. Barry Seldes, *Leonard Bernstein: The Political Life of an American Musician* (Berkeley: University of California Press, 2009), 19. Copland was not a member of the Group, but was an important collaborator during the Group's existence in that his studio served as one of their first meeting areas and his efforts to establish a new American music inspired the Group towards a similar movement in American theater. (Howard Pollack, *Aaron Copland: The Life and Work of an Uncommon Man* [Champaign-Urbana: University of Illinois Press, 2000], 258-59.)

8. David Thomson, "An Actor Prepares" in *On the Waterfront*, ed. Joanna E. Rapf (Cambridge: Cambridge University Press, 2003), 87.

9. Richard Schickel, *Kazan: A Biography* (New York: Harper Collins, 2005), 11.

10. Thomson, 87.

11. Robert Lewis, *Method—Or Madness?* (New York: Samuel French Inc., 1958), 15.

12. See for instance Elizabeth A. Wells, *West Side Story: Cultural Perspectives on an American Musical* (Lanham, MD: Scarecrow Press, 2011). 39-41.

13. Strasberg was famous for his svengali-like hold over actors, as Kazan recalled, "He carried with him the aura of a prophet, a magician, a witch doctor, a psychoanalyst, and a feared father of a Jewish home. . . . Everything in camp revolved around him. . . . He did this not only by his superior knowledge but by the threat of his anger" (Quoted in Thomson, 88). During filming of *Viva Zapata!* (1952) Kazan intentionally instigated a sense of suspicion between Marlon Brando and Anthony Quinn (the two played brothers in the film) that endured between the actors for the next ten years (Thomson, 103).

14. Quoted in Thomson, 89.

15. The chart is reproduced in *Method—Or Madness?* as a foldout insert in Chapter 2 between pages 34-35.

16. Lewis, 28.

17. Lewis, 35.

18. See Helen Smith, "*Peter Grimes* and Leonard Bernstein: An English Fisherman and His Influence on an American Eclectic," *Tempo* 60:235 (January 2006), 22-30.

19. Copland wrote scores for *The City* (1939), *Of Mice and Men* (1939), *Our Town* (1940), *The North Star* (1943), *The Cummington Story* (1945), *The Red Pony* (1949), *The Heiress* (1949), and *Something Wild* (1961). "New England Countryside" and "Sunday Traffic" from *The City*, "Barley Wagons" and "Threshing Machines" from *Of Mice and Men*, and "Grovers Corners" from *Our Town* comprise *Music for Movies* (1943). Excerpts from *Something Wild* are heard in *Music for a Great City* (1964) and "Song of the Guerrillas" (1943; lyrics by Ira Gershwin) for baritone solo, TTBB, and piano derives from *The North Star*. In addition *Our Town*, *The Red Pony*, and *The Heiress* have been fashioned into orchestral suites. For more complete information on Copland's film scores, please see Pollack, 558. For a fine representative recording of Copland's scores, please consult *Copland: Music for Films* featuring the St. Louis

Symphony conducted by Leonard Slatkin (RCA Victor Red Seal 09026-61699-2, 1994).

20. Humphrey Burton, *Leonard Bernstein* (New York: Doubleday, 1994), 236.

21. Elizabeth B. Crist, *Music for the Common Man: Aaron Copland During the Depression and War* (New York: Oxford University Press, 2005), 100.

22. See Neil Lerner, "Copland's Music of Wide Open Spaces: Surveying the Pastoral Trope in Hollywood," *Musical Quarterly* 85:3 (Fall 2001), 477-515.

23. Aaron Copland, *The Red Pony*: Film for Orchestra (New York: Boosey and Hawkes, 1951), 3.

24. Leo Braudy, "'No Body's Perfect': Method Acting and 50s Culture," *Michigan Quarterly Review* 35:1 (Winter 1996), 215n14.

25. Crist, 113.

26. Crist, 114-15.

27. Quoted in Lynn Garafola, "Making an American Dance: *Billy the Kid, Rodeo*, and *Appalachian Spring*," in *Aaron Copland and His World*, ed. by Carol J. Oja and Judith Tick (Princeton: Princeton University Press, 2005), 130.

28. Aaron Copland, *Billy the Kid*: Ballet Suite (New York: Boosey and Hawkes, 1941), 1.

29. Crist, 125.

30. Copland, *Billy the Kid*, 2-3.

31. Quoted in Garafola, 130-31.

32. Copland, *Billy the Kid*, 92.

33. www.imdb.com/title/tt0913761/. Last consulted 26 May 2012.

34. In addition, because Koussevitzky premiered the work, Bernstein would have been even more intimately familiar with the piece. One could argue a connection exists between the nostalgia inherent in Barber's music and Agee's text (see for instance Benedict Taylor, "Nostalgia and Cultural Memory in Barber's *Knoxville: Summer of 1915*," *Journal of Musicology* 25:3 [Summer 2008], 211-29) and the first appearance of Bernstein's Dignity theme; its simplicity, modal inflections, and melodic contour suggest longing for a time and place before Terry came under Johnny Friendly's control.

35. Honegger presents this material throughout the third movement, particularly from Rehearsal 13 until the end of the movement.

36. Arthur Honegger, Symphony No. 5 "Di tre re" (Paris: Éditions Salabert, 1951), 50.

37. Honegger, Symphony No. 5, 51.

38. Dmitri Shostakovich, Symphony No. 5 (New York: Leeds Music Corporation, 1945), 3.

39. Helen Smith also connected this movement with "A Boy Like That" from *West Side Story* when Anita lashes out at Maria (Smith, 27, especially Ex. 3a and 3b).

40. Benjamin Britten, Sea Interlude No. 4 "Storm" from the opera *Peter Grimes*, Op. 33a (New York: Boosey and Hawkes, 1945), 52.

41. Britten, Interlude No. 1 "Dawn," 1.

42. For instance, Keller, 82 and Burton, 236.

43. "Opera's New Face," *Time* 51:7 (16 February 1948), 63.

44. Burton, 237.

45. Quoted in Jack Gottlieb, "The Music of Leonard Bernstein: A Study of Melodic Manipulations" (D.M.A. diss., University of Illinois, 1964), 232.

46. Lewis, 17.

47. Helen Smith, *There's a Place for Us: The Musical Theatre Works of Leonard Bernstein* (Burlington, VT: Ashgate, 2011), 15, 18-19.

48. Anthony Bushard, "He Could've Been a Contender!: Thematic Integration in Leonard Bernstein's Score for *On the Waterfront*," *Journal of Film Music* 2:1 (Fall 2007), 48n22. This analysis and the ways in which I demonstrate how Bernstein derives themes in both Chapter 2 and Chapter 5 are in many ways influenced by Arnold Schoenberg's concept of the *Grundgestalt*. The term *Grundgestalt* (generally translated as "basic shape") originated during Schoenberg's early attempts at codifying his twelve-tone theory. According to Schoenberg, the basic shape is the fundamental motive that affects and governs musical events in a piece. He viewed themes, variations, and other structural entities as manifestations of the *Grundgestalt*. These "events" were usually considered thematic, but there is nothing intrinsic in the theory that confines it to pitch configurations. Furthermore, Schoenberg witnessed this phenomenon in his studies of the music of Bach, Beethoven, Brahms, and Wagner and therefore found justification for his emerging compositional theories as a continuation of that tradition. While the drama is the force that guides Bernstein to make musical decisions regarding this score, the way in which he manipulates (yet maintains) the basic shape(s) of important motives is consistent both with Schoenberg's principle of the *Grundgestalt* and with the cinematic narrative. For a good introduction to the concept of *Grundgestalt* see Patricia Carpenter, "*Grundgestalt* as Tonal Function," *Music Theory Spectrum* 5 (1983), 15-38 and David Epstein, *Beyond Orpheus: Studies in Musical Structure* (Princeton: Princeton University Press, 1979), 17-33.

49. Gottlieb, 188. For Gottlieb "musical concatenation" is another name for a musical process in which a theme "relates indirectly to a primary source through a series of linkages each dependent on the other" (Gottlieb, 151). For the rest of his analysis of the Symphonic Suite from *On the Waterfront*, see Gottlieb, 181-87.

50. Quoted in Gottlieb, 232.

51. Thomson, 96. Thomson goes on to mention that Kazan compared Stanley to Terry throughout his Production Notebook.

52. Bernstein appears to have based the dates in his log on his datebooks and written the entire "Log" at about the time that *West Side Story* opened (see Arthur Lurents, *Original Story By: A Memoir of Broadway and Hollywood* [New York: Alfred A. Knopf, 2000], 347 and Laird, 241). Portions of this section concerning *On the Waterfront*'s connection with *West Side Story* first appeared in Anthony Bushard, "From *On the Waterfront* to *West Side Story*, Or There's Nowhere Like Somewhere" in *Studies in Musical Theatre* 3:1 (August 2009), 61-75.

53. Bernstein (1982), 144-45.

54. Stephen Lias, "A Comparison of Leonard Bernstein's Incidental Music for the Film *On the Waterfront* and the Subsequent *Symphonic Suite* from

the Film, and an Original Composition—'Music for Theater'," (D.M.A. diss., Louisiana State University, 1997), 82-83.

55. David Bowman, "Bernstein: Songs from *West Side Story*," *Music Teacher* 71 (July 1992), 21.

56. Of course as demonstrated in the preceding section these same intervals factor prominently in the primary motivic material of *On the Waterfront*. Referring back to Ex. 2.6 and 2.7, the minor second and perfect fourth comprise the Pain motive (Ex. 2.6), which itself derives from the portion of the Dignity theme (2.7) that contains a tritone.

57. Leonard Bernstein, *West Side Story*, Full Orchestral Score (New York: Boosey and Hawkes, 1994), 6.

58. Leonard Bernstein, *West Side Story*, Piano/Vocal Score (New York: Boosey and Hawkes, 2000), 90.

59. Bernstein (2000), 163.

60. Joseph Peter Swain, *The Broadway Musical: A Critical and Musical Survey* (New York: Oxford University Press, 1990), 208.

61. Geoffrey Block, *Enchanted Evenings: The Broadway Musical from* Show Boat *to Sondheim* (New York: Oxford University Press, 1997), 260.

62. A further parallel could be drawn here between this scene and one in *On the Waterfront* following Terry's confession to Edie about his role in her brother Joey's death. She strikes Terry over and over, warns him saying, "I didn't say I didn't love you, I said stay away from me!" and relents as they embrace.

63. Swain, 224.

64. Bernstein (2000), 71.

65. Bernstein (2000), 211.

Chapter 3

1. Douglas T. Miller and Marion Nowak, *The Fifties: The Way We Really Were* (Garden City, NY: Doubleday, 1975), 3-4.

2. Miller and Nowak, 5-6.

3. Norman Vincent Peale, *The Power of Positive Thinking* (New York: Prentice-Hall, 1952), 124.

4. Samuel A. Stouffer, *Communism, Conformity, and Civil Liberties: A Cross-Section of the Nation Speaks Its Mind*, (Garden City, NY: Doubleday, 1955), 158-159.

5. Stouffer, 158.

6. Stouffer, 161-64.

7. Stouffer, 69.

8. Ellen Schrecker, *The Age of McCarthyism: A Brief History with Documents*, 2nd ed. (New York: Bedford/St. Martin's, 2002), 121.

9. Richard Hofstadter, *The Paranoid Style in American Politics and Other Essays* (New York: Knopf, 1966; Cambridge: Harvard University Press, 1996), 4.

10. Quoted in Hofstadter, 7.

11. Quoted in Hofstadter, 8-9.

12. Quoted in Schrecker, 125.

13. See Albert Fried, ed., *McCarthyism: The Great American Red Scare: A Documentary History* (New York: Oxford University Press, 1997), 25.

14. Hofstadter, 45-46.

15. For more on this subject see Larry Ceplair and Steven Englund, *The Inquisition in Hollywood: Politics and the Film Community, 1930-1960* (Garden City, NY: Anchor Press, 1980).

16. Ceplair and Englund, 286. The other nine witnesses who were cited with contempt (and comprised with Lawson the Hollywood Ten) are: Dalton Trumbo, Albert Maltz, Alvah Bessie, Samuel Ornitz, Herbert Biberman, Edward Dmytryk, Adrian Scott, Ring Lardner, Jr., and Lester Cole.

17. Quoted in Schrecker, 243. The statement's opening—and most important part—reads, "We will not knowingly employ a Communist or a member of any party or group which advocates the overthrow of the Government of the United States by force or by illegal or unconstitutional methods."

18. See Humphrey Bogart, "I'm No Communist," *Photoplay* 32:4 (March 1948), 53, 86-87.

19. Ceplair and Englund, 371.

20. Quoted in Schrecker, 69-70.

21. Quoted in Miller and Nowak, 131-32.

22. Quoted in Miller and Nowak, 130.

23. Gay Talese, "Gray-Flannel-Suit Men at Bat," *New York Times Magazine* (30 March 1958), 15, 17.

24. David Riesman, *The Lonely Crowd: A Study of the Changing American Character* (New Haven: Yale University Press, 1950), 7-8.

25. Riesman, 9-15.

26. Riesman, 19-22. Of course, as is the case with any such study, the actual lines of demarcation between types are not as clear as the study may suggest. Riesman admits that all human action is inner-directed, in that it is motivated and it is at the same time other-directed because its socialization depends on others. Moreover, no particular group is immune to the influences or opinions of the other group(s). In addition, similarities exist between different groups at different growth phases. Tradition-directed and other-directed individuals both rely on the opinions of others to shape their social development. However, the former depends solely on the signals received from family members within a tight unit and is therefore "culturally monotone." The latter relies on a vast array of different messages from a myriad of sources that must be deciphered at a fast pace. Finally, Riesman warns that an inherent problem in the S-curve is that one cannot know if the current phase is an arc in some other curve (Riesman, 25-27). Yet, one could argue convincingly that even in 2012, other-direction remains the dominant method of socialization.

27. For instance, construction of new single-family homes rose from 114,000 in 1944 to 1,692,000 in 1950 as a result of both programs (See Kenneth T. Jackson, *Crabgrass Frontier: The Suburbanization of the United States* [New York: Oxford University Press, 1985], 233-34). Jackson also argued

(219-30) that the Public Housing Act of 1937 was another factor that helped precipitate the suburban housing boom.

28. Jackson, 235.

29. Penn Kimball, "'Dream Town'—Large Economy Size," *New York Times Magazine* (14 December 1952), 36, 38.

30. Quoted in Miller and Nowak, 135.

31. Austin C. Wehrwein, "Crab Grass, Taxes and Tension Breeding Ailments in Suburbs," *New York Times* (8 August 1959), 1, 36-37.

32. Riesman, 84. As Riesman details, "progressive education," the dominant mode of education in the postwar United States, began as a quest to break down the walls between students erected in an inner-directed, intellectually stimulating curriculum. Rather, progressive education honed in on the many-sided, individual strengths of a child besides academic acumen. Young children became acclimated to school through play and instructors learned to be more aware of a student's social skills than with scholarly development. Progressive education even considered the arrangement and enhancement of the classroom. Boys and girls sat together and were further arranged by assumed peer pairings. Desks were often movable and usually the class took the form of a circle. Moreover, the walls were decorated with each other's art projects or posters from group studies in history. However, in its culmination, the style ceased to be progressive as people became more other-directed. In fact, what once was intended to emphasize one's individuality actually obscured it in favor of a group acceptance. For instance, children sacrificed individual identity through alphabetical seating by last name for a heterogeneous collective. The paintings, while seemingly honoring the creative spirit and downplaying traditional modes of evaluation, merely reinforced those modes by suggesting, "Mirror, mirror on the wall, who is fairest of all?" Even though the portraits showed vast imaginative potential at a young age, Riesman cautions that the school remained a place where fantasy must be abandoned for reality. Such use of the imagination fades by the teenage years. Only an assimilation of "taste and interest," witnessed in those early paintings, remained. The realism that took over manifested itself most noticeably in progressive education and in the stories the student read in later elementary years in which, "Caesar and Pompeii are replaced by visits to stores and dairies, by maps from *Life*, and the *Weekly Reader*" (Riesman, 60-62).

33. Miller and Nowak, 344.

34. Quoted in Rob Latham, "Subterranean Suburbia: Underneath the Smalltown Myth in the Two Versions of *Invaders from Mars*," *Science Fiction Studies* 22:2 (July 1995), 198-208.

35. "The Facts About A-Bomb 'Fall Out'," *Reader's Digest* 69:398 (June 1955), 24.

36. Richard Wilson, "Atomic Weapons . . . Will Save Money—They May Stop War," *Look*, 10 October 1950, 33-34. The article went on to point out that one atomic weapon costs five million dollars and if deployed in a populous area could create 100 million dollars in property damage and kill 25,000 people and "permanently disable" just as many for a cost of 100 dollars per casualty. On the other hand a conventional explosive device (5000 dollars each) activated in that same area would affect 200 people of which only 25 would be killed.

The authors of the article deduce that 1000 conventional bombs would be needed to inflict the same devastation that one atomic weapon could cause and at many hundreds of times the cost of delivering the atomic device.

37. John J. Balderston, Jr. and Gordon W. Hewes, *Atomic Attack—A Manual For Survival* (Culver City, CA: Murray and Gee, Inc., 1950), 26-27.

38. Quoted in Miller and Nowak, 54.

39. Edward Teller and Albert Latter, "The Compelling Need For Nuclear Tests," *Life* 44:6 (10 February 1958), 64-66, 69-72.

Chapter 4

1. For instance, the Motion Picture Alliance distributed a publication by Ayn Rand entitled *Screen Guide for Americans*. The pamphlet served as a guide to screenwriters concerning "appropriate" material. The booklet offered chapter titles like, "Don't Deify the Common Man," "Don't Smear Success," and "Don't Glorify Failure." In addition, this development manifested itself in several anti-Communist films that bordered on propaganda such as *I Was a Communist for the FBI* (1951), *The Steel Fist* (1952), and *My Son John* (1952). (See Douglas T. Miller and Marion Nowak, *The Fifties: The Way We Really Were* [Garden City, NY: Doubleday, 1975], 317-18.)

2. Miller and Nowak, 319.

3. Before 1952, the major production companies managed every facet of filmmaking from its creation, to its dissemination to theaters, and to the theaters that presented the films. They negotiated this model through actual ownership of a theater or some other contractual obligation on the part of the theater. Therefore, this guaranteed the studios that a set amount of films would reach the screen despite quality resulting in huge profits during the 1930s and 1940s. However, what was a stable market for the studio executives was considered a monopoly by the U.S. government. After a series of court battles beginning in 1938, the Supreme Court found in favor of the Justice Department and ordered the studios to rid themselves of theater ownership and from any sort of negotiation with theaters.

4. Jack C. Ellis and Virginia Wright Wexman, *A History of Film*, 5th ed. (Boston: Allyn and Bacon, 2002), 355.

5. Kenneth R. Hey, "Ambivalence as a Theme in *On the Waterfront* (1954): An Interdisciplinary Approach to Film Study," in *Hollywood as Historian: American Film in a Cultural Context*, ed. Peter C. Rollins (Lexington: University Press of Kentucky, 1983), 162. For a more detailed account of Kazan and Miller's work on *The Hook*, see Richard Schickel, *Kazan: A Biography* (New York: HarperCollins, 2005), 221-35.

6. Brian Neve, *Elia Kazan: The Cinema of an American Outsider* (London: I. B. Tauris, 2009), 76-77.

7. Also accompanying them during their meeting with Cohn was Miller's new love interest, Marilyn Monroe, whom Kazan and Miller introduced as their secretary, "Miss Baur" (Schickel, 228).

8. Brian Neve, "The 1950s: The Case of Elia Kazan and On the Waterfront," in *Cinema, Politics and Society in America*, eds. Philip Davies and Bri-

an Neve (Manchester, UK: Manchester University Press, 1981), 101-2. Richard Schickel speculates that given Brewer's connections to the FBI, his advice to adopt an anti-Communist perspective was designed to make Miller uncomfortable and expose him as a Communist (Schickel, 230-32).

9. Hey, 167-68. For a more in depth account of Schulberg's collaboration with Kazan, contribution to the film, and his intimate connection with the waterfront and its workers, see Dan Georgakas, "Schulberg on the Waterfront" in *On the Waterfront*, ed. by Joanna E. Rapf (Cambridge: Cambridge University Press, 2003), 40-60.

10. Georgakas, 41, 44.

11. Hey, 169.

12. Elia Kazan, *A Life*, (New York: Knopf, 1988), 499-500.

13. Thomas H. Pauly, *An American Odyssey: Elia Kazan and American Culture* (Philadelphia: Temple University Press, 1983), 187.

14. For a more complete account of Zanuck's contribution to the early drafts, see Rudy Behlmer, *Memo from Darryl F. Zanuck: The Golden Years at Twentieth-Century Fox* (New York: Grove Press, 1993), 224-30.

15. Schickel, 286-87.

16. Hey, 174.

17. William Baer, ed., *Elia Kazan: Interviews* (Jackson: University Press of Mississippi, 2000), 180.

18. Kazan, 518.

19. Kazan, 515.

20. Schickel, 289-90. The clinching part of the deal may have been when Spiegel allowed Brando to leave the set every day at 4:00 PM so that he could go across the river to Manhattan and meet with his psychoanalyst. In fact during close-up shots for the famous taxi scene, Rod Steiger was not actually speaking his lines to Brando because he had left for the day to see the analyst.

21. Hey, 173.

22. Young, 158-59.

23. Schickel, 296.

24. Young, 129.

25. Georgakas, 44. The workers received the same salary that they would have made working on the docks, with four hours per day minimum. Payment occurred each following day at noon. One particular day, the money was not there and the angry workers held assistant director Charlie Maguire over the water demanding compensation. Spiegel arrived shortly thereafter with the money and before any disasters occurred (Kazan, 521-22).

26. Hey, 176-77.

27. Jon Burlingame, "Leonard Bernstein and *On the Waterfront*: Tragic Nobility, A Lyrical Song, and Music of Violence," in *On the Waterfront*, ed. Joanna E. Rapf (Cambridge: Cambridge University Press, 2003), 125-26.

28. Kazan, 527.

29. Leonard Bernstein, "Interlude: Upper Dubbing, Calif.," in *The Joy of Music* (New York: Simon and Schuster, 1959), 66, 67. It is also quite possible that Bernstein empathized with the longshoremen's plight because it connected with the strong labor tradition on his mother's side of the family. Both Bernstein's mother Jennie and grandfather Samuel Resnick were involved in the

Lawrence, MA textile strikes in 1912 and as members of that guild, constituted an integral part of the Congress of Industrial Organization's (CIO) formation in the 1930s. (See Elizabeth L. Keathley, "Modernity and the Wife's Subjectivity: Bernstein's *Trouble in Tahiti*," *American Music* 23:2 [Summer 2005], 248-49.)

30. Burlingame, 127.

31. Bernstein, 67.

32. Burlingame, 128-30.

33. Bill Rosar, Personal E-mail Correspondence, 27 December 2006. However, despite Bernstein's suggestion of Skiles, Grau actually orchestrated the cue.

34. Bill Rosar, Personal E-Mail Correspondence, 15 April 2007.

35. Burlingame, 130-31.

36. Bernstein, 68.

37. Leonard Bernstein, "Notes Struck at Upper Dubbing: Tyro Film Composer Lauds Technicians' Marvels," *New York Times* (30 May 1954), X5.

38. Humphrey Burton, Leonard Bernstein (New York: Doubleday, 1994), 237.

39. Burlingame, 134, 144.

40. Burlingame, 144-46.

41. Neve (2009), 61-64. On 23 May 1951, Budd Schulberg gave similar testimony as Kazan in that he admitted membership, responsibilities, and also defended his reasons for joining the party. He stated that, "at the time I felt that the political issues that they seemed to be in favor of, mostly I recall the opposition to the Nazi [*sic*] and Mussolini and a feeling that something should be done about it" (Hey, 168). Schulberg left the party after they condemned drafts of his 1941 Hollywood exposé, *What Makes Sammy Run?* (Neve [1981], 102).

42. Neve (2009), 64-67.

43. For a detailed account of Bernstein's liberal political activities during the 1940s, see Barry Seldes, *Leonard Bernstein: The Political Life of an American Musician* (Berkeley: University of California Press, 2009), 25-52.

44. Quoted in Paul Boyer, "Leonard Bernstein: Humanitarian and Social Activist," in *Leonard Bernstein: American Original: How a Modern Renaissance Man Transformed Music and the World During His New York Philharmonic Years, 1943-1976*, Burton Bernstein, ed. (New York: Collins, 2008), 42.

45. Boyer, 39.

46. Seldes, 65-72. Moreover Seldes suggests that Bernstein's lawyer would have provided the composer's statement to the American Legion in order for Bernstein to be allowed by Columbia Pictures to begin composing his score for *On the Waterfront* (although his contract was with Spiegel's Horizon-American studio). Seldes also argues that Bernstein had already been blacklisted at CBS and because of interconnectivity between CBS and the New York Philharmonic led to a blacklist by the latter organization as well. Thus, the ultimate clearing of Bernstein's name and reputation in the passport scandal removed him from all blacklists, ultimately evidenced in his directorship of the New York Philharmonic in 1958. Seldes uses these blacklists going back to 1951—and his extended retreat to Mexico [to lay low?]—to surmise that the reason Bernstein took a conducting hiatus was not solely designed to allow him to finish compositional projects like *Trouble in Tahiti*, but also because he

wanted to escape further persecution. Based on the composer's FBI files, Seldes makes an interesting point but as Paul Laird notes (see Laird's review of Seldes's book in *Journal of the Society for American Music* 6:1 [February 2012], 127) because Bernstein was already planning to work on compositions before the supposed blacklist and because of the lack of evidence, such speculation on Seldes's part is impossible to prove.

47. See Joanna E. Rapf, "Selected Reviews and Commentary," in *On the Waterfront*, ed. Joanna E. Rapf (Cambridge: Cambridge University Press, 2003), 149-63.

48. Jeff Young, *Kazan: The Master Director Discusses His Films: Interviews with Elia Kazan* (New York: Newmarket, 1999), 118.

49. Lindsay Anderson, "The Last Sequence of *On the Waterfront*," *Sight and Sound* 24:3 (January/March 1955), 127-30.

50. Peter Biskind, "The Politics of Power in *On the Waterfront*," *Film Quarterly* 29:1 (Autumn 1975), 25-38. Biskind expanded upon this article in *Seeing is Believing: How Hollywood Taught Us to Stop Worrying and Love the Fifties* (New York: Pantheon, 1983).

51. For instance, Hey, 184.

52. David Riesman, *The Lonely Crowd: A Study of the Changing American Character* (New Haven: Yale University Press, 1950), 287.

53. Quoted in Seldes, 58.

Chapter 5

1. Budd Schulberg, "Foreword," in *On the Waterfront*, ed. Joanna E. Rapf (Cambridge: Cambridge University Press, 2003), xix.

2. Thomas H. Pauly, *An American Odyssey: Elia Kazan and American Culture* (Philadelphia: Temple University Press, 1983), 181.

3. William Hamilton, "*On the Waterfront*," *Film and TV Music* 14 (September-October 1954), 3. Yet Hamilton does imply that the music used for "The Accident" was supposed to be a repeat of the material that accompanies the opening scene of the film and Joey Doyle's death. In fact the short score manuscript of the cue at the Library of Congress does not contain any music.

4. Boxes 293 and 1043 comprise all materials related to *On the Waterfront* in the Sony Music Library. According to an inventory of materials conducted on behalf of the Society for the Preservation of Film Music in 1987, the boxes contained the full score, orchestra parts, sketches, conductor's score, and an orchestral chart that provided the breakdown of orchestra members required per cue (Bill Rosar, Personal E-mail Correspondence, 8 September 2010). However after personally examining the contents of those boxes in August 2011, all that remains from the above list is the conductor parts (which are essentially an annotated copy of Bernstein's Library of Congress short score). After extensive personal and e-mail communication with Raul Perez (Senior VP, Sony Pictures Entertainment, Music Administration) and Rod Davis (VP, Sony Pictures Entertainment, Music Affairs Group), they confirmed that the other materials have gone missing. As of this writing they are still trying to locate the missing materials.

5. Of course the score exists in another format, namely Bernstein's *On the Waterfront*: Symphonic Suite from the Film (New York: Boosey & Hawkes, 1955). Much of what Bernstein composed for the film remains intact (although there are some interesting omissions), albeit drastically reordered into a one-movement tone poem in which the film score's main title music serves as a sort of *ritornello* throughout the work. For a detailed comparison of the two scores one should consult Stephen Lias, "A Comparison of Leonard Bernstein's Incidental Music for the Film *On the Waterfront* and the Subsequent *Symphonic Suite* from the Film, and an Original Composition—'Music for Theater'," (D.M.A. diss., Louisiana State University, 1997). While much of Lias's study renders superfluous a detailed comparison of the two scores in this analysis, his musical examples were transcribed without consulting Bernstein's sketches at the Library of Congress and therefore do not take into consideration any potential differences between the full score of the film (orchestrated by Grau and Skiles) or suite. Such a study would prove to be quite useful but since the full film score is still missing (as of 31 July 2012), is sadly impossible.

6. Besides Hamilton's 1954 study and Lias's 1997 doctoral document, no sources provide any substantial musical analysis of Bernstein's score. Hans Keller ("*On the Waterfront*," *The Score and I.M.A. Magazine* 12 [June 1955], 81-84) touted Bernstein's score as among the best ever composed, even citing it as a perfect "synthesis" between German post-Romanticism and contemporary modernism, but refrained from musical analysis in favor of philosophical commentary. More recently (and referenced in Chapter 4) Jon Burlingame provided valuable "behind the scenes" commentary regarding Bernstein's decision to collaborate with Kazan and his experiences in Hollywood, but his musical discussion does not elevate the reader's understanding of the music beyond the level expected from program notes.

7. Jack Gottlieb, "The Music of Leonard Bernstein: A Study of Melodic Manipulations" (D.M.A. diss., University of Illinois, 1964), 10. Besides *On the Waterfront*, Gottlieb mentions: Symphony No. 1 "Jeremiah" (horn duet), *Facsimile* (oboe), Symphony No. 2 "Age of Anxiety" (clarinet duet), *Serenade* (violin), *Fancy Free* (snare drum [although "Big Stuff" that precedes is a vocal solo]), *Trouble in Tahiti* (clarinet), and Symphony No. 3 "Kaddish" (speaker). Helen Smith also notes this phenomenon in her study of Bernstein's musical theater works, specifically in the opening of *On the Town* and adds *Mass* (soprano and percussion) to Gottlieb's list (Helen Smith, *There's a Place for Us: The Musical Theatre Works of Leonard Bernstein* [Burlington, VT: Ashgate, 2011], 20).

8. In fact, Bernstein used as a tempo marking in the Symphonic Suite "Andante (with dignity)." The use of parentheses differs from the same marking found in the short score for the film: Andante, With Dignity.

9. Joanna E. Rapf, "Introduction: 'The Mysterious Way of Art': Making a Difference in *On the Waterfront*," in *On the Waterfront*, ed. Joanna E. Rapf, (Cambridge: Cambridge University Press, 2003), 13. Emphasis is Kazan's.

10. Leonard Bernstein Collection, Music Division, Library of Congress, "Waterfront"/Rough Sketches: "Waterfront Song," Typed lyric sheet with annotations in pencil; p. [14] yellow legal.

11. Leonard Bernstein Collection, Music Division, Library of Congress, "Waterfront"/Rough Sketches, "Waterfront Song," Piano-vocal score/sketch in pencil; p. [22-23].

12. Keller, 82.

13. In the score the second timpani represents the first point of imitation and the first timpani answers in measure 7 followed by the drums in measure 13. The entrances are stacked on top of each other in Ex. 5.5 for spatial considerations. In addition, the cymbal tremolo and crescendo in m. 19 has been omitted. Interestingly, although the piano is audible on the soundtrack doubling the second timpani in mm. 1-7, it is not notated in either the short score or the conductor part. Bernstein does indicate the piano in the Symphonic Suite so the piano must have been a late addition to the score at the recording session.

14. The Pain theme derives its name from Bernstein's notes for the Symphonic Suite in which he referred to the music as "a tugging, almost spastic motive of pain." Lias also refers to the theme similarly in his thesis.

15. Jeff Young, *Kazan: The Master Director Discusses His Films: Interviews with Elia Kazan* (New York: Newmarket, 1999), 146-47.

16. The Pain motive refers to the cell derived from the tritone passage of the Dignity theme (see Chapter 2, Ex. 2.6) and comprises the first four notes of the Pain theme, which is the entire passage as demonstrated in Ex. 5.6.

17. Moreover silent film cue sheet anthologies and manuals included pieces like Grieg's "Morning Mood" in their list of pieces designed to suggest "nature." See for instance Edith Lang and George West, *Musical Accompaniment of Moving Pictures: A Practical Manual for Pianists and Organists and an Exposition of the Principles Underlying the Musical Interpretation of Moving Pictures* (Boston: Boston Music Company, 1920), 27. Another prominent film that employs the oboe in an idyllic setting is Herrmann's score for *The Trouble With Harry* (1955) in which he uses the oboe against the backdrop of the Vermont countryside.

18. Quoted in Kenneth Hey, "Ambivalence as a Theme in *On the Waterfront* (1954): An Interdisciplinary Approach to Film Study," in *Hollywood as Historian: American Film in a Cultural Context*, ed. Peter C. Rollins (Lexington: University Press of Kentucky, 1983), 170-71.

19. In Bernstein's short score for the film there are two versions of the "Scramble" cue. The original version staggers the material in Ex. 5.13 by an additional measure and uses the second half of the Love theme in mm. 44-45 instead of the passage in Ex. 5.14. Both examples 5.13 and 5.14 reflect the conductor part version housed at Sony, which conveys Bernstein's "Scramble (revised)" cue from his short score at the Library of Congress.

20. Hey, 178.

21. The film was referred to as *Waterfront* until very late in production when *On the* was added at the last minute (Schickel, 282). In addition, on the Conductor Parts the film is also referred to as "Waterfront."

22. In fact, an interesting comparison could be made between the lyrics for "A Quiet Girl" and Edie's virtuous reputation. Yet as the film progresses, we discover that—like Ruth Sherwood—Edie is anything but quiet.

23. Leonard Bernstein Collection, Music Division, Library of Congress, "With All My Heart," Piano-vocal score in ink on transparencies; 3p., Signed and dated: "7 June 1954," Note: lyric by Mitchell Parrish [*sic*].

24. The song was also recorded in 1954 by Eve Boswell and the Ron Goodwin Orchestra and is available (although not in the United States) on a 2009 Naxos compilation (8.120887) of *West Side Story,* a sampling of themes from the film conducted by Morris Stoloff (taken from the original scoring session), and a treatment of some of the film's themes by the Goodwin Orchestra.

25. The cue is preserved in the Sony Music Library as Cue 5-AA, "Wedding March."

26. In the theatrical version and VHS versions, the whistling is heard on the soundtrack. However, on the DVD, the scene remains, but the whistling is omitted, rendering audible only Terry's footsteps and ship noises in the distance. A similar phenomenon of paranoia realized through transferal of a theme from the non-diegetic to diegetic space occurs in *High Noon* (1952). Throughout Dimitri Tiomkin mines the "Ballad of High Noon" for the score's thematic material. In one of several sequences depicting the Miller Gang waiting for their leader, Frank Miller, one of the gang is heard playing the ballad's theme on the harmonica. In this instance Tiomkin implies that the ballad's account of Will Kane's (Gary Cooper) failures to raise a posse is not just background commentary, but exists in the narrative as well. For more on the affective power of diegetic music, see Claudia Gorbman, *Unheard Melodies: Narrative Film Music* (Bloomington: University Press of Indiana, 1987), 21-26.

27. Leonard Bernstein Collection, Music Division, Library of Congress, Notes for Cue VI-A "Accident." "B" and "C" refer to rehearsal numbers (likely in the missing conductor's full score) where "B" is the repeat of the Pain theme in the woodwinds (which was cut in the recorded "Accident" cue) and "C" denotes the Violence theme *tutti*.

28. Lias, 47.

29. See Bernstein, Symphonic Suite (1955), mm. 220-221.

30. See *Gunmen from Laredo* (1959), 45:28-47:02.

31. Bill Rosar, Personal E-mail Correspondence, 28 June 2012. *Gunmen from Laredo* is not the only film that bears blatant cribbing from *On the Waterfront* on Bakaleinikoff's behalf. *Screaming Mimi* (1958), a Gerd Oswald *film noir* featuring Anita Ekberg, features the Dignity theme as conveyed in "The Challenge" (a cue that was never used in *On the Waterfront*) for its opening scene (see for instance http://www.youtube.com/watch?v=3Lkw07C1pW8, last consulted 5 July 2012) and reportedly lifted other cues from *On the Waterfront* for the film (see http://movies.nytimes.com/person/80425/Mischa-Bakaleinikoff, last consulted 5 July 2012). After researching ASCAP's list of materials that incorporate Bernstein's music (see https://www.ascap.com/ace-title-search/index.aspx, last consulted 5 July 2012), besides *Gunmen from Laredo* and *Screaming Mimi, The Case Against Brooklyn* (1958), and *Duel on the Mississippi* (1955) are credited to Bakaleinikoff and were released by Columbia Pictures. Television shows *Naked City, Dan Raven,* and *Tightrope* are all listed on ASCAP for Bernstein as well, but it is not clear if any of those shows in-

cludes music from *On the Waterfront* (the same holds true for *The Case Against Brooklyn* and *Duel on the Mississippi*).

32. While Bernstein intended this synchronization in the short score (The word "Piledriver" is written in the staff of the percussion line.), and his wishes were maintained on the conductor part, the way in which he notated the rhythm is *not* how the passage is heard on the soundtrack. In his dissertation, Stephen Lias did notate the passage correctly, but spelled enharmonic notes differently than Bernstein and placed the passage within a 2/4 meter instead of the 2/2 that Bernstein intended. Therefore, the material in Ex. 5.30 is a synthesis between Lias's accurate rhythmic transcription and Bernstein's intended note spellings, meter, and measure numbers (reflected in both the short score and conductor part).

33. Furthermore, the pitch collection (013679) is one of only three of the fifty hexachords that contains three tritones. The other two hexachords are (012678) and the whole tone collection (02468t). The chord is also a set class of the famous "Petrushka" chord, although here the C major and F-sharp major chords are replaced by F major and B major.

34. Bernard Herrmann, for instance, often achieved a similar effect in *The Day the Earth Stood Still* (1951), when he associated the tuba and contra-bass tuba with Gort.

35. See especially mm. 1-4 of "The Dirge" in Bernstein, Symphony No. 2 "Age of Anxiety" (New York: Boosey and Hawkes, 1965, 1993), 50. Of course Berg also employs an arpeggiating tone row in his Violin Concerto and later employs the row as a vertical sonority creating a highly dissonant effect depicting the tragedy surrounding Manon Gropius's death.

36. Leonard Bernstein, Symphony No. 2 "Age of Anxiety" (1965, 1993).

37. For instance, Brahms's Symphony No. 4, 2nd movement, particularly mm. 88-102.

38. Young, 143.

39. Further, Bernstein indicates in his notes on the first page of Cue IX-A (Coda—Accident) in the Library of Congress short score to "Use VI-A (Accident). Truck headlight should coincide with Bar 69 ["Opening Shot to Scream"]. Bars 79 to end should remain ff sempre." He went on to note that the final measure (m. 98) of "Opening Shot to Scream" should be the first measure of "Coda—Accident."

40. Compare Ex. 5.37 to the Introduction of Arthur Honegger's *Le roi David*, especially the horn passages in mm. 22-23, which feature a pedal tone in the harps and cellos and similar quartal harmonies in the horns.

41. I use Bernstein's short score here because he indicates violas for the opening of the cue and brings them back in to accompany the violins at m. 12. However, the conductor part (orchestrated by Grau) indicates violins throughout the first twelve measures and does not list the violas at all despite the obvious timbral differences between mm. 1-6 (violas) and mm. 7-9 (violins) and their juxtaposition in m. 12. In addition, the conductor part neglects to maintain Bernstein's subdivision of 5/4 meter into 3+2 indicated in the short score.

42. Bernstein's expressive instruction was omitted on the conductor part. The heroic connotations of E-flat major are voluminous, but its association with Beethoven (Symphony No. 3 "Eroica," Piano Concerto No. 5 "Emperor"),

Mahler (Symphony No. 8 "For a Thousand" and the finale of Symphony No. 2 "Resurrection"), and Richard Strauss (*Ein Heldenleben*) is particularly noteworthy in relation to Bernstein, his score, and Terry's journey, which culminates with the film's closing frames accompanied by music in E-flat major.

43. According to Bernstein's sketches, he had originally planned to introduce the Love theme above the sustained texture (Ex. 5.42, m. 35) and completely forego the Dignity theme, extending the Love theme past where "Dead Pigeons" eventually ended (when Mac blows his whistle at the shapeup). Bernstein crossed these measures out and attached an amended version of the final twenty measures of "Dead Pigeons" as it was represented in the conductor part.

44. The excerpt in the Symphonic Suite comprises 337-367 (five measures after Rehearsal 31 through Rehearsal 33). There are only minor differences between "The Challenge" and its corresponding excerpt in the suite. At two measures after Rehearsal 32 in the suite, Bernstein indicates strings only whereas at the same place in the conductor part ("The Challenge," m. 10) the score calls for strings and horns. Moreover some of the measures written in 4/4 time in the conductor part were changed to 3/4 in the Suite.

45. For more on the musico-dramatic implications of diegetic sound, see David Neumeyer, "The Musical Function of Sound in Three Films by Alfred Hitchcock," in *Indiana Theory Review* 19:1-2 (Spring/Fall 1998), 13-33, in which Neumeyer analyzes the psychological impact of different sounds and the role of sound as music in *Lifeboat* (1944), *Rope* (1948), and *Rear Window* (1954).

46. The repeated measures were omitted from the final version of the score, thus the first notes one hears after Ex. 5.47, m. 40 is Ex. 5.48, m. 44.

47. Young, 124.

48. Brian Neve, "The 1950s: The Case of Elia Kazan and On the Waterfront," in *Cinema, Politics and Society in America*, eds. Philip Davies and Brian Neve (Manchester, UK: Manchester University Press, 1981), 113.

Afterword

1. Kenneth R. Hey, "Ambivalence as a Theme in *On the Waterfront* (1954): An Interdisciplinary Approach to Film Study," in *Hollywood as Historian: American Film in a Cultural Context*, ed. Peter C. Rollins (Lexington: University Press of Kentucky, 1983), 184.

2. Hey, 162.

3. Elmer Bernstein quoted in Jon Burlingame, "Leonard Bernstein and *On the Waterfront*: Tragic Nobility, A Lyrical Song, and Music of Violence," in *On the Waterfront*, ed. Joanna E. Rapf (Cambridge: Cambridge University Press, 2003), 142. Bernstein went on to say that, "[Its tremendous energy] energized the film. It lent a dignity to the love interest instead of trivializing it. And forgetting everything else, it was just superior music on its own." In addition, Burlingame summarizes additional positive criticism for the score in his concluding remarks (see Burlingame, 139-46).

4. Consider for instance Williams's use of the perfect fifth as a pervasive unifying intervallic cell in his score for *E.T.: The Extra-Terrestrial* (1982).

5. Leonard Bernstein, *West Side Story*, Piano/vocal score (New York: Boosey and Hawks, 2000), 163.

6. *On the Waterfront* DVD (Culver City, CA: Columbia Tristar Entertainment 78409, 2001), Chapter 25, 1:33:50-1:33-54. Also see Chapter 22 (1:21:06-1:21:15) after Terry and Edie find Charley's body. Edie states, "Terry I'm frightened, let's get outta here please. First Joey, and then Dugan, and now Charley, and ne[xt]. . . . Please Terry someplace where we can live in peace."

7. e.e. cummings, "A Poet's Advice to Students," reprinted in *e.e. cummings: A Miscellany*, ed. by G. J. Firmage (New York: Argophile Press, 1958), 13.

APPENDIX

A listing of *On the Waterfront* manuscript materials at the Leonard Bernstein Collection in the Music Division at the Library of Congress and in the Music Library at the Sony Pictures Music Division.

Film Score to *On the Waterfront*

I-A main title; Short score in pencil with ann. in red and blue pencil; 3 p., [2] leaves
Note: signed in ink on cover
I-B Opening shot to scream; After titles; Short score/sketch in pencil; 6 p. Time sheet and notes in pencil; [1] p., yellow legal
Blue Goon Blues; Short score with vocal in pencil; [2] p. Notes in pencil; [2] p.
[Untitled]; Short score in pencil; p. 4-5
I-C Bar (Radio music [library]); Title page in pencil, no music included; [2] p.
II-A Roof morning; Short score in pencil; 2 p.
II-B Scramble; Short score in pencil; 4 p. Time sheet and notes in pencil; [1] p., yellow legal
Scramble (revised); Short score in pencil; 3 p.
III-A Riot in church; Short score in pencil; 6 p. Time sheet and notes in pencil; [1] p., yellow legal
3A-Revision; Short score in pencil; [1] p.
IV-A Glove scene; Short score in pencil; 3 p.
IV-B Pigeons and beer; Roof II; Short score in pencil; 6 p.
IV B Insert; Short score in pencil with ann. in red and blue pencil; 3 p.; 12" x 14"
Note on top: "(bars 1-10 as is)"
4-C Juke Box; Short score in pencil; 2p.
Note: "5X" crossed out on t.p.
V-A/"Saloon love" [insert]; Short score in pencil; [1] p.; 12" x 14"
VI-A Accident; Title page in pencil, no music included, notes on 2nd p.; [2] p.
VI-B After sermon; Short score in pencil; 2p.
VII-A Roof love; Short score in pencil; 2p.
7-A/Final authentic ending [insert]; Short score in pencil, 2m.; [1] p., 12" x 14"
VII-C Confession scene; Short score in pencil; 2p.
Note: Changed from "VII-B," a note on t.p. indicates now as "Organ music"

VIII-A Kangaroo court; Short score in pencil; 2p.
VIII-B Cab and bedroom; Short score in pencil; 7 p. + crossed out p. 6 at end; Time sheet and notes in pencil; [1] p., yellow legal
IX-A Charley's murder; Short score in pencil; 2p.
9-AA/Bars 20 and 21 [insert]; Short score in pencil with ann. in red and blue pencil, 2m.; [1] p., 12" x 14"
Note: page torn
Throwing the gun; Short score in pencil; 2p.
X-A (hallway, apartment, "dead pigeons"); Short score in pencil with annotations in red pencil; 5 p.
X-A (insert: p. 3, bar 34 + ff.); Short score in pencil; 2p., 12" x 14"
X-B Wild phrases; Melodic phrases and notes in pencil; [1] p.
XI-A The challenge; Short score in pencil; 3 p.
XI-B The fight; Short score in pencil; 3 p.
XI-C Terry unconscious; Short score in pencil; 3 p. On t.p.: "For Marlin Skiles"
XI-D The walk and end title; Short score in pencil; 2 p. On t.p.: "Gil Grau"
With all my heart; Piano-vocal score in ink on transparencies; 3 p. Signed and dated: "7 June 1954"
Note: lyric by Mitchell Parrish [*sic*]

"Waterfront"/Rough sketches; Sketches in pencil; [34] p., [15] items in total; Most items untitled, but titled and other works include:

Waterfront song; Typed lyric sheet with ann. in pencil; p. [14], yellow legal
[Tally of timings]; Notes in pencil; p. [15]
Hallway; Sketch in pencil; p. [17-18]
Cab brothers; Sketch in pencil; p. [20-21]
[Waterfront song]; Piano-vocal score/sketch in pencil; p. [22-23]
XI-A/XI-B; Sketch in pencil; p. [26-29]
XI-C (Terry unconscious); Sketch in pencil; p. [30-31]
XI-D (the walk); Sketch in pencil; p. [32-33]
Coda; Sketch in pencil, continuation of inside cover p. [2]; p.

Original manuscript (pencil) "Waterfront"; Original folder that contained above manuscript

Symphonic Suite from *On the Waterfront*; Full score in pencil on transparencies; 100p. Dated: "NewYork City, 4 July 1955, Hail Columbia!"

Conductor Part cues at the Sony Music Library listing reel/part number, cue title, total pages, total measures, and orchestrator (if given). Box 293 contained a small folder with conductor part cues while Box 1043 included a large folder with virtually every cue conductor part intact.

Large Folder
1A: Main Title; 2p. 19 mm. No orchestrator
1B: Opening Shot to Scream; 7p. 98 mm. Marlin Skiles
2A: Roof Morning; 2p. 35 mm. Gil Grau
2B: Scramble; 4p. 53 mm. Marlin Skiles
3A: Riot in Church (Rev. 4/19/54); 5p. 69 mm. Gil Grau
4A: Glove Scene; 3p. 38 mm. Marlin Skiles
4B: Pigeons and Beer (Rev. 4/20/54); 7p. 82 mm. Gil Grau
5A: Saloon Love; 2p. 25 mm. Gil Grau
5AA: Wedding March; 1p. 24 mm. Gil Grau
5B: Waterfront Love Theme; 3p. 42 mm. Gil Grau
5D: Blue Goon Blues; 3p. 33 mm. Gil Grau
6B: After Sermon; 2p. 18 mm. Marlin Skiles
7A: Roof 3; 2p. 23 mm. 1:29. Marlin Skiles
7C: Confession Scene; 2p. 30 mm. Gil Grau
8A: Kangaroo Court; 1p. 8 mm. Gil Grau
8B: Cab and Bedroom; 6p. 77 mm. Gil Grau
9A: Coda—Accident; 2p. 21 mm. Marlin Skiles
9B: Throwing the Gun; 2p. 24 mm. Gil Grau
10A: Dead Pigeons; 5p. 54 mm. Gil Grau
11A: The Challenge [Unused]; 2p. 31 mm. Gil Grau
11B: The Fight; 4p. 54 mm. Marlin Skiles
11C: Terry Unconscious; 2p. 17 mm. Marlin Skiles
11D: Walk and End Title; 3 p. 33 mm. Gil Grau

Small Folder: Each of these cues duplicate conductor part cues in the large folder, but in each case contain pencil markings that differ from the same cues in the large folder.

4A: Glove Scene; 3p. 38 mm. Marlin Skiles. "Waterfront Theme [Love theme] entire cue" marked in red pencil.
4B: Pigeons and Beer (Rev. 4/20/54); 7p. 82 mm. Gil Grau. "Waterfront Theme Starts at Bar 41 to end" marked in red pencil.
5A: Saloon Love; 2p. 25 mm. Gil Grau. "Waterfront Theme entire cue" marked in red pencil.
5B: Waterfront Love Theme; 3p. 42 mm. Gil Grau. "Fox Trot Arr." marked in red pencil.

7A: Roof 3; 2p. 23 mm. 1:29. Marlin Skiles. "Waterfront Theme entire cue" marked in red pencil.

8B: Cab and Bedroom; 6p. 77 mm. Gil Grau. "Waterfront Theme starts at Bar 49 to Bar 69 inc." marked in red pencil.

BIBLIOGRAPHY

Archival Materials

Bernstein, Leonard. *On the Waterfront*. Conductor Part. Culver City, CA: Sony Pictures, Music Library, Boxes 293 and 1043, 1954.

———. *On the Waterfront*. Short Score. Washington, D.C.: Leonard Bernstein Collection, Music Division, Library of Congress, 1954.

———. "'Waterfront' Rough Sketches: 'Waterfront Song'." Typed Lyric Sheet with Annotations in Pencil. Leonard Bernstein Collection, Music Division, Library of Congress, 1954.

———. "'Waterfront' Rough Sketches: 'Waterfront Song'." Piano-vocal Score/Sketch in Pencil. Leonard Bernstein Collection, Music Division, Library of Congress, 1954.

———. "With All My Heart." Piano-vocal Score in Ink on Transparencies. Leonard Bernstein Collection, Music Division, Library of Congress, 1954.

Print Sources

Andersen, Thom. "Red Hollywood." In *Literature and the Visual Arts in Contemporary Society*, ed. Suzanne Ferguson and Barbara Groseclose, 141-96. Columbus: Ohio State University Press, 1985.

Anderson, Gillian B. *Film Music Bibliography I*. Hollywood, CA: Society for the Preservation of Film Music, 1995.

Anderson, Lindsay. "The Last Sequence of *On the Waterfront*." *Sight and Sound* 24:3 (January/March 1955), 127-30.

Baer, William, ed. *Elia Kazan: Interviews*. Jackson: University Press of Mississippi, 2000.

Baber, Katherine. "Leonard Bernstein's Jazz: Musical Topic and Cultural Resonance." Ph.D. diss., Indiana University, 2011.

Balderston, Jr., John J. and Gordon W. Hewes. *Atomic Attack—A Manual for Survival*. Culver City, CA: Murray and Gee, Inc., 1950.

Barber, Samuel. *Knoxville: Summer of 1915*. New York: G. Schirmer, 1949.

Bates, Harry. "Farewell to the Master." *Reel Future*, ed. by Forrest J. Ackerman and Jean Marie Stine, 134-74. New York: Barnes and Noble, 1994.

Beebe, John. "The Notorious Postwar Psyche." *Journal of Popular Film and Television* 18:1 (Spring 1990), 28-35.

Behlmer, Rudy. *America's Favorite Movies: Behind the Scenes*. New York: Frederick Ungar and Company, 1982.

———. *Memo from Darryl F. Zanuck: The Golden Years at Twentieth-Century Fox*. New York: Grove Press, 1993.

Bekeny, Amanda Kriska. "The Trumpet as a Voice of Americana in the Americanist Music of Gershwin, Copland, and Bernstein." D.M.A. diss., Ohio State University, 2005.

Bell, Daniel. *The End of Ideology: On the Exhaustion of Political Ideas in the Fifties*. Cambridge, MA: Harvard University Press, 1988.

Bernstein, Leonard. "Notes Struck at Upper Dubbing: Tyro Film Composer Lauds Technicians' Marvels." *New York Times*, 30 May 1954, X5.

———. *On the Waterfront*: Symphonic Suite from the Film. New York: Boosey and Hawkes, 1955.

———. *The Joy of Music*. New York: Simon and Schuster, 1959.

———. *The Infinite Variety of Music*. New York: Simon & Schuster, 1962.

———. *Findings*. New York: Simon & Schuster, 1982.

———. Symphony No. 1 "Jeremiah." New York: Boosey and Hawkes, 1943, 1992.

———. Symphony No. 2 "Age of Anxiety." New York: Boosey and Hawkes, 1965, 1993.

———. *West Side Story* (Full Orchestral Score). New York: Boosey and Hawkes, 1994.

———. *West Side Story* (Piano/Vocal Score). New York: Boosey and Hawkes, 2000.

——— and John LaTouche. "On the Waterfront." New York: J.J. Robbins, 1954.

Biskind, Peter. "The Politics of Power in *On the Waterfront*." *Film Quarterly* 29:1 (Autumn 1975), 25-38.

———. *Seeing is Believing: How Hollywood Taught Us to Stop Worrying and Love the Fifties*. New York: Pantheon, 1983.

Block, Geoffrey. *Enchanted Evenings: The Broadway Musical from* Show Boat *to Sondheim*. New York: Oxford University Press, 1997.

Bogart, Humphrey. "I'm No Communist." *Photoplay* 32:4 (March 1948), 52-53, 86-87.

Boggs, Joseph M. *The Art of Watching Films: A Guide to Film Analysis*. Menlo Park, CA: Benjamin/Cummings Publishing Company, 1978.

Booker, M. Keith. *Film and the American Left: A Research Guide*. Westport, CT: Greenwood Press, 1999.

———. *The Post-Utopian Imagination: American Culture in the Long 1950s*. Westport, CT: Greenwood Press, 2002.

Bordwell, David. *Making Meaning: Inference and Rhetoric in the Interpretation of Cinema*. Cambridge, MA: Harvard University Press, 1989.

———. *On the History of Film Style*. Cambridge, MA: Harvard University Press, 1997.

Bowman, David. "Bernstein: Songs from *West Side Story*." *Music Teacher* 71 (July 1992), 20-25.

Boyd, Timothy W. and Carolyn Higbie. "Not So Much New Deal as Old Howard: Leonard Bernstein and Aristophanes' *The Birds*." In *Leonard Bernstein: The Harvard Years 1935-1939*, ed. Claudia Swan, 80-89. New York: Eos Orchestra, 1999.

Boyer, Paul. "Leonard Bernstein: Humanitarian and Social Activist." In *Leonard Bernstein: American Original: How a Modern Renaissance Man Transformed Music and the World During His New York Philharmonic Years, 1943-1976*, ed. Burton Bernstein. New York: Collins, 2008, 35-53.

Braudy, Leo. "'No Body's Perfect': Method Acting and 50s Culture." *Michigan Quarterly Review* 35:1 (Winter 1996), 191-215.

Britten, Benjamin. Four Sea Interludes from the Opera *Peter Grimes*. New York: Boosey and Hawkes, 1945.

Brown, Royal S. *Overtones and Undertones: Reading Film Music*. Berkeley: University of California Press, 1994.

Buhler, James, Caryl Flinn, and David Neumeyer, eds. *Music and Cinema*. Hanover: University Press of New Hampshire, 2000.

Burlingame, Jon. "Leonard Bernstein and *On the Waterfront*: Tragic Nobility, A Lyrical Song, and Music of Violence." In *On the Waterfront*, ed. Joanna E. Rapf, 124-47. Cambridge: Cambridge University Press, 2003.

Burt, George. *The Art of Film Music*. Boston: Northeastern University Press, 1994.

Burton, Humphrey. *Leonard Bernstein*. New York: Anchor/Doubleday, 1994.

Burton, William Westbrook. *Conversations About Bernstein*. New York: Oxford University Press, 1995.

Bushard, Anthony "Fear and Loathing in Hollywood: Representations of Fear, Paranoia, and Individuality vs. Conformity in Selected Film Music of the 1950s." Ph.D. diss. University of Kansas, 2006.

———. "He Could've Been a Contender!: Thematic Integration in Leonard Bernstein's Score for *On the Waterfront*." *Journal of Film Music* 2:1 (Fall 2007), 43-62.

———. "From *On the Waterfront* to *West Side Story*, Or There's Nowhere Like Somewhere." *Studies in Musical Theatre* 3:1 (August 2009), 61-75.

Butler, Jeremy G. "*Viva Zapata*: HUAC and the Mexican Revolution." In *The Steinbeck Question: New Essays in Criticism*, ed. Donald R. Noble, 239-49. Troy, NY: Whitston Publishing, 1993.

Butterworth, Neil. *The American Symphony*. Butterfield, VT: Ashgate, 1998.

Byron, Stuart and Martin L. Rubin. "Elia Kazan: Interview." *Movie* 19 (Winter 1971/1972), 1-13.

Bywater, Tim and Thomas Sobchak. *Introduction to Film Criticism: Major Critical Approaches to Narrative Film*. New York: Longman, 1989.

Cameron, Ian, ed. *The Movie Book of Film Noir*. London: Studio Vista, 1992.

Cameron, Kenneth M. *America on Film: Hollywood and American History*. New York: Continuum, 1997.

Cameron, Norman. "The Paranoid Pseudo-Community." *American Journal of Sociology* 49 (1943), 32-38.

———. "The Paranoid Pseudo-Community Revisited." *American Journal of Sociology* 65 (1959), 52-58.

Carpenter, Patricia. "*Grundgestalt* as Tonal Function." *Music Theory Spectrum* 5 (1983), 15-38.

Ceplair, Larry and Steven Englund. *The Inquisition in Hollywood: Politics in the Film Community 1930-1960*. Garden City, NY: Anchor Press, 1980.

Chown, Jeffrey. "Visual Coding and Social Class in *On the Waterfront*." In *On the Waterfront*, ed. Joanna E. Rapf, 106-23. Cambridge: Cambridge University Press, 2003.

Christensen, Terry. *Reel Politics: American Political Movies from* Birth of a Nation *to* Platoon. New York: Basil Blackwell, 1987.

Clurman, Harold. *The Fervent Years*, 2nd ed. New York: Hill and Wang, 1957.

Cohen, Lola, ed. *The Lee Strasberg Notes*. New York: Routledge, 2010.

Combs, James. *Movies and Politics: The Dynamic Relationship*. New York: Garland, 1993.

Cook, Pam and Mieke Bernink, eds. *The Cinema Book,* 2nd ed. London: British Film Institute, 1999.

Copland, Aaron. Piano Variations. New York: Boosey and Hawkes, 1930, 1959.

———. *Billy the Kid*: Ballet Suite. New York: Boosey and Hawkes, 1941.

———. Piano Sonata. New York: Boosey and Hawkes, 1942.

———. *The Red Pony*: Film Suite for Orchestra. New York: Boosey and Hawkes, 1951.

Crist, Elizabeth B. *Music for the Common Man: Aaron Copland During the Depression and War*. New York: Oxford University Press, 2005.

Crist, Elizabeth B. and Wayne Shirley, eds. *The Selected Correspondence of Aaron Copland*. New Haven: Yale University Press, 2006.

Crowdus, Gary, ed. *The Political Companion to American Film*. Chicago: Lake View Press, 1995.

cummings, e.e. "A Poet's Advice to Students." Reprinted in *e.e. cummings: A Miscellany*, ed. G. J. Firmage. New York: Argophile Press, 1958.

Darby, William and Jack Du Bois. *American Film Music: Major Composers, Techniques, Trends, 1915-1990*. Jefferson, NC: McFarland and Company, Inc., 1990.

Davison, Annette. *Alex North's A Streetcar Named Desire: A Film Score Guide*. Lanham, MD: Scarecrow Press, 2009.

Donnelly, K.J, ed. *Film Music: Critical Approaches*. New York: Continuum International Publishing Group, 2001.

Draft. Harry S. Truman to Joseph R. McCarthy; McCarthy, Joseph; General File; PSF; Truman Papers. Student Research File: "President Truman's Confrontation With McCarthyism." Harry S. Truman Library.

Editorial. "Pro Patria Mori." *Nation*, 30 January 1960, 89-90.

Ellis, Jack C. and Virginia Wright Wexman. *A History of Film*, 5th ed. Boston: Allyn and Bacon, 2002.

Epstein, David. *Beyond Orpheus: Studies in Musical Structure*. Cambridge: Massachusetts Institute of Technology Press, 1979.

"The Facts About A-Bomb 'Fall-Out'," *Reader's Digest* 69:398 (June 1955), 22-24.

Fine, Irving. "Young America: Bernstein and Foss." *Modern Music* 22:3 (March-April 1945), 238-43.

Flinn, Caryl. *Strains of Utopia: Gender, Nostalgia, and Hollywood Film Music*. Princeton: Princeton University Press, 1992.

Fried, Albert, ed. *McCarthyism: The Great American Red Scare: A Documentary History*. Oxford: Oxford University Press, 1997.

Fuery, Patrick. *New Developments in Film Theory*. New York: St. Martin's Press, 2000.

Fuller, Linda K. "The Ideology of the 'Red Scare' Movement: McCarthyism in the Movies." In *Beyond the Stars: Themes and Ideologies in American Popular Film*, ed. Paul Loukides and Linda K. Fuller, 229-48. Bowling Green, OH: Bowling Green State University Popular Press, 1996.

Garafola, Lynn. "Making an American Dance: *Billy the Kid, Rodeo*, and *Appalachian Spring*." In *Aaron Copland and His World*, ed. Carol J. Oja and Judith Tick, 121-47. Princeton: Princeton University Press, 2005.

Garber, Marjorie and Rebecca L. Walkowitz, eds. *Secret Agents: The Rosenberg Case, McCarthyism, and Fifties America*. New York: Routledge, 1995.

Gargrave, Wayne Eric. "The Use of the Saxophone in the Dramatic Music of Leonard Bernstein: A Guide for Informed Performance." D.M.A. diss. University of North Carolina, Greensboro, 2006.

Gentry, Philip. "Leonard Bernstein's *The Age of Anxiety*: A Great American Symphony during McCarthyism." *American Music* 29:3 (Fall 2011), 308-31.

Georgakas, Dan. "Schulberg on the Waterfront." In *On the Waterfront*, ed. Joanna E. Rapf, 40-60. Cambridge: Cambridge University Press, 2003.

Gledhill, Christine and Linda Williams, eds. *Reinventing Film Studies*. London: Arnold Publishers, 2000.

Gorbman, Claudia. *Unheard Melodies: Narrative Film Music*. Bloomington: Indiana University Press, 1987.

Gordon, Eric A. *Mark the Music: The Life and Work of Marc Blitzstein*. New York: St. Martin's Press, 1989.

Gregory, Charles T. "The Pod Society Versus the Rugged Individualists." *Journal of Popular Film* 1 (Winter 1972), 3-14.

Gutman, David. "Bernstein on Record." *Gramophone* 69:819 (August 1991), 41-42.

Gwiazda, Ron. "Leonard Bernstein at Boston Latin School." In *Leonard Bernstein: The Harvard Years 1935-1939*, ed. Claudia Swan, 38-45. New York: Eos Orchestra, 1999.

Hamilton, William. "*On the Waterfront*." *Film and TV Music* 14 (September-October 1954): 3-14.

Hapgood, Elizabeth Reynolds, ed. and trans. *Stanislavski's Legacy: A Collection Of Comments on a Variety of Aspects of an Actor's Art and Life*, 2nd ed. New York: Theatre Art Books, 1968.

Healey, Dorothy Ray and Maurice Isserman. *California Red: A Life in the Communist Party*. Champaign-Urbana: University of Illinois Press, 1993.

Hendershot, Cyndy. *Paranoia, the Bomb, and 1950s Science Fiction Films*. Bowling Green, OH: Bowling Green State University Popular Press, 1999.

———. *Anti-Communism and Popular Culture in Mid-Century America*. Jefferson, NC: McFarland and Company, Inc., 2003.

Hey, Kenneth R. "*On the Waterfront*: Another Look." *Film and History* 9:4 (December 1979), 82-86.

———. "Ambivalence as a Theme in *On the Waterfront* (1954): An Interdisciplinary Approach to Film Study." In *Hollywood as Historian: American Film in a Cultural Context*, ed. Peter C. Rollins, 159-89. Lexington: University Press of Kentucky, 1983.

Hickman, Roger. *Reel Music: Exploring 100 Years of Film Music*. New York: W.W. Norton, 2006.

Hill, John and Pamela Church Gibson, eds. *American Cinema and Hollywood: Critical Approaches*. Oxford: Oxford University Press, 2000.

———. *Film Studies: Critical Approaches*. Oxford: Oxford University Press, 2000.

Hobermann, J. "Paranoia and the Pod People." *Sight and Sound* 4:5 (1994), 28-31.

Hofstadter, Richard. *The Paranoid Style in American Politics and Other Essays*. New York: Knopf, 1966; Cambridge, MA: Harvard University Press, 1996.

Honegger, Arthur. Symphony No. 5 "Di tre re." Paris: Éditions Salabert, 1951.

Huntley, John. "Music in Films." *The Musical Times* 98 (December 1957): 662-63.

Jackson, Kenneth T. *Crabgrass Frontier: The Suburbanization of the United States*. New York: Oxford University Press, 1985.

Jayne, Edward. "The Dialectics of Paranoid Form." *Genre* 11:1 (1978) 131-57.

Joseph McCarthy to Harry S. Truman, February 11, 1950; OF 3371: McCarthy, Joseph R.: Truman Papers. Student Research File: "President Truman's Confrontation With McCarthyism." Harry S. Truman Library.

Kalinak, Kathryn. *Settling the Score: Music and the Classical Hollywood Film*. Madison: University Press of Wisconsin, 1992.

Kaskowitz, Sheryl. "All in the Family: Brandeis University and Leonard Bernstein's 'Jewish Boston.'" *Journal of the Society for American Music* 3:1 (February 2009), 85-100.

Kazan, Elia. *Elia Kazan: A Life*. New York: Knopf, 1988.

Keathley, Elizabeth L. "Postwar Modernity and the Wife's Subjectivity: Bernstein's *Trouble in Tahiti*." *American Music* 23:2 (Summer 2005), 220-56.

Keller, Hans. "Leonard Bernstein: *On the Waterfront*." *The Score and I. M. A. Magazine*, no. 12 (June 1955): 81-84.

Kimball, Penn. "'Dream Town'—Large Economy Size." *New York Times Magazine*, 14 December 1952, 12, 36-43.

Kostelanetz, Richard, ed. *Aaron Copland: A Reader: Selected Writings 1923-1972*. New York: Routledge, 2004.

Laird, Paul. "The Influence of Aaron Copland on Leonard Bernstein." M.A. thesis, Ohio State University, 1982.

———. *Leonard Bernstein: A Guide to Research*. New York: Routledge, 2002.

Lang, Edith and George West. *Musical Accompaniment of Moving Pictures: A Practical Manual for Pianists and Organists and an Explanation of the Principles Underlying the Musical Interpretation of Moving Pictures*. Boston: The Boston Music Company, 1920.

Latham, Rob. "Subterranean Suburbia: Underneath the Smalltown Myth in the Two Versions of *Invaders from Mars*." *Science Fiction Studies* 22:2 (July 1995), 198-208.

Laurents, Arthur. *Original Story By: A Memoir of Broadway and Hollywood*. New York: Knopf, 2000.

Ledbetter, Steven, ed. *Sennets & Tuckets: A Bernstein Celebration*. Boston: Boston Symphony Orchestra, Inc., 1988.

Lee, Lance. "*On the Waterfront*: Script Analysis Conventional and Unconventional." In *On the Waterfront*, ed. Joanna E. Rapf., 61-84. Cambridge: Cambridge University Press, 2003.

Lerner, Neil. "Copland's Music of Wide Open Spaces: Surveying the Pastoral Trope in Hollywood." *Musical Quarterly* 85:3 (Fall 2001), 477-515.

Lewis, Robert. *Method—Or Madness?* New York: Samuel French, Inc., 1958.

Lias, Stephen. "A Comparison of Leonard Bernstein's Incidental Music for the Film *On the Waterfront* and the Subsequent *Symphonic Suite* from the Film, and an Original Composition: Symphony No. 1—"Music for Theater." D.M.A. diss., Louisiana State University, 1997.

Limbacher, James L, ed. *Film Music: From Violins to Video*. Metuchen, NJ: Scarecrow Press, 1974.

Lipschutz, Ronnie D. *Cold War Fantasies: Film, Fiction, and Foreign Policy*. Lanham, MD: Rowman and Littlefield, 2001.

MacDonald, Laurence E. *The Invisible Art of Film Music: A Comprehensive History*. New York: Ardsley House, 1998.

Massey, Drew. "Leonard Bernstein and the Harvard Student Union: In Search of Political Origins." *Journal of the Society for American Music* 3:1 (February 2009), 67-84.

McCarty, Clfford, ed. *Film Music I*. New York: Garland, 1989.

Meares, Russell. "The Secret, Lies and the Paranoid Process." *Contemporary Pyschoanalysis* 24 (1988), 650-66.

Meyer, Leonard B. *Emotion and Meaning in Music*. Chicago: University of Chicago Press, 1956.

Meyler, Bernadette A. "Composing (for a) Philosophical Comedy." In *Leonard Bernstein: The Harvard Years 1935-1939*, ed. Claudia Swan, 71-79. New York: Eos Orchestra, 1999.

Michener, James A. "While Others Sleep." *Reader's Digest* 71:426 (October 1957), 70-243.

Miller, Douglas T. and Marion Nowak. *The Fifties: The Way We Really Were*. Garden City, NY: Doubleday, 1977.

Mirowsky, John and Catherine E. Ross. "Paranoia and the Structure of Powerlessness." *American Sociological Review* 48 (1983), 228-39.

Motion Picture Association of America, Production Code Academy of Administration Records. Special Collections, Margaret Herrick Library, Motion Picture Arts and Sciences.

Murphy, Brenda. *Congressional Theatre: Dramatizing McCarthyism on Stage, Film, and Television*. Cambridge: Cambridge University Press, 1999.

Murray, Edward. *Ten Classic Films: A Re-Viewing*. New York: Frederick Ungar, 1978.

Neumeyer, David. "The Musical Function of Sound in Three Films by Alfred Hitchcock." *Indiana Theory Review* 19:1-2 (Spring-Fall 1998), 13-33.

Neve, Brian. "The 1950s: The Case of Elia Kazan and *On the Waterfront*." In *Cinema, Politics and Society in America*, eds. Philip Davies and Brian Neve, 97-118. Manchester, UK: Manchester University Press, 1981.

———. "On the Waterfront." *In The Movies as History: Visions of the Twentieth Century*, ed. David W. Ellwood, 105-13. Stroud, UK: Sutton Publishing, 2000.

———. "The Personal and the Political: Elia Kazan and *On the Waterfront*." In *On the Waterfront*, ed. Joanna E. Rapf., 20-39. Cambridge: Cambridge University Press, 2003.

———. "Elia Kazan's First Testimony to the House Committee on Un-American Activities, Executive Session, 14 January 1952." *Historical Journal of Film, Radio and Television* 25:2 (June 2005), 251-72.

———. *Elia Kazan: The Cinema of an American Outsider*. New York: I. B. Tauris, 2009.

O'Connor, John E. and Martin A. Jackson, eds. *American History/American Film: Interpreting the Hollywood Image*. New York: Continuum, 1988.

Oja, Carol J. "Leonard Bernstein: *Trouble in Tahiti* (Review)." *American Music* 23:4 (Winter 2005), 526-28.

———. "*Wonderful Town* and McCarthy Era Politics." *Prelude, Fugue, And Riffs* (Spring/Summer 2007), 6.

——— and Kay Kaufman Shelemay. "Leonard Bernstein's Jewish Boston: Cross-Disciplinary Research in the Classroom." *Journal of the Society forAmerican Music* 3:1 (February 2009), 3-33.

On the Waterfront. DVD. Culver City, CA: Columbia Tristar Entertainment 78409, 2001.

Pauly, Thomas H. *An American Odyssey: Elia Kazan and American Culture*. Philadelphia: Temple University Press, 1983.

Peale, Norman Vincent. *The Power of Positive Thinking*. New York: Prentice-Hall, 1952.

Perrine, Toni A. *Film and the Nuclear Age: Representing Cultural Anxiety*. New York: Garland, 1998.

Platt, David. *Celluloid Power: Social Film Criticism from* The Birth of a Nation *to* Judgment at Nuremberg. Metuchen, NJ: Scarecrow Press, 1992.

Pollack, Howard. *Aaron Copland: The Life and Work of an Uncommon Man*. Champaign-Urbana: University of Illinois Press, 1999.

———. "Copland and the Prophetic Voice." In *Aaron Copland and His World*, ed. Carol J. Oja and Judith Tick, 1-14. Princeton: Princeton University Press, 2005.

Prall, David. *Aesthetic Judgment*. New York: Thomas Y. Crowell, 1929.

Pratt, Ray. *Projecting Paranoia: Conspiratorial Visions in American Film*. Lawrence: University Press of Kansas, 2001.

Prendergast, Roy M. *Film Music: A Neglected Art: A Critical Study of Music in Films,* 2nd ed. New York: W. W. Norton, 1992.

Quart, Leonard and Albert Auster. *American Film and Society Since 1945*, 3rd ed. Westport, CT: Praeger, 2002.

Rahn, Jay. "Coordination of Interval Sizes in Seven-Tone Collections." *Journal of Music Theory* 35:1-2 (1991), 33-60.

Rapf, Joanna E. "Introduction: 'The Mysterious Way of Art': Making a Difference in *On the Waterfront*." In *On the Waterfront*, ed. Joanna E. Rapf., 1-19. Cambridge: Cambridge University Press, 2003.

Riesman, David. *The Lonely Crowd: A Study of the Changing American Character*. New Haven: Yale University Press, 1950.

Robinson, Paul. *Bernstein*. London: MacDonald and Company, 1982.

Roffman, Peter and Jim Purdy. *The Hollywood Social Problem Film: Madness, Despair, and Politics from the Depression to the Fifties*. Bloomington: Indiana University Press, 1981.

Sarna, Jonathan. "Leonard Bernstein and the Boston Jewish Community of His Youth: The Influence of Solomon Braslavsky, Herman Rubenovitz, and Congregation Mishkan Tefila." *Journal of the Society for American Music* 3:1 (February 2009), 35-46.

Sayre, Nora. *Running Time: Films of the Cold War*. New York: Dial Press, 1982.

Schelle, Michael. *The Score: Interviews with Film Composers*. Los Angeles: Silman-James Press, 1999.

Schickel, Richard. *Elia Kazan: A Biography*. New York: HarperCollins, 2005.

Schrecker, Ellen. *Many Are the Crimes: McCarthyism in America*. New York: Little, Brown and Company, 1998.

———. *The Age of McCarthyism: A Brief History with Documents*, 2nd ed. New York: Bedford/St. Martin's, 2002.

Schulberg, Budd. "Foreword." In *On the Waterfront*, ed. Joanna E. Rapf, xv-xxii. Cambridge: Cambridge University Press, 2003.

Sefcovic, Enid M. I. "Cultural Memory and the Cultural Legacy of Individualism and Community in Two Classic Films About Labor Unions." *Critical Studies in Media Communication* 19:3 (September 2002), 329-51.

Seldes, Barry. *Leonard Bernstein: The Political Life of an American Musician*. Berkeley: University of California Press, 2009.

Shanet, Howard. *Philharmonic: A History of New York's Orchestra*. New York: Doubleday, 1975.

Shostakovich, Dmitri. Symphony No. 5. New York: Leeds Music Corporation, 1945.

Simeone, Nigel. *Leonard Bernstein: West Side Story*. Burlington, VT: Ashgate, 2009.

Simmons, Gary. "Conscience, Confession and Context in *On the Waterfront*." *Screen Education* 56 (2009), 91-96.

———. "Back to the Waterfront: A Close Reading of *On the Waterfront*." *Screen Education* 57 (2010), 137-43.

Smith, Helen. "*Peter Grimes* and Leonard Bernstein: An English Fisherman and An American Eclectic." *Tempo* 60:235 (January 2006), 22-30.

———. *There's a Place For Us: The Musical Theatre Works of Leonard Bernstein*. Burlington, VT: Ashgate, 2011.

Smith, Jeffrey P. "A Good Business Proposition: Dalton Trumbo, *Spar-*

tacus, and the End of the Blacklist." *Velvet Light Trap* 23 (Spring 1989), 75-100.

Stanislavsky, Constantin. *Building a Character*. Trans. by Elizabeth Reynolds Hapgood. London: Eyre Methuen, 1979.

———. *An Actor Prepares*. Trans. by Elizabeth Reynolds Hapgood. New York: Routledge, 1989.

———. *Creating a Role*. Trans. by Elizabeth Reynolds Hapgood. New York: Routledge, 1989.

Stokes, Melvyn and Richard Maltby, eds. *Identifying Hollywood's Audiences: Cultural Identity and the Movies*. London: British Film Institute, 1999.

Stouffer, Samuel A. *Communism, Conformity, and Civil Liberties: A Cross-Section of the Nation Speaks Its Mind.* Garden City, NY: Doubleday, 1955.

Strasberg, Lee. *A Dream of Passion: The Development of the Method.* Ed. by Evangeline Morphos. Boston: Little, Brown and Company, 1987.

Swain, Joseph Peter. *The Broadway Musical: A Critical and Musical Survey*. New York: Oxford University Press, 1990.

Swan, Claudia, ed. *Leonard Bernstein: The Harvard Years 1935-1939*. New York: Eos Orchestra, 1999.

Talese, Gay. "Gray-Flannel-Suit Men at Bat." *New York Times Magazine*, 30 March 1958, p. 15-21.

Taruskin, Richard. "Public Lies and Unspeakable Truth Interpreting Shostakovich's Fifth Symphony," In *Shostakovich Studies*, ed. David Fanning, 17-56. New York: Cambridge University Press, 1995.

Taylor, Benedict. "Nostalgia and Cultural Memory in Barber's *Knoxville: Summer of 1915*." *Journal of Musicology* 25:3 (Summer 2008), 211-29.

Teller, Edward and Albert Latter. "The Compelling Need For Nuclear Tests." *Life* 44:6 (10 February 1958), 64-66, 69-72.

Thomas, Tony. *Music for the Movies*. New York: A. S. Barnes and Company, 1973.

Thomson, David. "An Actor Prepares." In *On the Waterfront*, ed. Joanna E. Rapf., 85-105. Cambridge: Cambridge University Press, 2003.

Wehrwein, Austin C. "Crab Grass, Taxes and Tension Breeding Ailments in Suburbs." *New York Times*, 8 August 1959, 1, 36-37.

Wells, Elizabeth A. *West Side Story: Cultural Perspectives on an American Musical*. Lanham, MD: Scarecrow Press, 2011.

Wescott, Steven D. *A Comprehensive Bibliography of Music for Film and Television*. Detroit, MI: Information Coordinators, 1985.

Wilson, Richard. "Atomic Weapons . . . Will Save Money—They May Stop War." *Look*, 10 October 1950, 33-34.

Wolfe, Gary K. "*Dr. Strangelove*, *Red Alert*, and Patterns of Paranoia in the 1950's." *Journal of Popular Film* 5:1 (1976), 57-67.

Young, Jeff. *Kazan*: *The Master Director Discusses His Films: Interviews with Elia Kazan*. New York: Newmarket, 1999.

Zaniello, Tom. *Working Stiffs, Union Maids, Reds, and Riffraff: An Organized Guide to Films About Labor*. Ithaca, NY: Cornell University Press, 1996.

Websites consulted

digilib.nypl.org/dynaweb/ead/human/mssyaddo
hdl.loc.gov/loc.music/eadmus.mu998001
www.imdb.com/title/tt0913761/
www.youtube.com/watch?v=3Lkw07C1pW8
movies.nytimes.com/person/80425/Mischa-Bakaleinikoff
www.ascap.com/ace-title-search/index.aspx

INDEX

ABOUT THE AUTHOR

Anthony Bushard is associate professor of music history at the University of Nebraska, Lincoln, where he teaches courses in jazz history, film music history/analysis, world music, and specialized courses on American musical topics. He earned M.M. and Ph.D. degrees in musicology at the University of Kansas as well as a B.A. in piano (literature) at St. John's University (Collegeville, Minnesota). Dr. Bushard specializes in contemporary American music with a special focus on jazz, blues, and film music. He has contributed articles to *The New Grove Dictionary of Jazz*, second ed., *The Journal of Film Music*, *Studies in Musical Theatre*, *Notes*, *The Journal of Music History Pedagogy*, and *American Music*. In addition, he has lectured on jazz and film music at regional, national, and international conferences and symposia. Currently Dr. Bushard is co-editing and contributing two essays to *Anxiety Muted: American Film Music in a Suburban Age*, forthcoming.